Cindy Stiverson is leaving a legacy of love. Courageously rescuing me from childhood sexual abuse, she is not only my mom—she is my hero. *Woven* weaves her life experiences together with ministry tools to teach us how to step out on a journey with Jesus—and how to do this in community, with true compassion and authentic connection. Her transparency is what women crave, and it's what inspires us to get real ourselves. *Woven* will bring healing, grow you into a deeper relationship with God, and propel you into purpose. I encourage every church to adopt this book for their women's ministry!

Nicole Braddock Bromley,
author, international activist, founder of OneVOICE
(www.iamonevoice.org) and OneVOICE4freedom
(www.onevoice4freedom.org)

Woven is a profound and deeply moving book that will take you on a journey of self-discovery, healing, and genuine transformation in Jesus. Cindy Stiverson's compelling testimony, inspired teaching, and soul-searching exercises will keep you riveted from beginning to end. You will gain new insights and be moved to connect with other women to be "woven into a tapestry of love." This extraordinary book offers women everywhere a chance to be restored and made new by the Father's love as they move forward in His divine design for their lives.

Mary Kay Wagner, life-purpose coach, spiritual director,
speaker, and author of *Stepping Out: Nun No More*
and *Daisy Up: Begin Your Day in God's Embrace*

What Cindy Stiverson offers her readers is an understanding and practice of friendship that is critical for women in this age. Without friendships that run deep, we can feel marginalized and unsure of ourselves, our gifts, our calling. In telling her personal story, she attempts to reclaim friendship as something intimate, healing, and vital to our spiritual health as individuals as well as to our role in the Body of Christ. She weaves together her story of redemption within God's larger story of redemption in the world. Through this, we find that her "profitable trading" with the Lord has given her wisdom—wisdom she now offers to her readers.

Sarah Lehman, Woven leader, international
teacher, wife, mother

Being a therapist brings both privilege and responsibility. We may be the first person our client trusts with her story, and how we respond to that story may produce further shame or implement healing. I was honored to be Cindy's "safe place," as she describes it in this wonderful book. Watching her identify the lies she had believed and replace them with truth was like witnessing a battered little caterpillar emerge as the beautiful butterfly she was meant to be. The incredible joy is that her life's journey—the good and the bad—is impacting the lives of women everywhere through Woven. It is a delight to endorse this tender epistle.

Dr. Morven R. Baker, LPCC, contributing author,
international speaker, adjunct professor

It's as if author Cindy Stiverson read my mind (and probably yours too) when she wrote this book. Tired of superficial women's functions that left her feeling empty with a longing to connect, she realized other women struggled in this same area. God's response to Cindy's cries for intimate friendship resulted in Woven Women—a powerful international ministry. In *Woven*, Cindy describes her ministry, along with her remarkable personal testimony. Ready-to-use leader guides will assist in easily beginning your own Woven Women groups. God wants us woven into a tapestry of His love—and this book will show you how!

Connie Cameron, author of *God's Gentle Nudges*, *Christmas
Underdogs*, and *Stories of Faith and Courage from Prison*
(www.conniecameron.com), international speaker

I first met Cindy as a new Bible professor at Mount Vernon Nazarene University. She was leading a group of female students called to ministry while completing her BA in pastoral ministry. I came to appreciate her as a dedicated student who cared deeply about her fellow students. Five years later, she was starting a church in my neighborhood. I became part of that new start, appreciating Cindy's gifts as my pastor. This book comes from a person who loves her Lord most of all and cares deeply for everyone, and especially for women to find freedom in Christ. You will enjoy this book just because it is so interesting and uplifting. But as you study and internalize the biblical truths expressed so well by Cindy, you will find freedom to be the person God created you to be!

Rev. C. Jeanne Serrão, PhD, dean, school of theology and philosophy, professor of biblical literature

Many women (and men) are captured by their past, enslaved by their sin, chained up in their isolation, and jailed by their inability to escape. *Woven* offers a way out—a path toward freedom—by inviting women to gather together and be embraced by God's love. Cindy provides a resource that paints a clear picture of what Christian community can look like and how it can change everything about a person. *Woven* is an invitation to journey together with your wounds and worries into the heart of God for healing and hope. It will be a fruitful tool in gathering women and gleaning leaders for the harvest that God has in mind.

Rev. Don Ballard, pastor, Newark Church of the Nazarene

Cynthia K. Stiverson
is a contributing author to the following titles:

Breathe: Finding Freedom to Thrive in Relationships after Childhood Sexual Abuse (Moody, 2008)

Pearl Girls: Encountering Grit, Experiencing Grace (Moody, 2009)

The Ultimate Bird Lover (HCI Books, 2010)

The Ultimate Christian Living (HCI Books, 2010)

Mother of Pearl (Inspiring Voices, 2013)

Reflecting God Devotionals (NPH Spring 2014)

Reflecting God Devotionals (NPH Summer 2017)

Removing Masks, Reclaiming Identity,
Restoring Relationships, Reinventing Leadership,
Reaching the World

CYNTHIA K. STIVERSON

WOVEN
REMOVING MASKS, RECLAIMING IDENTITY, RESTORING RELATIONSHIPS, REINVENTING LEADERSHIP, REACHING THE WORLD

iUniverse books may be ordered through booksellers or by contacting:

iUniverse
1663 Liberty Drive
Bloomington, IN 47403
www.iuniverse.com
1-800-Authors (1-800-288-4677)

ISBN: 978-1-5320-4126-6 (sc)
ISBN: 978-1-5320-4125-9 (e)

Library of Congress Control Number: 2018903260

Print information available on the last page.

iUniverse rev. date: 07/10/2018

To my heavenly Father,
who lovingly created and healed me;
who called, equipped, and gifted me
to speak, write, and create;
and who inspired the writing of this book.

Also to the thousands of women
God has woven into this beautiful tapestry of love—
dedicated to *you*, my reader and new friend.

CONTENTS

FOREWORD

I met Cindy Stiverson, the author of this book—no, this *movement*—many years ago while seeking a women's retreat speaker for my church. I called Cindy, and she invited me, a perfect stranger, right into her home. I shouldn't have been surprised.

From the moment I sat across from her in her sweet kitchen nook, with steaming mugs of tea between us, I felt safe and deeply valued. There was something about her that reached out to my heart, linked arms with my soul, and drew me close, like a sister bursting with a happy secret. I booked her for the retreat because I wanted other women to catch what this girl had—her deep faith, a heart to build authentic community, and a courageous spirit that wasn't afraid to share her own painful experiences and hard life lessons if it meant helping someone else become free.

From that first meeting to the present day, Cindy has become a precious friend and sister. I continue to marvel at the many ways the Lord uses Woven, my friend, and the untold number of sisters who have caught the spirit of this amazing sisterhood of love. I have witnessed transformation in individual lives and entire communities through Woven's diverse connection opportunities. The monthly gatherings, retreats, community outreach and marketplace events, prayer vigils, quiet retreats, and mission trips all began with hearts that set their sights on authentic, godly sisterhood. I am thrilled that the blessing of Woven is now available in this book so more women can launch Woven groups where they live … and grow the love!

May the Lord use the book you now hold in your hands to transform your life and others, to transmit a spirit of love and purpose to your corner of the world, and to transcend all barriers to building Christ-honoring communities so that the Woven sisterhood will reach every woman on the planet for the glory of God.

Welcome to the family!

Kim Dent
retreat speaker and writer—DandelionWinds.com
care coach—Caring for the Heart Women's Ministry
(cfthwomen.com)

MY HEART SAYS "THANK YOU"

This book has been twenty years in the making, and I feel insufficient in my ability to acknowledge all the special people who have crossed my path and contributed to this beautiful journey. So I begin with my most precious gifts.

First, to my husband, Mark: This book could be considered an anniversary gift, celebrating our twentieth year of marriage. You have modeled strength, truth, patience, trust, and commitment. Thank you for always pointing me in the right direction and supporting every wild and crazy dream God has placed on my heart. Every woman wants a pillar of strength in her life, and you are exactly that for me. I love you always and forever. You are the man of my dreams.

To my daughter, Nicole: You were the wind beneath my wings before you were even born. Being your mom has always been the leading role of my life, and you are the star of my show. I love how God called you and is using your story for His glory. You are an inspiration to everyone you meet—and even those you've not met. I am so very proud of you and love you to the moon! Thank you for waiting for God's mate, Matthew, and for giving us three grandsons to spoil. Our life is complete.

To my sister, Pat: For setting an example of steadfast love and devotion to God through prayer, scripture, and church. Thank you for your consistent prayers, which led me to this amazing life in Christ. I love you, big sister!

To Mount Vernon Nazarene University, where I discovered

the love of God; received and accepted my call to ministry; and was surrounded by godly men and women who supported, strengthened, and affirmed my calling and the gifts and graces that accompany the call. Thank you, Dr. Lebron Fairbranks, Dr. Alex Varughese, Dr. David Cubie, Dr. Terrell Sanders, Dr. Lincoln Stevens, Dr. Bruce Petersen, and Dr. Jeanne Serrão for believing in me and for your gentle guidance and your open doors.

To the women who came alongside to help birth Women of Virtue: Anne Fairbanks, Rachel Archer, Mary Wiens, Inger Raymond, and Jackie Petersen. You looked to me as your leader when truly you were mentoring me in the process. I love you all so much. Thank you for your humility and grace, which continue to light my path.

To all the churches who placed their trust in me as their leader, pastor, preacher, speaker, and/or evangelist: Every experience has grown and empowered me to fulfill my calling. I couldn't have done it without you ... Homer Presbyterian Church, Mount Vernon First Church of the Nazarene, Lakeholm Church of the Nazarene, the Lamb's Manhattan Church of the Nazarene, the Shepherd's House, and innumerable denominations and invitations throughout the United States and Africa. *Thank you!*

To my church family at Newark Naz: I am so thankful to be a member of this dynamic group of people, a place where Mark and I have found a home. Thank you for providing the space and freedom to develop Woven Women into the ministry it is today. There are many beautiful women who have stepped up as leaders to make this happen. I cannot begin to mention all of you, but special thanks to Cheryl Simpson, who helped me launch Woven in this church. Kim Miller, Corky Morrow, Yvonne Hammond, Candy Link, Kathleen Benis, Kitty Roahrig, Julie Strong, Angie Lee, and Terri Shane: Our love for each other is contagious! I appreciate you all so much.

To my counselor, Morven Baker, and my prayer partner, Debbie Paxton: You both mean more to me than I can express. I thank God for choosing each of you as His healing hands.

Your prayers are priceless treasures—as is your friendship. I love you!

To my editorial team, who helped bear the burden of this book: Sarah Lehman, Terri Maxwell, Kathy Benson Wise, Nancy Stiverson, and Connie Cameron. You kept me going when I wanted to quit. Your input was invaluable.

To my international team: Pastor Charles and Agnes Mpagi and Pastors Joseph and Margaret Nsubuga for your obedience to God and open invitation to preach the gospel and for carrying the torch of empowering women and men through Woven Women International. Your love is overwhelming!

To Connie Cameron and Terri Shane, for following God and trusting me to lead you across the world. I am so thankful for both of you!

To Rose Apoya, Pastor Michael and Hellen Bitebe, and many others throughout East Africa and South Africa: Thank you for affirming my call to your continent. Thanks to John Forbes for initiating that first trip to South Africa, which spawned this global effort.

To Tash Horner, the brave young woman who began Woven Women in Japan: You make me proud. And to all the women who purchased my *Women of Virtue* workbooks in those early years and led Woven groups throughout the USA and South Africa. I praise God for you.

I want to give special honor to those on my journey who have been strong examples of living a life of love. My friend Mary Kay Moore: You are such a treasure trove of love. Wow! What a mentor you are. You lead by example, and your example is love, love, love! Thank you for loving me; I love you.

My precious friend Kim Dent: Love just oozes out of you. I hear it in your bubbly voice. I see it in your eyes. It shows up with every person you greet. You. Just. Love. And I love you!

My brother-in-law, Dr. Russell, and Nancy Stiverson: You personify God's love in family. We love our West Coast Stiversons so much! Thank you for your solid faith and strong ties.

Our beloved "God" parents, Elizabeth and (belated) John Haley: you have been pillars of support and treated Mark and me as though we were your own children. Thank you for the gift of unceasing prayers and unfailing love.

My mother-in-law, Esther Stiverson Esterline: On my very first visit, you grabbed my face with both hands, drew me in, locked eyes, and said, "I love you," with great enthusiasm. You have never failed to express love to me. I love you, my other mother. I praise God for you have taught me how to love freely. Thank you for raising a "perfect boy"!

To the lover of my soul, Jesus Christ: Your love has changed me from the inside out. Loving You with all my heart, soul, mind, and strength and leading others to do the same is my greatest joy. You complete me.

INTRODUCTION

I want you woven into a tapestry of love,
in touch with everything there is to know of God.[1]

We are experiencing the fallout of a major cultural shift. Instant information at our fingertips has changed the dynamics of relationships. We can accumulate thousands of friends and followers on Facebook or Twitter without ever meeting in person. Selfies and tweets portray lives we wish for but that are far from the truth of who we are and how we live. It is easier than ever to live life behind a facade, to show the good parts of our lives and leave out the bad. Scrolling through newsfeeds leaves us feeling empty if we compare our lives with others'. Women easily become entangled in a web of competition. Comparing our filtered looks and Instagram lives can diminish our unique identities, cause us to become unsatisfied with who God created us to be, and generate an ever-increasing void of true friendship.

Women are starving for vision and direction. We are hungry to be part of something bigger, something God inspired rather than goal driven. Each of us is tired of being just another body to accomplish someone else's agenda. We want to evolve into the people God intended for us to be. Women long to make a difference in the lives of others, and we are designed to do that *relationally.*

---

[1] Colossians 2:2 (the Message).

Are you longing for friendship? Searching for God? Wishing for godly girlfriends? We need one another more than ever. This book has a dual purpose with one goal in mind. The purpose is to grow leaders and gather women. The goal is to unite women by removing masks, reclaiming identity, restoring relationships, reinventing leadership, and reaching the world as we grow in relationship with God. Each chapter prepares you emotionally, spiritually, and relationally toward a deeper knowing of your true self through a deeper knowing of the one true God.

You can apply what you've learned by gathering women using the Woven group leader instructions and group handouts provided in the *Leader* section. Leaders are blessed with front-row seats to witness hearts slowly open and breathe new life in Christ. Together, we can break the cultural code of competition among women and become "woven into a tapestry of love, in touch with everything there is to know of God" (Colossians 2:2 MSG).

My prayer is for you to be tightly woven in your love for one another, as God divinely unites you with friends who understand you and know the intentions of your heart, so that you can prayerfully carry one another's burdens and help steer one another along God's path.

THE YOU-NESS OF YOU

Your you-ness is all that makes you *you*—your you-niqueness, your differentness, your giftedness, your one-of-a-kind fabulousness! God has gifted the world with you. Embrace your Maker; delight in the you-ness of you. He certainly does!

FREE TO BE— YOU AND ME

Two [women] are better than one, because
they have a good return for their work:
If one falls down, (her) friend can help [her]
up. But pity the [woman] who falls down
and has no one to help (her) up![2]

HELLO, FRIEND!

I am thrilled to finally greet you. My entire life has led me to this moment in time. Over the years God was performing major surgery on my heart and emotions. In the midst of my pain, He infused me with a wealth of wisdom through a plethora of experiences. I am excited to share the good, the bad, the ugly, and how beautifully God has woven all of it into a tapestry of love. There is so much to be said, and there are so many lies to be exposed and truths to be revealed. First and foremost, this is what I want you to know: I believe in you—the true you. My passion is to help you embrace your *you*-ness—the unique person God created you to be. I am convinced God has a powerful plan for your life, a purpose He implanted as He knit you together in your mother's womb.

I feel as though I know you, as if our paths have crossed. Maybe we've caught a glimpse of each other as harried moms,

---

[2]   Ecclesiastes 4:9–11 (NIV, adapted).

trying to keep it all together. Or perhaps we've sat quietly across the aisle on a subway, airplane, or bus. Maybe God used you or me to simply express a reassuring smile in the midst of a trial to say, "It's going to be okay." One thing is certain: We've been faced with hard places and tough times of searching and yearning. We are not immune to pain.

I don't know where you are in the course of your journey, but I confess I have made some major mistakes. I walked through devastating trials and experienced disappointments a woman prays never will happen. In the midst of it all, I learned to trust in a God of new beginnings. Sometimes I pinch myself to see if it's really true. He granted me the life I dreamed of but thought would never be. If He can do this for me, I know with certainty He can do this for you.

Have you already experienced this? Or are you still searching for someone to reach out and pull you from your storm? Have you found yourself in the deepest trench with a grueling, gut-wrenching, life-changing decision resting on your shoulders, crushing you under its weight? Maybe you are picking up the broken pieces of your life, sorting treasures from the trash so you can just move on. Perhaps you recognize there is more to friendship than shallow sharing. You can't rest because of the hollow feeling inside—an urgency that life is passing you by. God made you for more, and you want to embrace all He has for you.

Are you searching for a friend who understands, has gone before you, and is willing to listen to your heart's cry? Wherever you are on the road map of life, I am in your corner, praying you onward. More important, God sees you, hears you, knows you, and is whispering your name. It was no mistake that you picked up this book.

Are you ready to begin?

REMOVING MASKS—LET'S BE REAL

I've uncovered a deep desire that everyone shares. We want to be known by our best intentions instead of our past failures.

We want people to look beyond our outward appearances, beyond labels and titles, beyond our social status or family origins.

Painful labels—scabs and hurts covering our hearts and minds—affect how we see ourselves, our self-esteem. Our self-image affects how we perceive one another. We may not even realize how these labels affect us. Hurts and wounds are filters that create prejudices that separate and isolate.

We wear masks, attempting to look perfect, be perfect, and pretend we don't have any problems. It's our way of covering our insecurities and secrets, but it does not work. Our woundedness oozes out in our self-talk and in judgments we make about others. When we look at another woman, we think, *Who does she think* she *is?* It gets far worse from there. I'm sure you can relate; we constantly form tainted opinions of others, yet we all long for others to see our hearts—the very core of who we are.

My quest is to help you celebrate the incredible uniqueness of *you* so you can then embrace the uniqueness of each person God puts in your path. This requires compassion, to actually look people in the eye, consider the history behind their faces, listen to their stories, and recognize the God-given passion and purpose waiting to be birthed in them. It is to believe every human being is loved by God, and every person is your neighbor. It's obedience to the command Jesus has given us "to love your neighbor as yourself."[3]

How can we follow the commands of Christ if we never get beyond first impressions; if we are all hiding behind our insecurities, our comfy masks? How can we love each other if we loathe ourselves?

Most of us are waiting to be invited, to be pursued; waiting for friends to come to us. How's that working for you? That's right—*it's not!* I know this because I was *that woman* who longed for someone to see her heart. You name the circumstances; it's likely I have been there—done that. Deep down I knew I was not embracing the person or path

---

[3]   Mark 12:31.

God intended for me. My inner compass whispered, "You were meant for something more." Everything felt out of control because I allowed others to be in control. When I realized God saw my heart, understood my past, and had a plan for my future, I was set free![4]

We tend to think of love as a noun, an object, a possession. It is also a verb—love requires action. We are tentative when it comes to loving, not wanting to take the first step or make the first move. Love is scary! It requires being real, peeling off our labels, revealing our wounds and even secrets from our past. When we step outside our comfort zones, remove our masks, and extend love, the possibilities are endless. We become living breathing invitations for others to do the same.

RECLAIMING IDENTITY

God has given us the power to be free and the authority to set each other free. When a woman discovers her true self, something magical happens. She reclaims her identity and is empowered to be the person God intended her to be. No longer trying to be somebody else, she exudes the confidence we all seek. Her authentic self gives other women permission to embrace their true selves.

A major shift takes place when we refuse to align with cultural lies and give each other the freedom to be—you and me. We no longer view each other superficially. Like airbrushed models in a magazine, our best photoshopped selfies cannot compare with the beauty God planted in our souls. The world becomes alive because we see with new eyes. Looking beyond the surface, we see hearts and hurts and healing. We move beyond differences to a deep and mutual love. Our lives entwine to rewrite the story line.

Are you catching a glimpse of this vision? Woven Women are a powerful force. When God unites us, He also empowers us to go above and beyond what we could never do alone. We

---

[4]   Jeremiah 29:11.

CYNTHIA K. STIVERSON

become soul sisters journeying together on a rugged road we call *life*. Labels are lifted. Hearts are healed. Lives transform. Friendships are formed. Relationships are restored, and God is glorified!

RESTORING RELATIONSHIPS

Women were made for relationships. I'm not talking about the type of "friending" that is trending on Facebook or Twitter. This is not about virtual relationships based on your best filtered photos. On the contrary, it is an invitation to experience authentic heartfelt friendships that go beyond the surface, overcome fear, plant love deep into the heart, and restore broken trust. If we could capture this on YouTube, I guarantee our video would go viral. But God works in deep places we cannot reach on our own, in ways only He can see. The final product is a perfected inner person.[5]

Pause to think about this God of endless grace. Reflect on your personal growth. Appreciate how God has intervened throughout your life to perfect you. Consider how He is working with the women in your life, past and present.

I see my life in chapters, and in every chapter, God was there—preparing me for the next. When my daughter was in second grade, I was in desperate need of a friend. I remember walking into her classroom to meet her teacher. It was just one of many posters covering the wall, but it caught my eye like a billboard. A soft, snuggly kitten nuzzling in the warmth of a furry puppy shared this quote, which hit me head-on: To Have a Friend Is to Be a Friend.

I was very aware of my need *for* a friend, but I didn't know how to *be* one.

Those words turned over and over in my mind for weeks. To be a friend—what would *I* want from a friend? I wanted someone to talk to; someone to understand; to enter into my world; to share her thoughts, prayers, problems, and

---

[5] Hebrews 10:10–14.

dreams—and advise me in mine. So I determined to be a friend instead of waiting to be friended.

Fast-forward a few chapters in my life. My daughter was a senior in high school. I was a junior in college, a middle-aged newlywed. We moved from a ranch house in the country to a century-old Victorian home. It was my dream home—my groom's bachelor pad! During summer break, I shelved the textbooks and rolled up my sleeves. It was time to make his pad live up to my dream.

My hubby, Mark, worked long hours. My daughter was a busy girl. I felt very alone one July afternoon. I had spent several hot, humid days stripping wallpaper. A very long to-do list had few items checked off. My dream home felt more like a brick oven. I was overwhelmed and longed for a friend.

Then it happened: an unexpected knock on the door. It was the wife of my husband's friend, a new friend to me. Jeanine was a teacher, also on summer break. We talked a bit about our summer plans, hubbies, and hobbies. She could see I was knee-deep in renovations, so I shared my project list, which led us to the wool carpet in the parlor. Just looking at it made me sweat! It was like wearing an itchy sweater in midsummer. Jeanine agreed. Better yet, she knew what to do. By the time Mark returned home, there was not a hint of carpet or even a tack in that room. He was speechless when he saw the antique oak floor! I wasn't sure if that was a good thing, but in the end he was a happy man.

The rest of the summer Jeanine and I were a team. We redecorated her kitchen and bath. We papered and painted my walls. By working together on our to-do lists, we could accomplish so much more. Our work became play dates.

The lessons I learned that summer while doing life with Jeanine were not written in a textbook. They exposed a need to connect with other women. Though I made new friends at church, every Sunday was the same. We weren't moving beyond the mask of "Hi! How are you?" and "I'm fine! How are you?" I was weary of two-sentence conversations.

Week after week, I went to church with people I knew only

on the surface. I wanted to go beyond the clothes, the hair, and the makeup. I wanted to know the hearts of women. So I prayed and asked God to give me godly girlfriends. In answer to my prayer, God gave me Colossians 2:2 (KJV) as a mission statement: "That their hearts might be comforted, being knit together in love."

Once again, the message was "To have a friend is to be a friend." I envisioned women getting to know one another and growing in the Lord. Opening our homes, we would take our relationships to a personal level. We would become acquainted with spouses, children, pets, and hobbies and actually have something to talk about next time we passed in the church hallway. Most important, we could be an encouragement to one another and become "knit together" as allies instead of enemies. I began to dream about the potential of shedding the competitive stereotype of our gender and the resulting power of doing life together.

In January 1998, I hosted our first gathering as Women of Virtue. Little did I know the nine of us would become group leaders. I couldn't find teaching materials to match my vision, so I prayed my way through the writing of the first workbook. By October, we launched four groups with forty-four women, and a year later we doubled in size. The joy of connecting was contagious. One woman said she never really knew her sister-in-law of twenty-five years until they were in a Women of Virtue group together. A twenty-four-year-old college student became the dearest of friends with a ninety-year-old great-grandmother. We found a safe harbor—a place to share our fears, successes, and failures—and became a powerhouse of prayer support.

My heart's longing for friendship is universal. And it was the very heart of God to satisfy this need. My call to full-time ministry led me into churches throughout the United States and across the ocean. Over the years, Women of Virtue became Woven Women. God is using this ministry to connect thousands of women, weaving them into His beautiful tapestry of love.

I believe God is in the process of weaving you into this

tapestry of love too. Let's navigate through those hard places, past or present, as we journey inward and outward. Together, we will personally know God and communicate with His Spirit on a deeper level, embrace our true selves, and see our sisters through a new lens. The vision will come into focus as we pass this baton of love and encouragement, an invitation to be "woven into a tapestry of love."[6]

REINVENTING LEADERSHIP

Remember all those parties you were never invited to? How it left you feeling unwanted or unimportant? Well, here is your chance to do the inviting! Woven is an opportunity to share your faith and grow spiritually in a friendly fashion. I'm so thankful God gave me Woven because I have gained the most beautiful female friendships—beyond what I ever could have dreamed or imagined. You will be saying that too!

Women were designed to do life together. Each brings her various gifts, perspective, and personality. We truly need each other to weave balance and variation into the tapestry of our lives. Some are leaders. Others offer support and provide structure. Some are seeking a leader or a mentor. No matter the gifts you bring to the table, there is always someone who can learn from you, who looks up to you, and would love to spend time with you—yes, *you.*

There are also those who have journeyed ahead and long to share experiences and wisdom they have learned. As I encourage you to be a leader, I encourage you to also be led. We all have gifts and experiences to share. There is room for everyone at the table. So pull up a chair.

The *Leader* section in the back of this book is your toolbox for mentoring women. It contains Woven leader instructions and advice on leading a group. Take a peek at them now, if you like.

I've made it easy for you to focus on relationships. Simply

---

[6] Colossians 2:2 (the Message).

follow the script for leading your group. There is a group handout with the scripture and questions for your ladies to follow along. The handouts can be used totally on their own, without any homework or prep. Women can simply show up, relax, and contribute to the conversation. It's easy to draw women because it is also a small time commitment—one evening a month for seven months—but it pays huge dividends.

You don't have to know the Bible from cover to cover to lead a Woven group. You don't have to be an expert of any kind. (*Insert sigh of relief here!*) This is not about impressing one another with your knowledge. The leader is free to simply facilitate discussion based on scripture, using the lesson provided. When we lead with transparent hearts, we generate mutual sharing. Women feel safe to share their hurts and thoughts.

This modeling and mentoring type of leadership transforms lives and weaves hearts together. I have witnessed souls unfold like the petals of a rosebud, gently opening into full bloom. It's so beautiful! This is what happens when hearts find a safe place to rest and be heard. Your ladies will experience even more growth by reading this book and doing the personal study along with you. Before you know it, new leaders will rise up. Women will be waiting in line to join Woven groups when they see love growing and lives changing.

WOVEN: FREE TO BE—YOU AND ME

The theme for this set of lessons is *Free to Be—You and Me*. That's exactly what happens in our Woven groups. We give each other permission to be free, simply by allowing each person the freedom to share her heart and be heard without being judged. The Woven leader must create an atmosphere of trust and intimacy, where hearts feel safe and free to simply be. This is a rare gift we offer to our women.

The Woven purpose statement in Colossians 2:2 says that we are "woven together" by growing in our knowing, "in touch with everything there is to know of God" (the Message). Knowing is essential to loving. That's why our Woven groups implement three areas of relationship: Getting to Know Your Hostess, Getting to Know Each Other, and Getting to Know God.

The goal for Getting to Know Your Hostess is to have women host the group in their homes and share a bit about their lives. This provides an intimate setting for Getting to Know Each Other—an icebreaker that prompts each person to speak and introduce herself. Getting to Know God is our main focus—to transform hearts by making God's Word relevant to day-to-day life. The discussion is aimed at doing exactly that. The questions in each session begin broad and gradually become more personal. You can expect God to give each woman an individual message surrounding the same truth. The variety of responses opens our minds to new perspectives. God works through each personality to shape our life stories. When women come together and grow in these three areas—knowing your hostess, knowing each other, and knowing God—we come to a deeper knowing of our true selves. We are personally and spiritually transformed in the process.

Prayer provides an intimate closing, so we end our time by praying for one another. Prayer is simply having a conversation with God, using your own language. It doesn't have to be flowery or super-spiritual. Just be real. Just be you.

In *Free to Be—You and Me*, we become well acquainted with the "virtuous woman" in Proverbs 31, the woman who "surpasses them all." For many, she stirs the same reaction in our struggle with female relationships: feelings of inferiority, inadequacy, and fear of not measuring up to her seemingly perfect example. This makes her an excellent specimen for transforming our attitudes toward one another. Our goal is to see her as three-dimensional, one who knows firsthand the pressures and expectations women face, yet she has risen above and beyond. If we can come to love and appreciate *this* woman, we can love and accept *anyone*.

As we come to know the Proverbs 31 woman, we realize

we are not alone in our journeys. We also will walk alongside women of the Bible. Their stories will help us recognize our deep need for God and His presence in our lives. Though centuries separate us, these women speak directly into current situations. You will love them as sisters who have paved the path for our freedom.

THIS BOOK IS FOR YOU

This book will grow you as a person and as a leader. Even if you never gather women into a Woven group, God will use these pages to rewire your thoughts, emotions, and relationships. It has the capacity to change the way you live and love. There are three areas of *knowing* in each chapter: *Getting to Know Me*, *Getting to Know You*, and *Getting to Know God*. These sections in each chapter are for your personal study time. The insights you gain will heal you personally and bring spiritual depth from which you can share. This will prepare you to be an effective leader. Interpersonal relationships form naturally when you become confident of who you are and how much you are loved by God.

As author of this book, I am blessed to serve as your spiritual director. I invite you into my world in the *Getting to Know Me* section. In each chapter, I reveal life lessons through personal struggles, failures, successes, and relationships. By sharing the journey of discovering *my* true self, my prayer is that you will discover *your* true self. I have also invited other Woven Women to share their stories along the way. You'll enjoy these testimonies tucked into the fiber of each chapter. The hope is to shape your story so you, in turn, can help others shape theirs.

The *Getting to Know You* section is all about *you*. I will challenge you to see yourself in new ways, think new thoughts about your life journey, and help you process core issues that keep you from embracing God and embracing others. You will examine your underlying assumptions or judgments about women. We are easily wounded, so it can be a scary process to seek out new friendships. God wants us to pursue healthy relationships. This becomes a path to healing. So be brave, my friend. I am here in your prayer corner, coaching and cheering you forward as we seek to accomplish God's will—to love and know Him and one another. Feel free to email your questions along the way.[7]

The *Getting to Know God* section of this book will give you confidence to approach God, the Creator of the entire universe, the Creator of you. How well do you really know God? Are you convinced of His infinite love for you? Do you realize that He delights in the very essence of you and longs for you to receive, reflect, and respond to His love for you? He communicates through His Word (the Bible), His creation, His followers, and through His Holy Spirit. It's impossible for anyone to love us the way God, our heavenly Father loves us. He is the one who truly sees our hearts and knows us better than we know ourselves.

I like to think of the Bible as God's love letter to us. Our response to this amazing love and grace is to read God's Word and apply it to our lives. That's exactly what we will do.

GRAB YOUR JOURNAL—LET'S GET STARTED

Ever feel like your prayers get stuck somewhere between your head and heaven? Journaling is a great way to make your prayers more tangible and concrete, instead of just floating around in the clouds somewhere. This has been very formative in my spiritual journey and healing path. God wants us to heal and to grow. Before you go any further, pick up a journal for writing your answers to the personal reflections at the end of each chapter.[8] It's also a great place to make notes about things you'll want to share with your Woven group, so you'll want to keep it handy as you read and also when you lead.

I have a method of filing my thoughts as I journal. By

---

[7]   www.WeAreWovenWomen.com/contact.

[8]   Shop for my one-of-a-kind journals at WeAreWovenWomen.com.

writing prayers and reflections only on the right-hand page of the journal, the left-hand page is open for special insights from God and thoughts to share with my Woven group. Sometimes, my head is filled with a to do list, so I jot those nagging tasks on the left page to clear my head for journaling. After my prayer time, I go back to the list and start doing my to-dos. It's encouraging to look back through the journal and see how God has answered prayers.

I'm so excited for you! You are about to find out just how much we have in common. As we open our hearts, God sets us *free to be—you and me*!

GETTING TO KNOW ME—REACHING THE WORLD

As I reflect on the journey that has led me to this moment, I see the unlikelihood of *me* teaching *you*. Female friendships have always been a struggle for me. In my teens and twenties, I had wide circles of social friends but trusted very few. Even those special few would sometimes betray or disappoint me. I'm sure they probably felt the same about me.

When God called me to ministry in my thirties, the last thing I wanted to do was lead women. I had attended many women's ministry events over the years. I left feeling more friendless and alone than when I arrived. This was the very thing God used to move me to action. He told me, "Do something about it." First dubbed "Women of Virtue," Woven Women was born.

One thing is certain—God's plan is always bigger. Since those first roots in ministry, He has sent me to serve as lead pastor, staff pastor, church planter, adjunct professor, spiritual director, and revival and retreat speaker. God sent me to give spiritual counsel to the people of New York City after the terrorist attack on the World Trade Center in 2001 and opened doors for a multidenominational ministry throughout the United States, South Africa, Kenya, Uganda, and Rwanda as an evangelist.

All of this came to an abrupt halt in 2008, when my personal life collided with my professional life. I was prescribed a three-month sabbatical. It was a painfully beautiful season of healing. In the midst of that dismal season, God birthed "Her Cindyness," an art ministry of watercolor, words, and multimedia works. A few of my paintings are in this book. I never imagined I would be selling prints of paintings that revealed and relieved the deep pain in my heart or how those paintings would speak to the hearts of others. In the same season of healing, my writings were published in several books and blogs.

During my respite, we attended a church nearly an hour away. As I looked in the worship folder, God spoke to my heart: "Do you see anything for women in this church?"

It was as if He physically tapped me on the shoulder. I was quick to shoo Him away with my response: "No, but that's not my problem."

The question continued to pester me for weeks. I shared my ministry with the pastor. It was a shoo-in! Women of Virtue was launched anew as Woven Women. I had thoughts of this name change, which led me to look up our mission statement in The Message. Imagine my amazement when I read, "I want you *woven* into a tapestry of love, in touch with everything there is to know of God." I thought it was *my* thought but it was a God-thought!

This has been a spectacular relaunching with the deepest and most precious female friendships I have ever witnessed or experienced. The change of dynamics on Sunday mornings in our church became tangible, as women embraced, kissed, and were genuinely excited and joyful to greet one another.[9] Some gathered and prayed for each other—not just saying they would but actually doing it in the midst of the conversation. It changed our men because they are excited about the change they see in their wives. Our large congregation became the true sense of family.

Over the past ten years at this church, God has built a firm foundation for Woven. I'm blessed with a strong team

---

[9]   Romans 16:16 (ESV).

of women who help plan and implement the vision. Most important, we truly love one another and love *all* women. We punctuate our sentences with "I love you" and leave them open-ended.

Woven has expanded beyond the small–group experience to include a Woven Kick-Off, Woven Weekend Retreat, Woven Girls' Night Out, Woven Marketplace and Boutique, and Woven Quiet Retreat for spiritual formation. God has drawn His girls from near and far to our events via women inviting women. The Holy Spirit is wooing, healing, and uniting hearts.

Woven reaches women locally and around the globe. Locally, we have raised relief funds for women in transition, ministered to women in rehab through art therapy, provided personal care items, and included them in our Woven events. They bless our hearts beyond measure as we affirm they are loved beyond measure.

Globally, we encourage and grow the body of Christ in Africa through annual mission trips. We unite women by launching international Woven Women groups, and we support efforts to establish small enterprises. We seek to meet the needs of oppressed people, especially women, children, and pastors around the globe as God guides, provides, and directs. A major thrust is to address the need of underwear and sanitary pads for women and schoolgirls.

Through the Woven blog and online devotionals, we've reached women from countries I've never visited, including the launch of a Woven group in Japan. We praise God for His equipping and vision for the threads of our hearts to be woven into a tapestry that reaches the world. His vision sees no boundaries, and *you* are a beautiful face in this picture.

GETTING TO KNOW YOU

I remember a time when I was so timid and self-conscious that even saying my name to someone felt weird. It was awkward to say, "Hi, my name is Cindy. What's yours?" I wanted to be known. I wanted to know others. But I couldn't get past "Hello, my name is …"

Names are important. They have meaning and may even predict your future. We love it when people remember our names, right? So, what's *your* name?

- Begin by writing down your full name. Look at it. Think about it. Speak your name out loud as if you were introducing yourself to me. How does it feel to say your name?
- Do you like your name? If it were someone else's name, how would you envision her? What would your expectations be of her?
- What is the meaning of your name? Look it up online. Read all the derivatives and variations. Do you feel this describes you? Why, or why not?
  - o Now that we've been formally introduced, write about your first visit to your current church or community. What circumstances led you there?
  - o Who were the first women you noticed, and why? To whom were you introduced, and what were your first reactions? Do you remember their names?
  - o How have your perceptions changed since those first visits and first impressions? What brought about these changes?

First impressions can be so deceiving. We have inhibitions and untended hurts from past relationships. Lack of forgiveness and bitterness can taint our reactions to each other. God heals our hearts through healthy relationships. The only way to overcome these judgment calls is to seek to build relationships and to go deeper than that initial introduction. If there are women in your current circle whom you feel uncomfortable around, give them the benefit of the doubt. Give them another chance. This is not an invitation to return to a relationship that has improper boundaries. Pray and ask God to prepare the way. Seek ways to break the ice.

Begin to cultivate a healthier way of relating with the women God has planted in your path. He may have put them there just to stretch you, heal you, and set you free.

GETTING TO KNOW GOD

The poem of the virtuous woman found in the book of Proverbs 31 provides a backbone for this book. Read this passage and reflect on its meaning and purpose. You may want to read it in several biblical translations. Write your first impressions about this woman in your journal.

10 Who can find a virtuous woman? for her price is far above rubies.
11 Her husband has full confidence in her and lacks nothing of value.
12 She brings him good, not harm, all the days of her life.
13 She selects wool and flax and works with eager hands.
14 She is like the merchant ships, bringing her food from afar.
15 She gets up while it is still dark; she provides food for her family and portions for her servant girls.
16 She considers a field and buys it; out of her earnings she plants a vineyard.
17 She sets about her work vigorously; her arms are strong for her tasks.
18 She sees that her trading is profitable, and her lamp does not go out at night.
19 In her hand she holds the distaff and grasps the spindle with her fingers.
20 She opens her arms to the poor and extends her hands to the needy.
21 When it snows, she has no fear for her household; for all of them are clothed in scarlet.
22 She makes coverings for her bed; she is clothed in fine linen and purple.
23 Her husband is respected at the city gate, where he takes his seat among the elders of the land.

24 She makes linen garments and sells them, and supplies the merchants with sashes.
25 She is clothed with strength and dignity; she can laugh at the days to come.
26 She speaks with wisdom, and faithful instruction is on her tongue.
27 She watches over the affairs of her household and does not eat the bread of idleness.
28 Her children arise and call her blessed; her husband also, and he praises her:
29 "Many women do noble things, but you surpass them all."
30 Charm is deceptive, and beauty is fleeting; but a woman who fears the LORD is to be praised.
31 Give her the reward she has earned, and let her works bring her praise at the city gate.

(Proverbs 31:10 KJV; Proverbs 31:11–31 NIV)

If we were reading this poem in Hebrew, we would view it as an acrostic poem. This means each line begins with the next letter in the Hebrew alphabet, which made the poem easy to memorize for Jewish families.

- Why would they memorize this poem?

It seems that Jewish families placed great value in the role of women in the household, so they recited this poem at the dinner table on Friday nights. They praised her for her skills. And in case you didn't notice, this woman has skills. She was much more than a cook and maid. She expanded her domain beyond domestic goddess. She managed a business and was a compassionate caregiver, craftsman, and teacher. She provided food and clothing, all while juggling the roles of wife and mother. Sound familiar? The woman of virtue pulls it off with great ease and finesse because she is "a woman who fears the Lord" (Proverbs 31:30). She is praised for her godly character and wisdom.

- How does the role of the proverbial woman of virtue compare to women's role in society today? How does her role compare to your role in the family, community, and society?
- Upon what qualities and virtues does today's culture place value and emphasis? Describe the woman that our culture would consider "perfect," virtuous, or valuable.
- Is this an adequate representation or treatment of women? Do you feel valued? By your family? By your employer? By your church or community?
- Take time to write about how you are treated. What makes you feel valuable? What causes you to feel as though your work or input is unappreciated? How could others treat you in a way that gives you value or honor?
- Now, turn that around: How can you extend honor and value to those you love and/or those in need of love? How well do you honor the skills and gifts of other women? How much thought do you give to honoring your husband or the men in your life?
- If your family were to write a poem in your honor, what do you suppose they would say? Just for fun, ask them to write one. Share the woman of virtue poem with them, and challenge them to write something about you. Have them read it out loud to you. It would be a great discussion over dinner, don't you think? How does it compare to what you thought they would say? (*Oh, how I wish I could read what they wrote! Send me an email, if you'd like, or share it on our Facebook page.[10]*)

---

[10] facebook.com/WeAreWoven.

A PRAYER FOR YOU

What is most frustrating or stressful to you as a woman of the twenty-first century? Write about it in your journal and turn it into a prayer, asking God to change what needs to be changed in our culture, in our gender, in your female and family relationships. Ask Him to begin with you.

Heavenly Father,

I pray for my Woven sister. Provide a friend she can trust with her heart, who gives her permission to be her true self. Enrich her circle with women who understand one another and pray for each other. Heal their hearts through healthy friendships. Lord God, overwhelm them with your love for them and their love for each other.

Grow my friend as a leader. Affirm her as a woman You have chosen. Reveal Your plans and direct her decision about beginning a Woven group. Make clear Your calling and Your timing to grow a team and gather women.

Most of all, assure her that You love her exactly as she is, and set her free to be the person You created her to be.

I pray these things in Jesus's name.

Amen.

LIVING WATER

She walked a lonely path. Vulnerable. Used. Abused. Tossed aside. Longing for someone who would look beyond the surface to see her hurting heart and love her for who she was.

She was the woman at the well, but she could be your neighbor, your mother, your daughter, your friend. She could be you.

Jesus knows everything about us and loves us just as we are. He loves us so much that He doesn't leave us the way He finds us. He washes away the shame of our past, leaving us with a testimony: "Come meet a man who told me everything I ever did."

"WHAT MAKES THIS CHICK TICK?"

Satan's greatest psychological weapon is a gut-level feeling of inferiority, inadequacy, and low self-worth. This feeling shackles many Christians, despite wonderful spiritual experiences, despite their faith and knowledge of God's Word. Although they understand their position as sons and daughters of God, they are tied up in knots bound by terrible feelings of inferiority, and chained to a deep sense of worthlessness.
—David Seamands[11]

I know what you're thinking: *This woman of virtue is way too perfect for me.* Women like her make us want to run in the opposite direction. They trigger our insecurities. And this Proverbs 31 woman—she has way too much going for her. Who wants to hang out with someone who is attractive, well-to-do, and puts us to shame with her multitude of gifts, abilities, and accomplishments? How in the world does she do it? How does she find the time? She has to have at least *one* flaw!

That's exactly how we are wired to think, isn't it? When we meet a woman who is truly remarkable, we find something wrong with her. On the other hand, when we meet a woman who is quite the opposite, we delight in judging and looking

---

[11] David Seamands, *Healing for Damaged Emotions* (Colorado Springs, Colorado: David C. Cook, 1981).

down on her. We don't take time to look beyond the surface to find something right with her. In our minds we ask, *What's her deal? What makes this chick tick?* The tone is derogatory. We don't really want to know her. We look for faults in an effort to boost our own egos.

What if we decided to truly understand *what makes this chick tick?* Could we look beyond actions and assumptions and see her heart instead? Imagine the friends we would make, the help we could offer, the healing that could take place, and fresh perspective we would gain. I believe it's what God is urging us to do in Colossians 2:2, "I want you woven into a tapestry of love."

When we see a tapestry, we are drawn to the multiple threads and colors meticulously woven into a beautifully detailed design. If we consider the time and talent required to create this piece of art, we cannot neglect the heart and love necessary to bring it to completion. When we reverse the tapestry to look at the back, we are even more astonished. Threads are strewn from one end to the other, making no sense at all. It truly is a mess.

God uses this great illustration in Colossians to woo us into a life of love. We are *one hot mess* when we choose to go solo. When we invite His love to be woven into the very heart of our lives and our relationships, we behold the glory of His craftsmanship. We see ourselves and each other through the lens of love. Fully aware that every one of us has a messy life, we choose to see the God-potential in every person.

God is not asking for cookie-cutter women. He is longing to enhance our individual attributes by collectively weaving us into His beautiful masterpiece. Then, we *all* look amazing as we bring out the best in one another! Imagine how colorful this tapestry must be in God's eyes: our diverse and beautifully battered lives *woven* into one story for His glory. And to think it all depends on what we're thinking about each other. Now that's a thought worth thinking about.

Before we look more closely at the virtuous woman in Proverbs, let's take a peek at a woman who is quite the opposite.

A NOT-SO-VIRTUOUS WOMAN: JOHN 4:1–42

There is a woman in the Bible whose story begins much the same as the story of Cinderella. You may remember the scene when the prince was traveling home to the castle. As fate would have it, he stopped at the home of Cinderella for a drink of water. Ironically, the Samaritan woman also had an unexpected encounter with a man who was traveling and thirsty and asked her for a drink. At face value, we would all agree that this woman was no *virtuous* woman. Unlike Cinderella, she had no idea this man was the Prince. Perhaps you'll want to read John 4:1–42 before going any further. Go ahead—I'll wait for you. Let's check her out and see *what makes this chick tick.*

The scene unfolds in the year AD 27. It was early in Jesus's ministry, and He was traveling with his disciples. They became hungry and tired, as fate would have it, near a certain Samaritan woman's hometown of Sychar in Samaria. Typically, the Jews would not step foot on Samaritan ground, even though it provided a shorter route from Jerusalem to Galilee. Samaritans, according to Jewish culture, were unclean half-breeds or lowlifes. But John 4:4 says Jesus "had to go through Samaria." He had to go this way because he had a mission to accomplish there, a divine appointment with the Samaritan woman. While the disciples ventured into town to buy some groceries, Jesus decided to lie down and rest near a well.

He was at the exact well at the exact time the Samaritan woman came to draw water every day. This day was no different. She came alone at noon, the hottest hour of the day. She had adapted her schedule to avoid any possibility of being seen, to avoid interacting with other women. The well was a place where the local women met in the cool of the evening to socialize, exchange news of the day, and develop friendships—but not this woman. Scorned and shunned, she was tormented by the guilt and shame of her lifestyle. She had few friends except the men who used her, abused her, and left her. In search of love and acceptance, she went running into the arms of another and another and another, only to be disappointed.

The Samaritan woman's life was about to make a dramatic change. On *this* particular day, *this* particular man would change her life forever. His unashamed love for her had caused Him to walk miles and miles in the heat of the day. He crossed all the social boundaries of their time. He was a Jew speaking to a Samaritan, a man speaking with a woman. This was not culturally acceptable! On an even deeper level, this was a man of integrity, spending time alone with a promiscuous woman.

The conversation went something like this: He asked her for a cup of water; she questioned His motives. He made promises, and she challenged His logic. He spoke to her need; she asked for relief. Then Jesus spoke directly into her life:

> He told her, "Go, call your husband and come back."
>
> "I have no husband," she replied.
>
> Jesus said to her, "You are right when you say you have no husband. The fact is, you have had five husbands, and the man you now have is not your husband. What you have just said is quite true."
>
> "Sir," the woman said, "I can see that you are a prophet!"[12]

She challenged His religion. He opened her eyes to the truth of who He was and the truth of who she was in His eyes.

Meanwhile, the disciples returned with groceries and their preconceived notions about Jesus carrying on a conversation with a Samaritan woman, alone, in the middle of the day—a woman with a bad reputation. They were all very familiar with a rabbinical rule that a man should not have a conversation

---

[12] John 4:16–19 (NIV).

with any woman in the street, including with his wife, because it could cause other men to gossip. (*Men? Gossip? Hmm ...*)

In the midst of the interchange between Jesus and the disciples, the Samaritan woman left her vessel at the well. This was very symbolic. Along with her vessel for carrying water, she left her other baggage too—her shame and guilt; her fear, pain, and disgrace. At the very place where she was daily confronted with her loneliness and sinful lifestyle, the Samaritan woman left her burdens with Jesus.

Then, this woman who avoided everyone and was considered an outcast, an exile with low self-esteem and little respect, *ran* down Main Street of her hometown. She called out in the streets, inviting everyone, "Come, see a man who told me everything I ever did. Could this be the Christ?"[13] Her life was changed, and everyone knew it.

Now, ladies, let's picture this: The local promiscuous woman invites all the neighbors to come and meet yet another man who had the inside scoop on her life. Imagine what a scandal *that* would stir!

Do you see their raised eyebrows?

Do you hear the whispers?

This time it was no scandalous love affair. This was the extravagant, unconditional love of God Himself. She had met the Messiah, the Christ!

Like Cinderella, she had a face-to-face encounter with her Prince. But this was no fairytale. This was the real deal. In a single conversation with Jesus, the Samaritan woman was set free. She opened her heart to receive this unconditional, no-strings-attached, unblemished love of God. It was a miraculous transformation. She could now freely talk about the very things that, as recently as an hour earlier, had shamed her into a life of solitude and exile. Head held high, eyes sparkling, and heart set free, she shared her testimony. As you can imagine, the neighbors were all ears!

---

[13]   John 4:29 (NIV).

Many of the Samaritans from that town believed in him because of the woman's testimony, "He told me everything I ever did."

So when the Samaritans came to him, they urged him to stay with them, and he stayed two days. And because of his words many more became believers.

They said to the woman, "We no longer believe just because of what you said; now we have heard for ourselves, and we know that this man really is the Savior of the world."[14]

One woman, one conversation with Christ, and an entire town was transformed!

The Samaritan woman was living as an exile but was destined to be an evangelist. "Come. Meet a man who told me everything I ever did." It was the only way the woman at the well could describe what had happened. It was what she remembered most in her conversation with Jesus.

The impact was bigger than the fact that Jesus was able to prophetically tell her everything she ever did. It was His way of seeing beyond her sin and mistakes; His ability to look deep into her heart. Perhaps it was the first time in her life that a man looked at her with respect instead of lust. Jesus looked beyond her actions and understood the reasons behind them. He was not only aware of *her* sin; He saw the sins that had been committed against her.

The Lord doesn't see things the way you see them. People judge by outward appearance, but the Lord looks at the heart. (1 Samuel 16:7 NLT)

---

[14] John 4:39–42 (NIV).

TRUE OR FALSE?

Honestly, if we are willing to give the Samaritan woman—or *any* woman—a chance, we've got to stop judging one another on appearances. The only way it will happen is by seeing each other in 3-D—looking beyond the surface and into the heart. If we are honest about our own situations, it's easy to see how she ended up with half a dozen men or more. Our hearts turn a corner when we compassionately consider what makes this chick tick. In other words, what initiated the journey that led her on an endless search for love and affection? What was her childhood like? Was she rejected by her parents or betrayed by previous husbands? Was she physically, sexually, or emotionally abused? Did she grow up in an alcoholic home? Was she coping with deep emotional wounds, untapped grief, or pent-up emotions? It's really not hard to imagine what motivated her because we know what it is to suffer. Whether we admit it or not, we all long to be transformed, to be set free from our pasts.

When we read about the Samaritan woman, we wish it could happen to us. And it can! This same Prince who set her free wants to set us free too! It's the process Paul wrote about in Ephesians 4:22-25:

> You were taught, with regard to your former way of life, to put off your old self, which is being corrupted by its deceitful desires; to be made new in the attitude of your minds; and to put on the new self, created to be like God in true righteousness and holiness. Therefore each of you must put off falsehood and speak truthfully to his neighbor, for we are all members of one body. (NIV)

Picture this interaction between the Samaritan woman and Jesus as He spoke into her personal life. I see Jesus looking deeply into her eyes and piercing her very heart. It was difficult to look Him in the face as He talked about her lifestyle. Yet there was something so engaging about this stranger. She could not look away. She looked into His eyes and embraced what Jesus had to say. What she saw behind those eyes was total acceptance. It was worth the risk to go to those deep places, to examine her past openly and honestly. She didn't argue or deny what Jesus showed her; she simply surrendered to the truth.

The Samaritan woman's false self led her to become a promiscuous woman. She was ready to "put off [her] old self" and submit to this process of transformation. She put on the new self. Jesus exchanged her "deceitful desires" for "righteousness and holiness." Then, she "put off falsehood and [spoke] truthfully to [her] neighbors."

This public announcement—"Come, meet a man who told me everything I ever did"—brought the transformation into immediate reality. It served as a baptism of sorts. She declared publicly, "I am a new woman, a true woman." When Jesus looked into her heart, He saw this virtuous woman waiting to be birthed anew. It was true for the Samaritan woman, and it can be true for you and me. We can be made new.

This "new self" in Ephesians 4 is our true self, inner child, or inner being. Psalm 139:13 speaks of God knitting us together in our mothers' wombs. Each of us is individually handcrafted by God as His one-of-a-kind child with a purpose and destiny imagined only by the mind of our Maker. These are our wonderfully made true selves. Before we can embrace the persons God destined us to be, we must identify and put off our false selves, the persons we have created in our own images. We do this by allowing God to search our hearts and personally reveal "what makes *this* chick tick."

In his book *Abba's Child,* Brennan Manning identifies three core values of the false self: placing our confidence and self-worth in (1) what I have, (2) what I can do, and (3) what others think of me. We begin to create and shape this false self in childhood, as we learn how to cope with pain and rejection. We learn what pleases people and what will win our parents' approval and acceptance. We develop our personal strategies for success—our false selves—based on performance and outward appearances. The false self denies or represses pain, thrives on compliments and accomplishments, and avoids being alone. It's the mask we wear in public. Satan uses our false selves to lie to us, saying we will not be accepted without the facade. It leads to pride, self-righteousness, deception, divisiveness, stress, anxiety, and burnout, just to name a few. The false self is, in fact, a lie. Yet we come to believe the false self to be our true selves.[15]

Listen to the words Jesus spoke to the Samaritan woman, words that were a turning point in their conversation. These words carved a path to her true heart, exposed her false self, and set her free:

> It's *who you are* and *the way you live* that count before God. Your worship must engage your spirit in the pursuit of truth. That's the kind of people the Father is out looking for: those who are simply and honestly themselves before him in their worship. God is sheer being itself—Spirit. Those who worship him must do it out of their very being, their spirits, *their true selves*, in adoration.[16]

So how do we embrace our true selves? Instead of what we have, what we can do, and what others think, we change our core values to focus on *who we are* and *the way we live.* This is important to God and brings value to our lives. As the passage says, Christianity is a life of simplicity, honesty, and worship of God. We don't have to work to earn His love and acceptance. He already loves us unconditionally. God wants to be our first love. His only requirement is to love and love and love, and we can't even do *that* without Him! When we

---

[15] Some content taken from *Abba's Child: The Cry of the Heart for Intimate Belonging* by Brennan Manning. Copyright © 1994, 2002. Used by permission of NavPress. All rights reserved. Represented by Tyndale House Publishers, Inc.

[16] John 4:23–24 (TM, emphasis mine).

surrender to this love of God, nothing will ever be the same. We are well on our way to embracing our true selves.

Go ahead—take a moment right now to pray a prayer of surrender, Ask God to fill you with His love.

GETTING TO KNOW THE VIRTUOUS WOMAN

When we read the passage of the woman of virtue described in Proverbs 31 we could easily just dismiss her, accusing her of operating from her false self. At a glance, she appears to be performance-driven and goal-oriented, running her life like a clock and trying to impress everyone, even trying to impress us, centuries later. I've met women who are irritated by the implication of the virtuous woman being "so perfect." They feel pressured to fit into her mold. My friend Jill shares her journey of getting to know the virtuous woman.

My Love/Hate Relationship with the Proverbs 31 Woman

I had been sensing God's call into a women's fellowship for a couple of months and couldn't have been more thrilled when I was approached to participate in Woven. At our first leadership meeting, I was stunned when our leader and author, Cindy Stiverson, introduced us to the Proverbs 31 woman as our subject matter. I felt like an absolute hypocrite. How in the world could God expect me to *lead* others in a study of my least favorite (would it be a sin to say *detested*?) book in the Bible?

When it was my turn to share which strength my life most exemplified of this more-than-real woman, I found maybe just one: honesty. So I poured out my heart and honestly admitted that for years I rejoiced when there were *not* thirty-one days in the month so I wouldn't need to feel guilty about not reading the thirty-first chapter of Proverbs, not wanting to be confronted by that "overachieving woman." I felt convicted and knew I'd need to repent before I went any further. And, within moments, that's exactly what I was doing.

As we met each month, I found others felt as I did—avoid this woman at all costs! However, something else happened. As we progressed, lesson by lesson, we were introduced to another aspect of this successful and caring wife, mother, and entrepreneur. She had a spiritual side, a deep connection and dependence on her Lord. She had learned not to dwell upon her weaknesses but to trust God to guide her through the days *and* seasons of her life. The walls of fear and prejudice were beginning to crumble, along with the personal shame I'd endured since I was introduced to her as a new Christian—the shame of not measuring up to the church's and my husband's expectations and to the defeat I felt whenever confronted with her. We were learning a lot about her from the lessons and the godly women in our group.

Then, it happened. It was early in the morning at my kitchen table. I was reading through the passage, as Cindy had instructed us, in preparation to lead our groups. I found my heart becoming tender and grateful we have a God who loves women so much that He would plant, in the middle of his Word, an example of what a godly woman—one who puts Him first—can accomplish in a personal relationship with Him: to live in peace, joy, service, and the contentment of a life well lived.

I praise God that His Word is new every morning, and no matter how many times we've read a portion of scripture, He can make it fresh and teach us new lessons. I thank Him also for

the inspiration He gave to His servant Cindy Stiverson, for her prayerful openness, obedience and presentation of the Proverbs 31 woman and the Woven ministry.
—Jill, a Woven Woman of virtue

GETTING TO KNOW ME

Did you catch the moment that transformed Jill's attitude toward the virtuous woman? It was a moment of truth and honesty before God, the very words Jesus spoke to the Samaritan woman in John 4:23-24.

Now, I have to be honest with you. This story of the Samaritan woman could be my story. Are you feeling it too?

When I divorced at age twenty-three, my status instantly changed from accepted to outcast. I was surprised to discover how this splitting of ways with my spouse created a broad chasm of division. Suddenly, I felt divorced from family members and friends. Everyone chose sides. At a time when I needed them more than ever, it seemed my own family struggled to understand me or love me, no matter what. Honestly, *I* didn't understand myself. My relationships were strained, estranged. Groups who formerly embraced me now rejected or avoided me. Being single *and* a mom didn't grant an entrance into many social circles.

When I was widowed at the age of thirty-six, I discovered this severing of relationships doesn't just happen with divorce. A loss or change of any kind changes relationships: the death of a loved one, moving to a new community, a job loss, a breach of trust, misunderstandings or lack of communication, hurtful words, unforgiveness, family feuds. Life changes create chasms that leave us feeling empty, used or abused, unloved or unaccepted. We long for a second chance—to be understood from the inside out. Like the Samaritan woman, we want to be loved for who we are, in spite of what we do or have done, no matter if we're married or to whom we are married, or how important our parents are.

That was me: longing for unconditional love, wanting someone to look beyond the circumstances of my life and see my heart. When I finally came to the end of myself, I discovered God could take all the broken parts and pieces of this messy life and transform them into something beautiful and useful.

I was the Samaritan woman. I had been living in exile but was destined to be an evangelist. Six months after my husband's death, I enrolled in college to become a math teacher. But instead, God called this misfit into ministry. I couldn't imagine it! Why, of all people, would God choose me? But He did! This has been a glorious journey of growing in love, which led me to this very moment of sharing life with you.

We are *woven* with a thread consistent with women of all ages and generations. We share common experiences. Some have parents whose love was hollow, emotionless. Some have had men who promised a forever love, yet rejected or abused them. We've had friends who betrayed our trust. We long for someone to look beyond our outward appearances, beyond our faults and failures, to look deep into our hearts.

Whether you realize it or not, this inner yearning is your inner child, your true self waiting to be acknowledged, to be heard, healed, and released. She is the woman God created in your mother's womb. Once you get a glimpse of her, you will love what you see. She is the person you really long to be. You might be thinking, *I think I'm already there. God has already set me free.*

Let me tell you, friend, it's impossible to exhaust or fully realize the expanse of God's loving and immense "plans to prosper us ... to give us hope and a future."[17]

> As it is written: "No eye has seen, no ear has heard, no mind has conceived what God has prepared for those who love him." (1 Corinthians 2:9)

---

[17] Jeremiah 29:11.

A few years ago, I suffered from burnout. After four years of planting and pastoring a new church, I was forced to totally shut down, to rest and recuperate. I started seeing a counselor, who recommended three months off. It was a slow, painful process of letting go of things I felt were important. As a pastor and church planter, it was beyond my imagination how the church would survive without me. I was afraid everything we had worked to build would collapse; I would be considered a failure. My false self—my fear of failure, my need to be perfect, to perform for others—is what led to burnout in the first place. That was only part of the picture.

To my surprise, this transition was triggered with the death of our beloved dog Chloie. This little white ball of fur had been a treasured family member for seventeen years. I remember sitting in the church office thinking to myself, *This doesn't have to affect me. It's only a dog. I can just keep going. It's no big deal.*

God interrupted my little pep talk. "You've been doing that your entire life. It's time to stop and grieve all the losses in your life." The weeping began, whether I wanted it to or not. I couldn't control it. Tears came like a flood. Getting to the office each morning was a chore. The grief accompanied me out of bed. It took me forever just to get showered and dressed. If you've ever tried, you know that putting on makeup with tears running down your face is counterproductive.

I discovered that three months of rest was not enough. Upon my return as pastor and after much prayer, God called me to resign my position. My counselor gave me permission to simply *be*. She helped outline my new job, which was to allow God time and space to nurture and heal my inner child. She helped me take inventory of the losses of my life.

Memories had been surfacing for over a year—repressed memories of childhood sexual abuse. It was amazing to realize I was in survival mode from the day I was born: near brushes with death, growing up in an alcoholic home, the loss of innocence through sexual abuse, divorce, death of my father and the resulting division between siblings, death of my husband. The list went on and on and on. There was never time to grieve in the midst of my circumstances. I survived by pushing forward; survival status was my norm.

Finally, I found a soft, safe place to land. God carved out this time for deeper healing, grieving, and rest. It was time to simply allow God to be God in my life—to nurture and lavish me with His love. Parts of the journey were extremely painful, but it was necessary to go back and walk through the pain to reach the freedom on the other side. It laid a foundation for embracing my destiny and moving toward the God-dreams planted in the very DNA of my heart.

A climactic moment of transformation took place a year later. It was a Sunday morning. We were attending a large church that was nearly an hour from home. As I got dressed that morning, I made a conscious decision to be low-key in how I presented myself, to let my hair down, so to speak. No masks. No pretenses. No fear of rejection. I determined to initiate conversations and not hold back. Wow! It truly was transforming. In my mind's eye, I had a visual of a snake shedding its skin. The crusty outer layer fell off, my true self was revealed, and my inner child danced with delight!

> And we, who with unveiled faces all reflect the Lord's glory, are being transformed into his likeness with ever-increasing glory, which comes from the Lord, who is the Spirit.[18]

This process of transformation is unending. I praise God because I hardly recognize the twenty-three-year-old who was divorced or the thirty-six-year-old who lost her husband. I'm not the same person I was twenty years ago. Even better, I am not the same person I was ten years ago, five months ago, or even two weeks ago because this is a day-by-day journey with Jesus. I am committed to seeking all the freedom and healing and all the plans and dreams God has for me. This is the very heart of God, to "transform us into his likeness with ever-increasing glory." This is my heart's longing for *you*.

---

[18] 2 Corinthians 3:18 (NIV).

GETTING TO KNOW YOU

Allow yourself quiet time to reflect on your life. Open your journal, and grab your favorite pen. Let's get in touch with your true self—this beautiful woman you long to be.

- Write down the titles, responsibilities, and roles you fill now and those you've had at various times throughout your life. Are you surprised at the number of things you were able to come up with?
- Which responsibilities have been especially fulfilling and accurately define who you are as a woman and person?
- What are you most passionate about? What brings out a sense of a calling, a need for change in this world? What makes you tick as a chick?
- Does your relationship with God affect your other relationships and all that you do? How do you integrate God into your work, play, family, and day-to-day life?
- Take a few minutes to take this survey, based on Proverbs 31, "What Makes This Chick Tick?"

PERSONAL SURVEY: WHAT MAKES THIS CHICK TICK?

Rate yourself in the following areas from Proverbs 31, using the scale:

0 = Not at all; 1 = Infrequently; 2 = Sometimes; 3 = Often; 4 = Almost Always

I. "She is worth far more than rubies. Her husband has full confidence in her and lacks nothing of value" (Proverbs 31:10b–11).

____I have confidence in me.
____Others have confidence in me and trust my word/work.

II. "She gets up while it is still dark ... She sees that her trading is profitable, and her lamp does not go out at night" (Proverbs 31:15, 18).

____I spend time in prayer daily.
____I spend time in scripture daily.
____I keep God first in my daily routine.
____I trust the Lord to provide the grace to sustain me in my work.

III. "She sets about her work vigorously; her arms are strong for her tasks" (Proverbs 31:17).

____Strength: I possess the inner strength necessary to tackle a task.
____Endurance: I remain steadfast in my commitment and press on to the goal.
____Commitment: I see things through to completion.

IV. "She opens her arms to the poor and extends her hands to the needy" (Proverbs 31:20).

____Compassion: I am sensitive to the needs of others and am willing to meet those needs.
____Empathy: I am able to feel what others are feeling; I can relate to them in their circumstances.
____I am active in community service/outreach.

V. "When it snows, she has no fear for her household; for all of them are clothed in scarlet" (Proverbs 31:21).

____I am thrifty: I am a good provider for myself and/or my family while maintaining a budget.
____I do not live above my means by overspending.
____I love a good bargain!

VI. "She makes coverings for her bed; she is clothed in fine linen and purple" (Proverbs 31:22).

____I take care of myself and am attentive to my appearance.

VII. "She is clothed with strength and dignity; she can laugh at the days to come" (Proverbs 31:25).

____Faith: I trust in the Lord to supply my needs.

VIII. "She speaks with wisdom, and faithful instruction is on her tongue" (Proverbs 31:26).

____I think before I speak.
____I am conscious of not offending others when I speak to them.
____I give God the glory for what He has done in my life.
____I nurture others in the way of the Lord.
____I seek out opportunities to witness.
____I refrain from using offensive language.
____I refrain from speaking critically of others.

IX. "Her children arise and call her blessed; her husband also, and he praises her" (Proverbs 31:28).

____ I model biblical characteristics as an example for others.
____Next to God, I am careful to keep my family as first priority in my life.

X. "Charm is deceptive, and beauty is fleeting; but a woman who fears the LORD is to be praised" (Proverbs 31:30).

____It is not a secret that I love the Lord.
____My emphasis and desire is more focused on growing spiritually than on acquiring more things.

XII. "Give her the reward she has earned, and let her works bring her praise at the city gate" (Proverbs 31:31).

____My life shows evidence of "good fruit."
____Others recognize the hand of God in my life.

_____I have been awarded/rewarded for specific areas of ministry or productivity in my work.

Reflect on your answers to this survey. How do you measure up as a virtuous woman?

- Write about it in your journal.

- Consider the life of this virtuous woman:
    o What roles and responsibilities does she fill?
    o Can you find seasons of a woman's life represented?

    o Does the idea she is accomplishing this over a lifetime rather than simultaneously make her more approachable and believable?

    o What clues do you find that reveal her relationship with her true self?

    o What important relationship sums up the entire passage?

    o What do you have in common? Could the passage describe *you*?

The last question brings us full circle; the answer is *yes*! The virtuous woman is not just an ideal. She is me. She is you. She is every woman who commits to make God her most important relationship. Jesus turned the Samaritan woman's brokenness into beauty. She proves our potential for transformation too. As Jill and I have shared our stories, don't you see? Any woman—every woman—can be free!

GETTING TO KNOW GOD

The women in this chapter share examples of getting to know God. Let's take some time to reflect on the Samaritan woman's story in John 4, the godly example of the woman of virtue in Proverbs 31, Jill's testimony in the Woven letter, and my story in the *Getting to Know Me* section.

- What did you learn about God and His character through each of our stories?
- How did these stories speak into *your* life story, your journey with Jesus? What have you discovered about yourself through our lives and testimonies?
- Revisit the story of the Samaritan woman and imagine walking in her shoes.
    - o What was she thinking and feeling when she made the trip to the well?
    - o How did her interaction with Jesus change her perspective of herself, of God, of others?
    - o Why do you suppose she left when the disciples arrived?
    - o Why would she leave her vessel of water?

Could she have experienced what Jesus promised in John 4:13–14?

> Jesus answered, "Everyone who drinks this water will be thirsty again, but whoever drinks the water I give him will never thirst. Indeed, the water I give him will become in him a spring of water welling up to eternal life."

The Samaritan woman's thirst had been quenched! She immediately asked for this living water. "Sir, give me this water so that I won't get thirsty and have to keep coming here to draw water." This was her heartfelt prayer to God. She was asking for this miracle of transformation from the inside out—and she received it! She walked away from that well as a virtuous woman. It was just that simple. She became a "woman who fears the Lord."

The woman of virtue is confident. She knows who she is and whose she is. Free of anxiety, she sees no need to keep striving to impress others. She simply walks in God's grace. "She has no fear for her household ... she can laugh at the days to come." Verse 30 reveals her most sacred secret to success: "charm is deceptive and beauty is fleeting; but a woman who fears the Lord is to be praised."

Don't let this word *fear* scare you away from God. To fear God is to respect Him, to revere Him, and to be in awe of Him and aware of His sovereign position. The virtuous woman gives glory to God for her every attribute, accomplishment, and ability. There is no doubt in her mind—He is the source of her stability, her strength, and her excellence.

Being a virtuous woman is simply surrendering to a deeper dependence on God instead of operating in performance mode. As Jesus explained to the Samaritan woman, "'That's the kind of people the Father is out looking for: those who are simply and honestly themselves before him in their worship" (John 4:23).

- What do you need to change in order to rely more on the Lord's strength and less on your own abilities? To come in touch with your true self?

- Which area in your life is most in need of work/repair/ attention/surrender?
  o relationship with your self
  o family relationships
  o relationships with women
  o work relationships
  o relationship with the Lord

- Ask the Lord to help you set practical and spiritual goals for how you will make these changes. Write them down.

A PRAYER FOR YOU

Thoughtfully read and pray this prayer adapted from Romans 12:2, 1 Samuel 16:7, Jeremiah 29:11, and 2 Corinthians 3:18:

> Dear Father God,
>
> I do not want to conform any longer to the pattern of this world. I want to be transformed! Help me to renew my mind. Teach me how to do this.
>
> Lord, I am tired of doing things my way. Show me the things in my life I need to let go of, areas in my life that are in need of healing, and unhealthy relationships I need to surrender. Help me see others as You see them and to look upon the heart instead of judging outward appearances. Teach and instruct me, so I may be able to test and approve what Your will is—Your pleasing and perfect will, Your one-of-a-kind plans and purposes for my life. May I truly be engaged in a forever journey of being transformed, with ever-increasing glory through Your Holy Spirit.
>
> I pray this in Jesus's name. Amen.

AN ISSUE OF BLOOD

She had "an issue of blood." Sick. Unclean. She had consulted every doctor. No one could heal her. No one could help. She had no hope until she reached out in faith and touched the hem of Jesus's garment. She was set free.

We have an issue of blood. We need a divine blood transfusion. Only the blood of Jesus Christ can heal us, cleanse us, and set us free.

WHO DOES SHE THINK SHE IS?

There is only one problem on which all my existence,
my peace, and my happiness depend:
to discover myself in discovering God.
If I find Him I will find myself and if I find
my true self I will find Him.
—Thomas Merton[19]

If you are like me (and I'm guessing you are), you've looked at another woman with this initial reaction—*Who does she think she is?* Maybe she made you angry. You were disgusted by her attitude. She triggered your inner critic. In all fairness, it may have seemed legitimate to feel this way. She intentionally or unintentionally said or did something to offend you.

There are also times when it's not her fault at all. A woman who walks with confidence and speaks with grace arrives on the scene, and we can't help but think, *Just* who *does she think she is?* This woman is self-assured, at peace with her true self. Her joyful spirit points an invisible finger at our own self-loathing. We think, *Boy, she really thinks she's something*—even worse, we open mouth and insert foot by saying it.

What is really bothering us sounds more like this:
I wish I were more like her.
She's the real deal!

---

[19]   Thomas Merton, *New Seeds of Contemplation* (New York: New Directions, 1961).

She is a living example of what it is to be free.

The pain of our hearts speaks a well-worn message: *I'm not good enough* or *I'm not as good as this remarkable woman.* Satan has a heyday reminding us of every manipulative lie inscribed on our souls. Stirring old wounds and attacking our self-worth, he accomplishes his goal. He convinces us we are unworthy of healthy relationships. We pull away to isolate and insulate ourselves. Being "woven into a tapestry of love" becomes only an ideal. We are frozen in fear of female friendships.

The woman of virtue radiates qualities that make us feel inadequate. She seems too good to be true. How can we arrive at this place of peace and contentment in you being you and me being me? The Proverbs 31 woman challenges us to go further, to look deeper, to stretch outside our comfort zones:

> She gets up while it is still dark ... She sees that
> her trading is profitable, and her lamp does not
> go out at night. (Proverbs 31:15a, 18)

I know she's really got your panties in a bunch now. You're all stirred up, wondering, *Just exactly what kind of trading is she doing ... at night?* She gets up early *and* stays up late? She's obviously bragging about it if everyone knows her schedule. Most of us are either morning people or night people, but she claims to be both. When does this woman sleep?

Let's look at her from another perspective. Suppose this woman's "profitable trading" is with the Lord, and *that's* why she is up early and goes to bed late. What if her routine is to begin and end her day by spending time alone—with God? Now *that* is a different story!

WE HAVE ISSUES

Friend, our issues are not with each other. People are not the enemy. Our battle is between our false self and our true self. Our enemy is Satan, and our issue is with God. We construct a defensive roadblock, forcing God to take a detour around those deep places where our false selves store up fear, rejection, insecurity, envy, bitterness, and emotional pain. It seems easier to bury our issues than to deal with them. The truth of our reality is that we need an attitude adjustment that can only come through profitable trading with the Lord.

There is a woman in Mark 5:21-34 who knew what it was to have "issues." Although she was labeled by society as an unclean woman, she was confident that her trading with Jesus would be profitable. Go ahead and read about her in the book of Mark. I'll grab a cup of tea and join you!

SHE HAS ISSUES

There is a common language among our gender that we all understand—it's *that* time of the month. Over the centuries, this feminine issue has acquired many nicknames: menses, nature's course, Eve's curse, the monthly curse, ragging, on the rag, Aunt Flo's visit, on my period, having a period, period, and just simply "dot."

Medical experts now recognize there's even a period before the period: premenstrual syndrome. PMS is just an attempt to explain that our hormones are very much in charge of our emotions, no matter what time of the month it is. Regardless of what we call it, women everywhere share a common experience of what it means: cramping, irritability, chocolate, mood swings, bloating, depression, and more chocolate. (Yes, you have permission to eat chocolate. Aunt Flo said so!)

After reading this passage in Mark 5, let's imagine a period that was truly unending. Try to fathom what it would be like if Aunt Flo showed up at your door unexpectedly and stayed for weeks without any indication of leaving. The weeks turn to months, and months become years. This truly *would* be a curse!

The woman with the issue of blood had suffered for twelve years with nonstop bleeding. You thought you had issues? This woman had *issues*! The social implications of her era compounded her problem. She was considered culturally unclean, unable to be seen in public. Constant bleeding left her barren. Her "issue of blood" disqualified her from marriage because anyone who associated with her would be considered unclean too. She was totally alone.

Imagine the physical strain on her body, the exhaustion and anemia from losing so much blood. She also must have felt physically unclean. There were no tampons, minipads, or maxipads. Being "on the rag" was not just a figure of speech; it was literal. She was doomed for gloom.

Where could she turn? She exhausted all hope in medicines and physicians. For her, it was "been there, done that." The doctors couldn't come up with a reason or a remedy. They just took her money and sent her home, emotionally scarred and secluded.

If you have been afflicted with a chronic illness, you can relate to this woman's dilemma. Life was out of her control. Her body had betrayed her. Disease had taken over and had become her identity. Can you hear them whispering? *"She is the woman with the issue of blood!"*

Trapped inside her body and an outcast of society, she was hopeless and helpless, but she had not given up. Oh-h-h no! This woman refused to accept this as her doom. "Woe is me" was not her attitude. She was certain it was not God's plan for her life. She was made for more.

Good news about healings and miracles and love and acceptance delivered hope to her door. Jesus's preaching reached her ears and touched her heart. He was not caught up in religious rules and regulations. Jesus was an invitation to come out of hiding and be healed; to shake off her false self, uncover her true self, and reclaim her identity.

HER TRADING WAS PROFITABLE

It took courage for this woman to risk being seen in the crowd that day. According to Jewish law, it was illegal for a menstruating woman to even appear in public. (Yes, I'm wondering the same thing you are—how did the keepers of the law keep track of every woman's time of the month?) In this woman's case, we can be certain that people knew. They recognized her. We can read their minds: *Who does she think she is? She has no business being in public. She's unclean!*

She didn't let them stop her. Joining throngs of anxious people who wanted to see Jesus, she worked her way through the thick crowd. Weaving her way among this jungle of legs, she got close enough to stretch out her arm and ever so slightly brush her hand across the threads of Jesus's robe. By simply touching the hem of His garment, "Immediately her bleeding stopped and she felt in her body that she was freed from her suffering."[20]

Try to picture the sights, smells, and sounds in this crowd of people as though you are an eyewitness at the scene. Watch what Jesus does. Listen carefully to what He says.

> At once Jesus realized that power had gone out from him. He turned around in the crowd and asked "who touched my clothes?"
>
> "You see all the people crowding against you," his disciples answered, "and yet you can ask: 'Who touched me?'"
>
> Then the woman, knowing what had happened to her, came and fell at his feet and, trembling with fear, told him the whole truth. He said to her, "Daughter, your faith has healed you. Go in peace and be freed from your suffering." (Mark 5:28–34 NIV)

I love how discreet Jesus is. He does not identify this woman. We have no idea of her name; we only know her shame. She's written in the pages of history simply as the "woman with the issue of blood." He protects her confidentiality.

---

[20]   Mark 5:29 (NIV).

Jesus calls her "daughter," implying she is a child of God, a follower of Christ. Though He had never met her, Jesus knew her. Twelve years of pain and suffering. What had she been doing in this unending time alone? How did she muster up the courage this particular day to step out of her home?

I believe this woman had learned the secret of being a virtuous woman. "She knew that her trading was profitable."[21] She had been "trading" her sorrows, pain, and disease in prayer to the Lord. He was changing her from the inside out. This day in history culminated with a great exchange. The woman with the issue of blood traded her fear for faith. Her prayers were answered. She was healed!

Reading this passage, you might think, *Jesus didn't seem concerned about discretion when He demanded to know who touched Him.* True, she couldn't leave as discreetly as she had hoped. I see a much greater point to His purpose. Imagine if Jesus allowed our sweet friend to slip back into the crowd and go home—alone and unnoticed. Would she truly have been free to live the life she wanted? I don't think so!

She still would have been labeled as the woman with the issue of blood. She still would have been banned from appearing in public. Jesus went beyond healing her physical pain. By publicly affirming her physical healing, He set this woman free, socially and emotionally. She got the total package! She was truly *free.*

"The woman ... came and fell at his feet and, trembling with fear, told him the whole truth."

Our sister could have just slipped further into the crowd and disappeared. Instead, she faced her fear, fell at His feet in surrender, and spilled out the truth before Jesus. This brought completion to her healing. It served as a public confession of faith. Jesus affirmed her, "Daughter, your faith has healed you. Go in peace and be freed from your suffering." Together, they spoke her healing into existence. The trade was made.

The same Jesus who was sensitive to her is sensitive to

---

[21] Proverbs 31:15 (NIV).

us. He knows our issues. In fact, nothing about our lives goes unnoticed. He hears our every whisper and knows every thought that crosses our minds. He is aware of the tiniest movement we make toward Him. The moment we stretch out and reach for "the hem of His garment," He acknowledges and affirms us. He longs for us to come to Him but never forces Himself on us. A true gentleman, Jesus honors our freedom to choose. He is looking for those who, like the woman of virtue, the Samaritan woman, and the woman with the issue of blood, are "simply and honestly themselves."[22]

FEAR OR FREE?

The woman with the issue of blood was living in fear. She was destined to be free. What does she teach us? Ashamed of our pasts and anxious about the future, we spend much of our lives afraid of failing. We are consumed with thoughts of what others will think. This flood of fears points us to one common fear. We are afraid of pain. Fear is a roadblock in our spiritual journey. Our reaction to emotional pain is to avoid it, so we stuff it, squelch it, pray it away, do anything but allow ourselves to face it and feel it. All the while, our inner child longs to hear, "Daughter, your faith has healed you. Go in peace and be freed from your suffering." God wants us to be free. Pain can be our path to healing.

Let's think about how we are wonderfully made by God—to the extent that He wired us with an alarm system. When something or someone invades our bodies, it triggers the alarm and we begin feeling the symptoms—physical or emotional pain and discomfort. Imagine having chest pains and shortness of breath. We would waste no time getting to the ER in lieu of a heart attack. There is no shame in that, and we are quick to take steps to get help. We go to the doctor or hospital when we suffer physically. A cold or other virus requires rest to heal, but we don't take time to rest. We ask the

---

[22]   John 4:23 (the Message).

doctor for a prescription because we're simply too busy. We refuse to be still and wait it out. Believing we are invincible, we want to be known as one who keeps going—no matter what.

This resistance to rest is even more evident when it comes to emotional pain. Emotional pain is also a warning, but we react much differently. Our hearts are hurting, in need of healing, yet we tend to ignore, repress, or deny it. Most often, we seek the world's solutions for our emotional heart problems by filling our emptiness with physical and virtual relationships, cell phones, exercise, food, alcohol, work, social status, social media, family, television, shopping, volunteerism, good causes—endless busyness. All the while, we are playing hide-and-seek with God.

We lack the faith or courage to reach out and touch the hem of Jesus's robe. We avoid His still small voice wooing us to embrace our vulnerable inner child. Our false self and full calendar may divert our pain for a while, but eventually we wear ourselves out trying to bury our hurts and keep our plates spinning. It is only a matter of time until our self-constructed worlds implode. We cannot continue to live a lie.

Let's follow the example of the woman with the issue of blood. Imagine if she had not reached out in faith to Jesus that day. If she had allowed her fear of rejection, her false self to be in control, she would have been doomed to live the rest of her life alone with her pain and shame. Instead, she invested in profitable trading. Her pain became a gift that led her to Jesus.

This woman's situation was different than most. She was forced into solitude; we must voluntarily choose to enter. Lamentations 3:28 advises,

> When life is heavy and hard to take, go off by yourself. Enter the silence. Bow in prayer. Wait for Hope to appear. (MSG)

There is no need to recreate ourselves. God created us uniquely one of a kind. Morning, evening, anytime of the day or night, we can place our faith in Him and trust Him with our fears, and He will lead us to our *free me*—the person we are meant to be!

"WHO DOES HE THINK HE IS?"

Would it surprise you to know that Jesus gets this reaction too? Take a look at what took place on the Sabbath, shortly after our friend was healed from her issue of blood.

> On the Sabbath, he gave a lecture in the meeting place. He made a real hit, impressing everyone.
>
> "We had no idea he was this good!" they said. "How did he get so wise all of a sudden, get such ability?" But in the next breath they were cutting him down: "He's just a carpenter— Mary's boy. We've known him since he was a kid. We know his brothers, James, Justus, Jude, and Simon, and his sisters. **Who does he think he is?**" They tripped over what little they knew about him and fell, sprawling. And they never got any further.
>
> Jesus told them, "A prophet has little honor in his hometown, among his relatives, on the streets he played in as a child." Jesus wasn't able to do much of anything there—he laid hands on a few sick people and healed them, that's all. He couldn't get over their stubbornness. He left and made a circuit of the other villages, teaching. (Mark 6:1-6 MSG)

There it is, bold and brazen: *Who does he think he is?* Can you believe the audacity of these people to question the authority of Jesus? It's exactly what we have been discussing in regard to our reaction to women. They weren't criticizing Jesus because He was inferior. He superseded their expectations! First, they were impressed by His wisdom and ability to preach. Then they started fault-finding, unwilling to look beyond the surface. "They tripped over what little they knew about him ... and never got any further."

Haven't *we* done that with God? We get just close enough to hear some nuggets of truth and then get tripped up. It's too much for us. *Who does He think He is?* He is our ticket to freedom, but we are stuck in fear and lacking in faith.

"Jesus ... couldn't get over their stubbornness."

WHO DO YOU THINK YOU ARE?

I hope you are picking up this truth: being "free to be—you and me" is totally *not* what our culture would say it is. The freedom we're talking about has nothing to do with how many Facebook friends we accumulate, how full our closets are, what our career status is, where our children attend school, or how good we look. Being "free to be—you and me" does not follow the philosophy "If it feels good, do it!"

Many of the things on which we place false importance actually *don't* make us feel good, do they? They create unnecessary busyness and stress. We put this pressure on ourselves! Why is it so hard to just be who we are? We dress for other women, seeking compliments because we believe the lie that we are in competition. We send Christmas letters reporting the "highlights" of our year. We prefer to talk about our kids' achievements but not their disappointments or needs. We post something online, waiting eagerly for others to notice and acknowledge how great our lives must be. Becoming caught up in our own insecurities, we spend precious time and energy trying to hide them. *Why is it so important to us?* We are consumed with what others think.

God's value system is totally different from the world's standard. The "free me" we are talking about is the freedom of being the person God intended *you* and *me* to *be*! No more insecurity because we are secure in the Father who created us. He wants each of us to embrace the unique individual He has woven together—with His own hands—in our mothers' wombs.[23] God wants us to be consumed with His thoughts. He is the one who made you and loves you beyond measure.

> Don't copy the behavior and customs of this world, but let God transform you into a new person by changing the way you think. Then you will learn to know God's will for you, which is good and pleasing and perfect.[24]

Do you realize there has never been a single person like you since the very beginning of humankind? You are *one of a kind*! We live in a world where there are few original thoughts, where people protect their copyrights. Companies put a patent on their products and register their trademarks, only to discover someone else has copied it or maybe even had the same idea. It's an open market for exploitation of words, photos, products, and even people. People hack into our accounts and pretend to be us. We are bombarded with social media and sound bites—messages that have traveled so far from their source they become little more than gossip. If they had any original value at all, they have depreciated to untruth, yet we regard them as truth.

This, my friend, is truth: In the midst of this repetitive, competitive world, God created *you* as His masterpiece. You are His one-of-a-kind creation who has never been and never will be duplicated. This is a powerful truth! Listen carefully to God's Word:

> How blessed is God! And what a blessing he is! He's the Father of our Master, Jesus Christ, and takes us to the high places of blessing in him.
>
> Long before he laid down earth's foundations, he had us in mind, had settled on us as the

---

23   Psalm 139.
24   Romans 12:2 (NLT).

focus of his love, to be made whole and holy by his love.

Long, long ago he decided to adopt us into his family through Jesus Christ. (What pleasure he took in planning this!) He wanted us to enter into the celebration of his lavish gift-giving by the hand of his beloved Son.

Because of the sacrifice of the Messiah, his blood poured out on the altar of the Cross, we're a free people—free of penalties and punishments chalked up by all our misdeeds.

And not just barely free, either. Abundantly free!

He thought of everything, provided for everything we could possibly need, letting us in on the plans he took such delight in making. He set it all out before us in Christ, a long-range plan in which everything would be brought together and summed up in him, everything in deepest heaven, and everything on planet earth.

It's in Christ that we find out who we are and what we are living for. Long before we first heard of Christ and got our hopes up, he had his eye on us, had designs on us for glorious living, part of the overall purpose he is working out in everything and everyone.

It's in Christ that you, once you heard the truth and believed it (this Message of your salvation), found yourselves home free—signed, sealed, and delivered by the Holy Spirit. This signet from God is the first installment on what's coming, a reminder that we'll get everything

God has planned for us, a praising and glorious life.

I ask—ask the God of our Master, Jesus Christ, the God of glory—to make you intelligent and discerning in knowing him personally, your eyes focused and clear, so that you can see exactly what it is he is calling you to do, grasp the immensity of this glorious way of life he has for his followers, oh, the utter extravagance of his work in us who trust him—endless energy, boundless strength! (Ephesians 1:3–19 MSG)

Every one of us has "an issue of blood." Ever since Adam and Eve sinned in the garden of Eden, both men and women have been cursed with death. We have unclean blood. God offers us a divine blood transfusion.[25]

Because of the sacrifice of the Messiah, his blood poured out on the altar of the Cross, we're a free people—free of penalties and punishments chalked up by all our misdeeds ... Abundantly free! (Ephesians 1:7 MSG)

GETTING TO KNOW ME

I can relate to the woman with the issue of blood. Divorce left me feeling unclean, ashamed, and isolated, with a precious toddler to care for. I needed a friend and a job. Let's face it—*I needed a new life.* When options seemed limited, I remarried.

Shame and fear accompanied me into my second marriage. My husband "Vince"[26] and I were self-employed; we each grew our own businesses. We worked together, played together, and did everything as a family. We became financially comfortable

---

[25] For more info, visit www.peacewithgod.net, or see chapter 7.
[26] Not his real name.

and were respected in our community. Our relationships were loving and understanding, and life seemed perfect.

When my daughter, Nicole, was preparing for high school, we began discussing her college options. In our conversations, my husband shared his dreams for us as empty-nesters. This made me increasingly uncomfortable, but I didn't understand why. When I finally acknowledged my feelings, I was shocked to discover, after ten years of marriage, I was afraid to be alone with my husband. Something was terribly wrong with our picture-perfect world!

So I began a prayer vigil of walking the perimeter of our seven-acre property, crying and seeking answers for my life and marriage. Once, twice, sometimes three times a day, I would walk until my legs could barely carry me. I was awakened to my situation and forced to admit how miserable I had become.

At first, I thought it was me, that I was weary of the stress required to run my business. As an artist, I could sell everything I produced, which had pushed me to fourteen-hour workdays and landed me at the point of burnout. I began to dream about going to college and starting a new career. When I shared my dream with Vince, I was surprised at how calmly he responded. But a few minutes later, he became violent—I heard dishes breaking, yelling, cursing, and items hurtling across the kitchen. My prayers and cries began exposing the lies.

In my desperation for an answer, God slowly unveiled the truth of our marriage. Over the years, Vince had drawn me away from friends and family, isolating and monopolizing me. He scrutinized every minute of my time; even going to the grocery store was stressful, as I knew he was watching the clock. I felt like I was constantly walking on eggshells, afraid of upsetting him. The pressure and stress became tangible. I knew things just weren't right, but I still could not pinpoint what was wrong.

My prayers initiated an unstoppable force that brought forth truth and light. I noticed strange behavior—things he said and did just didn't make sense. When I questioned him, he made me feel like an idiot, accusing me of being suspicious or jealous. He drilled me with words until I was emotionally limp and then left me feeling guilty, stupid, and ashamed. Life as we knew it was a carefully constructed deception.

The situation escalated when we took Nicole and Anna, Vince's daughter, on a family vacation to the Bahamas. Being away from his controlled environment, he reverted to inflammatory remarks and embarrassed me by publicly expressing that I was his "property." At the beach, I sensed he had offended my daughter in some way. When I questioned her, she said guardedly, "I'll tell you later."

After returning home, I shared my concerns with one of my few remaining friends. As we talked, it became obvious—I needed to schedule a mother-daughter talk with Nicole as soon as possible.

It was a Friday night when I shared my thoughts of going to college and asked how Nicole felt about it. I told her how Vince reacted; how I was struggling to figure out what was wrong. I asked if she had noticed anything or if he had frightened her in any way. This opened a door to her deepest, darkest secret. As her story unraveled, my worst fears were acknowledged. My husband had been sexually abusing my daughter.

Despite all the questions and concerns I already had, Nicole's response to my questions brought shock, confusion, and even fear. It made perfect sense, yet I wondered why I hadn't seen this offense. The pieces fit like a sinister puzzle. As strange as it sounds, my prayers were answered in this one mother-daughter conversation. I knew there was only one right thing to do and that was to protect my daughter. With absolutely no idea what to do or how to do it, I made a vow to her: "Don't worry; I will take care of it." I had no idea how I was going to fulfill that promise.

This was new territory for me. Despite the fact that my heart was broken to pieces, I made it through the weekend by planning our escape. In my husband's presence, I pretended nothing had changed. When he left the room, I wept silently, grieving the loss of my daughter's innocence and my husband's betrayal.

On Monday, I saw an attorney, knowing Vince was going

out of town for several hours that evening. I returned home and followed the attorney's advice. As soon as Vince left for his appointment, I packed our minivan and went to my parents' house. He returned to a note on the counter, telling him where I was and that I needed some time away. Vince came knocking on the door at ten o'clock that night, attacking me with words. When he realized I was not backing down, he finally left. I called Children's Services and reported my husband for childhood sexual abuse. When Nicole and I went to bed that night at my parents' house, I told her, "We have to pray and believe together that whatever happens, it will be God's best for everyone involved." I clung to our prayer with faith, believing God would honor it.

It was the first day of my most frightening week, and it was destined to become the defining moment of my life. The next morning we were interviewed by the police and Children's Services. Later in the day, I received a call from the police detective. She said they had interviewed my husband. Concerned for our safety, she urged me to leave town with Nicole for the night. We went to a hotel in the city.

I couldn't believe how incredibly freeing it was just to go to a movie and dinner with my daughter. Most mothers do this all the time with their children. For me, it was a first! Walking across the parking lot into the theater, I felt so light. With every step I took, I saw a vision of shackles and chains falling from my arms and legs. I had no idea how complicated and controlled my life with Vince had been. I was imprisoned, but God was leading me to freedom.

Because this injustice occurred under my own roof and to my own daughter, an inner strength moved me beyond my circumstances. It was so very hard: The walls came down and pain came crashing in. All week Vince relentlessly questioned friends and relatives, trying to find us. We were hiding, afraid for our lives. God so clearly protected us. Toward the end of the week, I received a call from my attorney. She said a hearing had been scheduled. Checking the date, I noticed it was Nicole's first day as a freshman in high school. My daughter would face him in court and be interrogated to prove her innocence and his guilt. I cried out to God, "This cannot be the answer to our prayer that whatever happens, it will be the best for everyone involved!"

I didn't see it on the horizon, but there would be no trial. In the midst of this tragedy came another tragedy. The next day, he committed suicide. The case was closed, and we received a letter stating that the charges had been substantiated. He had proven his own guilt. He was gone—completely out of the picture. No more fear of retaliation. No more hiding from him. Instead, we had a funeral to arrange in the midst of a huge realm of emotional pain.

In the case of a suicide, everyone wants someone to blame. I shouldered the blame to protect my daughter's innocence, leaving everyone to believe he took his life because I had left him. Sometimes I felt so alone, yet I had to persevere for my daughter's sake. He left me holding his bag of rubbish, the guilt and shame of his life and death. I was the one who had to face relatives and friends. He left me wondering, *How did life drop me off at this doorstep?*

Endless questions circled like a flock of buzzards in my mind. Everything I had believed and trusted about my husband and our life together was suddenly a lie, a cover-up for his sexual sin. I'd been living in fear for nearly eleven years without even realizing it.

Like the woman with the issue of blood, God heard my prayers in my years of seclusion. He increased my faith, giving me strength to take my issue public. When we touched the hem of His garment, Jesus said to me and my girl, "Go in peace and be freed from your suffering."[27]

We had been living in fear. We were destined to be free.

GETTING TO KNOW THE VIRTUOUS WOMAN

My husband's death left me a crumpled mess. Now a widow and again a single mom, my life seemed barren and as dry

---

[27] Mark 5:34.

as a desert. My future felt like shifting sand beneath my feet. I cried out to God for wisdom. He led me to the book of Proverbs, one of five wisdom books of the Bible (Job, Psalms, Proverbs, Ecclesiastes, and Song of Songs) and also to the home of the virtuous woman. He spoke so clearly to me through Proverbs 3:5-6:

> "Trust in the LORD with all your heart and lean not on your own understanding; in all your ways submit to him, and he will make your path straight."

This verse became my mantra for survival. I continually rehearsed it in my mind, allowing it to soak into my heart. Reading this passage as a word from God enabled me to truly trust Him with every decision in every aspect of my life and future.

God blessed me abundantly for my step of faith. I was willing to give up my husband, home, marriage, livelihood, reputation—everything to protect my daughter. I could never have imagined how God would move on my behalf. I inherited everything. But I also had to quickly learn how to manage our property and financial affairs. Even buying a new lawn mower took me out of my comfort zone. So I determined to make no decision without praying and seeking God's answer. When I gave Him this level of control over my future, the transformation was amazing. At a time when I trusted no one, I placed my trust in God. It was the greatest decision I have ever made. He is a trustworthy God.

I didn't have to wallow in a state of confusion, listening to the multitude of opinions on how to pick up the pieces of my life. He *made my paths straight*. His path led me straight to His good and perfect plan.

> "For I know the plans I have for you," declares the LORD, "plans to prosper you and not to harm you, plans to give you hope and a future. Then you will call on me and come and pray to me,

and I will listen to you. You will seek me and find me when you seek me with all your heart."[28]

I sought Him with all my heart and discovered it truly was His plan for me to go to college. Six months later, I became a college student. In those months following Vince's death, I spent much of my time grappling with the big picture of life. I wanted answers—and I wanted them directly from God.

How did life lead me to this dead-end road?

Why me, Lord?

How could all these things happen to me?

The more I sought Him, the more I truly found Jesus. The more I found Him, the more I discovered my true self. Thomas Merton's quote at the beginning of this chapter rings true. I would never have found myself if I had not discovered God. Submitting to this time of solitude and seeking led me to my God-planned destiny.

God was calling me into ministry. It became common for me to wake in the middle of the night, impressed to journal what I was hearing in my head. Often it was a word of prayer for someone I knew, sometimes someone I barely knew. The prayers of my own heart and answers to my questions came forth as I wrote. The Bible became so alive to me! I found myself writing what seemed to be sermons. One such morning, I asked God, "Is this really you, Lord? Are you waking me so energized at three o'clock every morning? Are these words from you or just my imagination?" When I opened my Bible in the next moment, my eyes fell upon these words in Isaiah 50:4:

> The Sovereign LORD has given me an instructed tongue, to know the word that sustains the weary. He wakens me morning by morning, wakens my ear to listen like one being taught. (NIV)

---

[28] Jeremiah 29:11–13 (NIV).

My trading was profitable. The Lord was affirming that I was becoming a woman of virtue.

"Who does this virtuous woman think she is?" She is a woman who spends time in prayer, seeks the Lord's wisdom and direction in her life, and listens for His answers "like one being taught."

> She gets up while it is still dark ... She sees that her trading is profitable, and her lamp does not go out at night ...[29]

The only way we overcome circumstances in our lives and attitudes of the heart is in prayer and the Word of God. There lies the straight road to becoming this woman of virtue. God wants you, me, and every woman to be at peace with who He created us to be, what He has destined us to do, and to do so with confidence and courage because of His Spirit living in us.

Those of us who've tasted what it means to be *free to be me* can encourage and mentor those who are waiting for someone to pass them a permission slip to be free.

It is my pleasure to introduce you to Kay, a woman God sent my way.

> I can identify with the woman who needed to get to Jesus to touch the hem of his garment. She needed physical healing. I needed mind, body, and soul healing.
>
> Like this woman who exhausted everything humanly possible, I tried everything. She pursued physicians. I pursued counselors, psychiatrists, drugs, and alcohol, with several respites on a mental health floor. No one could heal the pain in my heart. I needed to get to Jesus.
>
> I had been a Christian for years, taught Bible study, and even spoke at women's retreats. But then life happened—thirty years of abuse

---

[29] Proverbs 31:15, 18.

from my husband, doubts, disappointments, a terminal illness, my husband's death, and bankruptcy. My friends deserted me. My church let me down. After years of ongoing battering, I began to argue with God. After humbly submitting these events to Him, I decided the Christian life just didn't work—at least not for me.

After a seven-year sabbatical from Christ, His love, grace, and mercy began to woo me back. I had no idea how to go there. I asked God to somehow deliver me from the hurts and brokenness of the past and reveal Himself in a new way. Then I encountered Woven Women.

Six months later (though I was still on the sidelines), someone paid for me to go to the Woven Quiet Retreat, "Hello Love." I went reluctantly, thinking it was no use. But *wow*!

Cindy had us create a scrapbook page to share our journeys. Everyone created these beautiful pages, but mine was a black piece of paper with the word BROKEN written in glitter glue. I found a picture of a vase of flowers, cut it into many pieces, and glued it on the paper.

Somehow through the process of making my BROKEN paper and honestly going through the different prayer and journaling stations, God began to saturate my spirit. His Holy Spirit fell on me with such power that I could do nothing but respond to His love, mercy, and grace. Each station went from my brain to my heart and came out through my hand. As I wrote in my journal, God completely healed and restored my soul.

Woven Women has been a life-changing experience for me. My friend Cindy Stiverson was God's woman, in God's place, in God's time, doing God's will, and the results brought tremendous eternal value.

I love you, Cindy, and will be forever grateful.
—Kay, a Woven Woman of virtue

God wasted no time at all in putting Kay to work applying her lifetime of experience in His Word. She is actively writing and leading Bible studies for women. I am so proud of her.

If you are a woman of virtue in waiting, I, Cynthia K. Stiverson, give you, _____ [*your name*] permission to be *free to be you*. God created you for greater things than these![30]

GETTING TO KNOW YOU

My friend, we've touched on many things in this chapter that may have stirred up hurts and past pain. Reflect on your reading of the woman with the issue of blood and the story behind the story of my husband's death. What is the pain of your heart? Journal those feelings and ask God to lead you during this time of profitable trading. I'm praying for you as I write.

Let's refer back to the section in this chapter called *Fear or Free?*

- Ask God to help identify your biggest fear in life.
  - o   Write it down.
  - o   Describe it.
- Ask God to take you to the very source of that fear and pain.
  - o   How did it begin, and how did it gain control?
  - o   How did that initial incident snowball into a series of incidents over the years?
  - o   Have you surrendered this to God and conquered this fear?
- How has your fear of pain prevented your healing from wounds of the past?

---

[30]   John 14:12.

o   What are the vices you've used to numb your pain, fill the hole in your soul, and feed your false self?
o   Will you trust God to trade your fear for faith?
o   Can you draw the courage to reach out and just brush your hand against the hem of Jesus's robe?

Without rushing this time with the Lord, close your eyes in prayer as you focus your entire attention on Him. Envision yourself as the woman with the issue of blood touching the hem of His garment. Ask for His healing. Wait for His answer. Allow Him to speak to you. Write down the words, images, and impressions that come to you in this still, quiet moment with the Lord. Thank Him for His presence in your life, His power to heal, and His desire to dwell in those innermost places of your soul.

I pray that your trading is profitable.

GETTING TO KNOW GOD

We tend to think that "getting to know God" is about reading and memorizing scripture, growing in our knowledge of God's attributes and the history of His people, and studying His Word. This is great and important, but unfortunately we can do these things and still not know God personally and intimately. We can be tempted to fill our heads with knowledge *about* God without ever coming close to having a vital relationship *with* God. This intimate relationship with God is necessary because He is the only one who can fill the hole in our souls with His unfathomable, unending love. He leaves us breathless for more of Him and less of what this world has to offer. This is my longing for you, my friend: "to know this love that surpasses knowledge—that you may be filled to the measure of all the fullness of God" (Ephesians 3:19).

So let's take another look at Proverbs 31:15 and 31:18,

which have set the stage for this chapter. Take a few minutes to compare and contrast them with Psalm 55:16–17, below.

> She gets up while it is still dark … She sees that her trading is profitable, and her lamp does not go out at night. (Proverbs 31:15, 18)

> But I call to God, and the LORD saves me. Evening, morning and noon I cry out in distress, and he hears my voice. (Psalm 55:16–17)

What do you see? How do these verses relate to each other? Do you see how this psalm further illustrates how the woman of virtue spends her time? No wonder her trading is profitable! She's totally dependent upon the Lord to guide and give meaning to her life.

One of my favorite passages of scripture is the first few chapters of Proverbs. I love this metaphor that wisdom is a woman. As you read, visualize this woman. Listen with your heart to these verses and take note of phrases that touch you to the core of your being:

> Wisdom calls aloud in the street, she raises her voice in the public squares; at the head of the noisy streets she cries out, in the gateways of the city she makes her speech: How long will you simple ones love your simple ways? (Proverbs 1:20–22a NIV)

> Lay hold of my words with all your heart;
> keep my commands and you will live.
> Get wisdom, get understanding; do not forget my words or swerve from them.

> Do not forsake wisdom, and she will protect you;
> love her, and she will watch over you.
> Wisdom is supreme; therefore get wisdom.
> Though it cost you all you have, get understanding.

Esteem her, and she will exalt you;
embrace her, and she will honor you.
She will set a garland of grace on your head and
present you with a crown of splendor. (Proverbs
4:4–9 NIV)

Picture this beautiful woman, Wisdom, who stands at the intersection of your busy life. She expects that you will acknowledge her presence and respect her advice. Wisdom's soft voice beckons you to slow down, to stop and listen. She wants to warn you of things to come, to help you through this busy day, and to bring divine appointments your way. Yet you whiz right past her.

Can you see this woman in your mind? Read this passage again. Then close your eyes and imagine her.

I see a beautiful woman of virtue, this woman of wisdom, standing on the street corner. She is the most beautiful being, dressed in sheer-white clothes that blow lightly in the wind. She is angelic—soft-spoken, gentle, and so unobtrusive that she is almost invisible. Yet she is certainly there. She is by no means weak. She is exceptionally strong, but her strength rises from within. Wisdom doesn't force herself on you, but her words are profound. She longs to share all that she knows about your life—insights that would heal your past and forewarnings that will guide you through today, tomorrow, and the next day. She holds the answers of your heart's questions about your past, present, and eternity.

Wisdom stands at the main intersection of life and cries out as you pass, yet you just go about your business and do things in your own power and strength, according to your limited understanding and human ability. Do you hear her whispering? "If you'll just touch the hem of my garment ... you ... will ... be ... free."

This woman is a beautiful metaphor of the Holy Spirit of God who lives within us when we give our hearts to Him. The Spirit of God is the inner voice that never pressures us but gently guides us if we take time to listen. This is a reminder that our trading with God is always profitable. Her hope is for us to truly cry out to Him "evening, morning, and at noon."[31]

- Let's go back to your journal entries in the *Getting to Know You* section.
  - o Confess to God your sin of making gods of other things (your schedule, your past, your family, your pain) by putting them first, ahead of Him. Ask Him to cleanse you of everything in your heart, your home, and your life that is attached to that sin. Allow Him to show you what those things are. If there is something in your home that needs to be removed, take it to the trash so the enemy cannot use it to tempt you.
  - o Now pray and surrender whatever God is showing you to surrender.
  - o Ask Him to fill the hole in your soul with His Holy Spirit.
- Read the verses about wisdom again.
  - o Observe all the benefits of beginning your day with wisdom. You'll discover even more if you open your Bible to Proverbs and read with an open heart and ears.
  - o Write yourself a note in your journal, a commitment to not forsake Wisdom but to embrace her with all of your heart and life.[32]

Make it your goal to receive this "garland of grace and crown of splendor."[33] Women will see you and say, "Who does she think she is?" And someone who knows your heart will affirm, "Why, she's a woman of virtue! Isn't she fabulous?" Imagine how being free to be you can set other women free too. Pray that by your example of truly knowing and loving God, others will long to know God and become their true selves.

I'm sending you a hug today. You've come a long way!

---

[31] Psalm 55:16-17.
[32] Proverbs 4:5.
[33] Proverbs 4:9.

A PRAYER FOR YOU

Today we are praying my favorite prayer. It is the prayer that the apostle Paul prayed for the church at Ephesus, recorded in Ephesians 3:14–21 (NIV). I want you to first read it as it is written, for the church. Then read it again for *you* by changing the pronouns to first person (for example, change the *you* to *me* or *I*). I pray this will become the prayer of your heart before God.

> For this reason I kneel before the Father, from whom every family in heaven and on earth derives its name. I pray that out of his glorious riches he may strengthen you with power through his Spirit in your inner being, so that Christ may dwell in your hearts through faith. And I pray that you, being rooted and established in love, may have power, together with all the Lord's holy people, to grasp how wide and long and high and deep is the love of Christ, and to know this love that surpasses knowledge— that you may be filled to the measure of all the fullness of God.
>
> Now to him who is able to do immeasurably more than all we ask or imagine, according to his power that is at work within us, to him be glory in the church and in Christ Jesus throughout all generations, forever and ever! Amen.

"FREE TO BE ME"

Buried beneath the debris and demands of life, your true self awaits. Hurting. Yearning. Longing to emerge from the ashes; to become the person God created in your mother's womb; to fully embrace your destiny.

Jesus is pleading, "Come out. Be healed. Be free!"

WHERE DID SHE GET THAT OUTFIT?

4

It's you I like.
It's not the things you wear.
It's not the way you do your hair.
But it's you I like, the way you are right now,
the way down deep inside you.
Not the things that hide you ...
It's you I like.
—Mr. (Fred) Rogers

"Where did you get that outfit?" How many times have you been asked that question? I tend to hear this often because the free me loves to express myself artistically. The question is usually followed with, "Well, *you* can pull it off!" (I'm never quite sure if that's a compliment.)

For me, getting dressed is like applying paint to a fresh canvas. Sometimes women ask where I shop and how I find things that coordinate so well. What's my secret? When I see something I feel connected to and the price seems like a bargain, I buy it. The real magic happens when I bring an item home to discover it perfectly completes an ensemble. I love when it all comes together. It was worth waiting for!

The secret behind my secret is bigger than the outfit. I have come to know who I truly am. There is no need to imitate someone else's style. I aim to reflect my own uniqueness—what makes me *me*. When I try something on, even if it looks great, I ask myself, "Is this really me, or do I like it because my friend would like it?" If I can't honestly say it's my style, it goes back on the rack. Otherwise, it hangs in my closet, unworn, with tags included, until years later. Have you "been there, done that"?

Being true to being me has become a front-row seat to the beauty of watching women step out in their own styles. My courage empowers others to embrace their own style of different; to step out of the dressing room in the uniqueness of their true selves. We all possess this precious gift, to give each other permission to be *free to be—you and me*!

WHERE DID SHE GET THAT OUTFIT?

I'm sure that just as someone has asked you "Where did you get that outfit?" as a compliment, there have been times when the question tormented your mind as a derogatory thought towards your rival. Whether the outfit is in poor taste or good taste, whether the gal looks dynamite or disgusting, the vicious thought cycle begins.

If we could meet the woman of virtue in Proverbs 31, I'm guessing we would ask, "Where did she get that outfit?" This woman "is clothed with strength and dignity; she can laugh at the days to come."[34]

A virtuous woman dresses with integrity because royal blood runs through her veins—the blood of Christ. She uses discretion in how she dresses to avoid giving the wrong cues. This is much bigger than the clothes she wears and the way she struts her stuff. The virtuous woman exercises discernment in her relationships. She is cautious with her body language and carefully chooses her words, especially with men. She seeks God's protection over her emotions to prevent unhealthy attachments. Everything about her is an expression of her relationship with Christ. This is what it says about her wardrobe:

---

[34] Proverbs 31:25.

When it snows, she has no fear for her household;
for all of them are clothed in scarlet.

She makes coverings for her bed; she is clothed
in fine linen and purple.[35]

Sounds like this woman is dressed like royalty—because she is! In biblical times, linen was worn by the wealthy because it allowed the air to circulate, keeping the body cool. In the Middle Eastern climate, this would have been quite a luxury. There were different types of linen, but the finest linen was used for priests and worn by kings, queens, and members of their royal courts.

The color purple is also connected to royalty. The color was achieved by making a dye from mollusks, a shellfish in the Mediterranean Sea. It was a pricey dye, as it took 250,000 mollusks to make one ounce of dye. Purple was the color God required in the tabernacle. The color purple was reserved for royal robes and garments of the wealthy.

Aren't you curious? Where did she get that outfit? How can she afford to dress like this? Who is this woman anyway? She is not your typical female. Where do we find a woman like this?

WHO CAN FIND HER?

"Who can find a virtuous woman?" This question begins the poem in the King James Version of Proverbs 31:10. The poem is believed to have been written by the mother of King Lemeul, advising her son of the type of woman he should seek for his bride. Being the only place in the Bible where this king is mentioned, Lemeul could possibly be a pet name for King Solomon. If so, the author would be Bathsheba, who had a not-so-perfect life. She speaks from the heart of one who knows the forgiving grace of God.

If you are the mother of boys, you can likely relate to

---

[35] Proverbs 31:21–22.

the king's mother. In reading this list of qualifications, it is obvious—not just any woman is good enough for her son. It's no surprise this poem begins with the question of whether she can even be found. This is not your average woman. She is rare but worth the search.

It reminds me of the story of *Cinderella.* The king and queen are getting older, preparing to retire. They decide it is time for their son to find a wife. In the story of *Cinderella*, it was the prince who was very particular. His mother could not understand what he was waiting for. He had his pick of every available woman in the kingdom. As for the prince, not just any wife would do.

No matter how many times I watch the movie, the prince's struggle to find a bride entrances me, even though I *know* how it's going to turn out. My favorite version is Rodgers and Hammerstein's *Cinderella* that I watched annually as a little girl, starring beautiful Lesley Anne Warren. She brings to life the question posed in Proverbs 31: "Who can find a virtuous woman?"

In the opening scene the prince was traveling and stopped to rest, as fate would have it, at the home of Cinderella. His first impression was probably, *Where did she get that outfit?* She was dressed in rags, and her clothes and face were dirty from the cinders, yet the prince was taken by her countenance.

He noticed she was frightened to approach him, yet she offered him a drink of water. As she went for the cup of water, he said to his horseman, "Her kindness has overcome her fear." When she returned, the prince was intrigued and began asking questions about her family. When he asked about her father, she replied, "He sleeps in heaven."

I believe the prince's search for Cinderella began long before he found the glass slipper. His search began in this initial meeting, the moment he came face-to-face with this virtuous woman. Cinderella was unassuming, having the innocence of a child. Her gentle spirit set her apart from every woman he knew. It was as if he had seen an angel. He would never settle for just any woman; he was searching for a woman whose outward beauty reflected the beauty of her heart. He was searching for a woman of virtue.

We are all familiar with how the story goes. The king and queen hold a ball so the prince can choose his bride among all the young ladies in the land. Despite Cinderella's wicked stepmother's and stepsisters' attempts to keep her from attending, the fairy godmother appeared and miraculously transformed Cinderella. It was the ultimate makeover from head to toe, the most beautiful outfit and accessories a girl could imagine. Her dream of going to the ball came true. She even had her own regal coach and drivers.

Arriving fashionably just in time, she entered the palace. It was as if the whole world stood still. Everyone stopped and stared. She was so radiant and glowing; she lit up the entire ballroom. Imagine what the other maidens were thinking: *Where did she get that outfit?* Little did they know she had a divine intervention. The transformation was so amazing that even her stepmother and stepsisters had no clue who she was. But oh, were they bitterly jealous and threatened by this unknown beauty. Cinderella was the total package!

You couldn't help but love her, and the prince obviously did. It was the ultimate love story. Their eyes met, and the spark was lit. They swept the dance floor in perfect unison until the clock struck twelve. There was one stipulation. Cinderella could only stay until midnight because at midnight, her clothes would again turn to rags, the horses to mice, and the coach to a pumpkin. As she ran up the steps and out of the castle, she lost her tiny glass slipper. The heart broken prince was left holding the slipper. Thus, his search for a bride became a search for the woman whose foot could fit into the tiny glass slipper.

"Who can find a virtuous woman?" The question haunts each line like a mystery novel as we read Proverbs 31. We feel we have been cast as a character in the Cinderella story. We read this passage of scripture, wondering, *Who does this shoe fit? Could it possibly be me? Or am I just one of the average ho-hum women in the palace? Could I be the bride he is looking for? Could I possibly be Cinderella? Would the prince choose me?*

One thing always bothered me—the size of the glass slipper. It was never too big for any of the women; it was always too small. I felt awkward and clumsy because I knew my feet were big. Even as a little girl, I remember thinking, *There is no way that slipper would* ever *fit my foot!*

Reading this poem in Proverbs, you may have that same reaction. With each verse, the glass slipper appears to shrink smaller and smaller, eliminating more women and making us question if it would actually fit anyone. Let's take another look at this princess in Proverbs.

10 Who can find a virtuous woman? She is worth far more than rubies.
11 Her husband has full confidence in her and lacks nothing of value.
12 She brings him good, not harm, all the days of her life.
13 She selects wool and flax and works with eager hands.
14 She is like the merchant ships, bringing her food from afar.
15 She gets up while it is still dark; she provides food for her family and portions for her servant girls.
16 She considers a field and buys it; out of her earnings she plants a vineyard.
17 She sets about her work vigorously; her arms are strong for her tasks.
18 She sees that her trading is profitable, and her lamp does not go out at night.
19 In her hand she holds the distaff and grasps the spindle with her fingers.
20 She opens her arms to the poor and extends her hands to the needy.
21 When it snows, she has no fear for her household; for all of them are clothed in scarlet.
22 She makes coverings for her bed; she is clothed in fine linen and purple.
23 Her husband is respected at the city gate, where he takes his seat among the elders of the land.
24 She makes linen garments and sells them, and supplies the merchants with sashes.

25 She is clothed with strength and dignity; she can laugh at the days to come.

26 She speaks with wisdom, and faithful instruction is on her tongue.

27 She watches over the affairs of her household and does not eat the bread of idleness.

28 Her children arise and call her blessed; her husband also, and he praises her:

29 "Many women do noble things, but you surpass them all."

30 Charm is deceptive, and beauty is fleeting; but a woman who fears the LORD is to be praised.

31 Give her the reward she has earned, and let her works bring her praise at the city gate. (Proverbs 31:10–31 KJV)

Sounds like the happily-ever-after life of Cinderella, doesn't it? It seems easier to just pretend the virtuous woman is only a fairytale or a fantasy. That would certainly relieve us of the pressure of filling her shoes. But then, there is the fact that this *is* the Bible we are reading. So where do we find this virtuous woman?

FROM PEASANT TO PRINCESS

Beloved, have you noticed? There is a real-life Cinderella story tucked right in the middle of the Old Testament between Nehemiah and Job—an entire book of the Bible devoted to a woman of virtue. The book of Esther is the story of an unknown orphaned Jewish girl who arose from among all the other women in the kingdom and became queen.

The scene opens with a huge banquet in the palace of King Xerxes the Great. He went all out for this banquet. It was extravagant. He even dressed the courtyard in fine linen and purple.

> For six months he put on exhibit the huge wealth of his empire and its stunningly beautiful royal splendors. At the conclusion of the exhibit, the

king threw a weeklong party for everyone living in Susa, the capital—important and unimportant alike. The party was in the garden courtyard of the king's summer house. The courtyard was elaborately decorated with white and blue cotton curtains tied with linen and purple cords to silver rings on marble columns. Silver and gold couches were arranged on a mosaic pavement of porphyry, marble, mother-of-pearl, and colored stones. Drinks were served in gold chalices, each chalice one-of-a-kind. The royal wine flowed freely—a generous king! (Esther 1:4–7 the Message)

While King Xerxes the Great was holding his banquet, his wife, Queen Vashti, was holding a banquet for all the women in the palace. In reading what happens next, it seems there was some real bonding taking place among these women. They were discovering beauty was more than skin deep, and their hearts were being *woven* together in love.

On the seventh day, the king called for Queen Vashti to put on her royal crown and come to his banquet. He wanted to display her beauty to all who attended his party, to show off his wife as though she were a trophy. For the first time in their marriage, the queen refused to come and expose her beauty before the people.

As might be expected, the king was very angry. More than angry, he was worried. He called in his legal advisers. What if the other women heard about this? What would happen if the women bonded together and became disobedient to the whims and wishes of the men? The men were incensed by Queen Vashti!

When the women hear it, they'll start treating their husbands with contempt. The day the wives of the Persian and Mede officials get wind of the queen's insolence, they'll be out of control. Is that what we want, a country of angry women who don't know their place?[36]

They convinced King Xerxes that he had only one choice. He had to put Vashti in her proper place to set an example to all women. Taking the men's advice, the king banned Queen Vashti from his presence and ordered a search for a new queen.

> Let us begin a search for beautiful young virgins for the king. Let the king appoint officials in every province of his kingdom to bring every beautiful young virgin to the palace complex of Susa and to the harem run by Hegai, the king's eunuch, who oversees the women; he will put them through their beauty treatments. Then let the girl who best pleases the king be made queen instead of Vashti.[37]

Like the story of Cinderella, all the young women were vying for the prize of becoming the new queen, and the most *unlikely* woman arose as the most likely candidate. Her name was Esther, and like Cinderella, she was an orphan, a peasant Jew whose ancestors stayed in Persia following the Babylonian exile. Esther's cousin Mordecai raised her as his adopted daughter after her parents died ... and she was stunning!

Even though the young women selected for the contest were naturally beautiful, they had to go through a regimen of beauty treatments:

> Before a girl's turn came to go in to King Xerxes, she had to complete twelve months of beauty treatments prescribed for the women, six months with oil of myrrh and six with perfumes and cosmetics.[38]

---

[36] Esther 1:17–18 (the Message).
[37] Esther 2:2–4 (the Message).
[38] Esther 2:12.

Can you imagine a twelve-month makeover? An entire year of living the life of luxury, but only one would win the title. Esther became the Cinderella of this contest. She was chosen to be the new queen.

> The king fell in love with Esther far more than with any of his other women or any of the other virgins—he was totally smitten by her. He placed a royal crown on her head and made her queen in place of Vashti. Then the king gave a great banquet for all his nobles and officials—"Esther's Banquet." He proclaimed a holiday for all the provinces and handed out gifts with royal generosity.[39]

"The king fell in love with Esther ... he was totally smitten by her." If this was just another Cinderella story, it could end right here, and we would assume Esther lived happily ever after. If it had only been about her outward appearance, the story would basically be over because there would be nothing more to tell. Who would want to hear about Queen Esther aging and putting on a few pounds or how the king grew weary of her and began a search for a younger, more beautiful replacement? But Esther had much more to offer than just a face and figure. This story is far from over!

Esther, now queen, kept silent about her Jewish heritage. King Xerxes had no idea she was a Jew. Four years later, he appointed Haman as his top-ranking noble. Haman demanded the lesser nobles and servants bow down to him as he passed by the King's Gate. Mordecai, Esther's Jewish cousin (who became her father), blatantly refused. Bowing down to Haman was to bow down to the Amalekites, a long-standing enemy of the Jews. Haman was furious, and he sought revenge by plotting to have the entire Jewish population eliminated— massacred! This was to take place in every province of the

---

[39] Esther 2:17–18.

kingdom on an appointed day, and all Jewish property would be seized.

When Mordecai discovered the consequences of his actions, he dressed in sackcloth and mourned publicly. His last hope for the Jews was his adopted daughter, who had become queen. Mordecai's famous appeal to Queen Esther to act on behalf of her people is found in Esther 4:14.

> For if you remain silent at this time, relief and deliverance for the Jews will arise from another place, but you and your father's family will perish.
>
> And who knows but that you have come to royal position for such a time as this? (NIV)

Esther was in a precarious situation, to say the least. The king had no idea that Esther was a Jew. She could easily have been hanged and killed as an imposter, especially since Haman was the king's most trusted adviser. More than that, Esther was not permitted to present herself to the king unless he initiated the meeting. What was she to do? This was Esther's response:

> Then Esther sent this reply to Mordecai:
>
> Go, gather together all the Jews who are in Susa, and fast for me. Do not eat or drink for three days, night or day. I and my maids will fast as you do. When this is done, I will go to the king, even though it is against the law. And if I perish, I perish.[40]

The results of their fasting created a tsunami of events in favor of the Jews. Esther was respected, favored, and trusted by the king. He was willing to do whatever she asked. You'll be amazed to read in the book of Esther 5-8 that every evil

---

[40]   Esther 4:15-16 (NIV).

Haman planned was divinely intercepted and even reversed in favor of the Jews. Take a few minutes now to read those chapters so you can savor the grandness of this victory!

Haman was hanged on the very gallows he had ordered built for Mordecai's punishment. King Xerxes appointed Mordecai as his new second in command, lavishing him with wealth. He "left the king's presence wearing royal garments of blue and white, a large crown of gold and a purple robe of fine linen."[41] There it is again—purple and fine linen.

Esther's plea to the king did not stop with overthrowing Haman's plan. She approached Xerxes again on behalf of future generations to protect the Jews. Listen to the grace in her voice as she speaks to the king. Hers is the voice of virtue.

> "If it pleases the king," she said, "and if he regards me with favor and thinks it the right thing to do, and if he is pleased with me, let an order be written overruling the dispatches that Haman … devised and wrote to destroy the Jews in all the king's provinces. For how can I bear to see disaster fall on my people? How can I bear to see the destruction of my family?"
>
> King Xerxes replied to Queen Esther and to Mordecai the Jew, "Because Haman attacked the Jews, I have given his estate to Esther, and they have hanged him on the gallows. Now write another decree in the king's name in behalf of the Jews as seems best to you, and seal it with the king's signet ring—for no document written in the king's name and sealed with his ring can be revoked."
>
> So Queen Esther, daughter of Abihail, along with Mordecai the Jew, wrote with full authority to confirm this second letter concerning Purim.[42]

---

[41]   Esther 8:15.
[42]   Esther 8:5–8; 9:29 (NIV).

Esther was more than just a pretty face in the palace; she was the wealthiest woman in the kingdom. She was also the only woman to be given full authority to write an edict on the king's behalf. The future of the entire population of Jewish people in the kingdom was secured. Wow! What an amazingly virtuous woman!

> For the Jews it was a time of happiness and joy, gladness and honor. In every province and in every city, wherever the edict of the king went, there was joy and gladness among the Jews, with feasting and celebrating. And many people of other nationalities became Jews because fear of the Jews had seized them.[43]

The Lord chose His beloved Esther to intervene on behalf of his people. Her beauty was a foot in the door to the palace, but her inner strength and determination—her virtue—brought honor to her, to Mordecai, and to the Jews and changed the course of history. Esther brings the woman of virtue to life:

> She has no fear for her household; for all of them are clothed in scarlet ... fine linen and purple.
>
> Her husband is respected at the city gate, where he takes his seat among the elders of the land.
>
> She is clothed with strength and dignity; she can laugh at the days to come.[44]

Going back to the beginning of Esther's story, when Queen Vashti held a seven-day banquet for all the women in the palace, it seems it all began with a Woven Women's retreat! This may have been the first time these women really spent

---

[43]   Esther 8:16–17 (NIV).
[44]   Proverbs 31:21–23, 25.

time getting beyond their superficial relationships and petty competition for first place in the beauty contest.

When they got beyond the clothes, hair, and makeup, they found meaningful relationships. Looking into one another's hearts and listening to one another's hurts, they were "woven into a tapestry of love." They became unstoppable—a threat to the king and his advisers!

Cinderella and Esther were living like peasants, but God intervened. They were destined to be queens.

GETTING TO KNOW ME

As a little girl watching the movie, I could relate more to the Cinderella with cinders on her face, hands, and clothes than to the princess she became. I felt dirty, unworthy, and unloved. I accepted Christ at the age of eight, but shame was in charge of my life. My alcoholic father placed this legacy of shame on my shoulders as a family mantle. Add childhood sexual abuse, and shame gained control. I adopted pride as my BFF to hide shame. Pride created a false persona that said if I would just do everything perfectly or at least better than most, then I could control shame; I could put shame to shame!

I clearly remember a warm summer day in our small country church. It was Vacation Bible School and we all walked single file, like a row of ducklings, into the sanctuary. Sitting way in the back with my class, lined up on a wooden pew, I raised my hand in response to an invitation to accept Christ. Accepting Christ did not remove pride and shame from my heart that day. It seems unimaginable at age eight, but pride told me I should be ashamed of myself for pretending to be saved in an effort to be good enough in the eyes of the church.

The sense that I was not good enough was a stumbling block in my Christian walk. In my mind, God was sitting on a throne in heaven, waiting for me to mess up so He could point His huge finger at my mistake. The sermons every Sunday assured me—I was a sinner. Boy, did I make mistakes; I was always messing up.

Though I was living like a peasant, I sensed deep inside that God's little princess was longing to come out, to be free. It seemed like a fairytale, an impossible dream. I chased that dream in relationships. Six months after my high school graduation, I recited wedding vows by candlelight with my high school sweetheart in front of several hundred witnesses. It was a beautiful Christmas ceremony, with white velvet, red roses, and holly—the type of wedding dreams are made of. Four years later, we were blessed with a beautiful baby girl. Everything was seamlessly moving toward happily-ever-after. But one year later, our bubble burst. After five years of marriage, we filed for dissolution of our marriage. Shame grew deeper roots.

I became a single mom during a deep recession. It was difficult to find a job. I settled for the least amount of child support, just wanting to hang on to my baby girl. At only twenty-three, I was still a vulnerable little girl myself—still searching for my Prince Charming, still longing to be loved and accepted for who I was inside, still walking around with a hole in my soul no human could fill. I wanted others to know the real me, when in truth even *I* didn't know my true identity.

Within two years I remarried, this time to a man seven years older with three children, ages eleven, nine, and three. Life was hard. It was not the dream, not what I had envisioned or planned. Convinced this was my destiny, I thought if I worked hard enough it could become my Cinderella story. Over the years, we became knit together as a family. We built two businesses while loving, supporting, and encouraging our children to be all that they could be. But, quite honestly, it was counterfeit. Eleven years later, our empire crumbled when I discovered my husband's secret life, which led to his suicide.

As I picked up the remnants, feelings of betrayal led me to the only one I knew I could trust. I surrendered everything— the pain, the pride, the shame—to God. He totally cleansed me from my past and gave me a new vision of myself. Dressed as a bride in a beautiful gown of white, I stood before the Lord as a spiritual virgin, ready to marry my forever Bridegroom—Jesus!

My Cinderella story came true. I allowed the Prince of Peace to fill that hole in my soul. His love was overwhelming, overflowing, and more than enough for me. I saw everything and everyone differently. My tears of pain became tears of joy as I viewed the world through the eyes of Christ—with love and compassion. I was complete, content to live out my life as His bride.

God had yet another plan. In His perfect timing, God united me with my perfect match: a forty-year-old bachelor who loved God with all his heart. He was waiting for a woman of virtue. Not just any woman would do for this gentleman. Fully surrendered and waiting for God's choice, I was the reluctant yet fortunate woman God hand-selected and presented to Mark. (He is the one whose bachelor pad renovation I mentioned in chapter 1.)

At a time when I struggled to ever trust another man, God demonstrated through Mark that there are trustworthy men. This relationship brought Jesus to me in the flesh. Through his gentleness and patience, God healed my wounded soul. We are truly living happily ever after because, separately and jointly, we chose Christ as our first love. Our intention is to live in this continual state of surrender to Him. This doesn't mean life is perfect. We still have struggles and face trials, but we seek God first and trust Him for the answer. This is an ever-evolving and forever-growing relationship. It truly is a beautiful life, our dream come true!

The truth is, married or single, it could still be happily ever after for each of us. Living wholeheartedly for Christ is a beautiful life, a life dreams are made of. Jesus is our perfect companion when we commit to Him as our first love.

GETTING TO KNOW THE VIRTUOUS WOMAN

Cinderella and Esther were living like peasants but were destined to be queens. God intervened because they consciously chose to be different than the average woman. They were committed to godly virtues. We can make the same choice. I love this testimony from our friend Terri, who is so brave to share her story:

> I am sixty-nine years old. I gave my life to Jesus at the age of six after hearing a preacher share the gospel in Boca Raton, Florida. I knew, as much as a six-year-old could know, that God was the answer to everything in my life. He was my love, my life, and I could trust Him more than anyone. I stayed close to Him for a while, but because my family didn't have Jesus at the center of their lives and I wasn't strong enough at that age, I slowly became intoxicated by the world. My father was an alcoholic, and he traveled a lot with other women. I quickly learned that the most important things in the world were for a man to love and adore me and take care of me financially.
>
> I had no idea what pit I was about to fall into, but the evil one did. I met and fell in love with my Prince Charming—a very wealthy married man, who I thought adored me. We were together for many years. I struggled between wanting to know and live in God's truth, and wanting to believe Satan's lie that this man really loved me but just couldn't leave his family.
>
> About seven years ago, I began attending a Nazarene Church where I witnessed God's love and truth for the first time. I began growing in His Word and started to trust in Christian fellowship. I could see that these people were real and were full of love and they meant what they said.
>
> Then, I started attending the Woven Women events. Because of what I was learning, I could feel myself becoming stronger in my faith.

Hope began springing up inside me. The man I was with wanted to control me, so he never encouraged me to have women friends. This was threatening to him, and because I was ashamed of what I was doing, I was afraid to have close friends. I knew they wouldn't approve.

But God used Woven Women to demonstrate what real Christian women are about—they love unconditionally. This ministry and these women showed me Jesus, up close and personal. Through Woven, I became strong enough to end the relationship, which had me in chains for most of my life. I will forever be grateful for Woven Women.

I am free!

—Terri, a Woven Woman of virtue

God offers everyone the opportunity to change her status from peasant to princess. Christ is our Prince, the Prince of Peace, and He is searching for a bride. In this relationship, we don't have to wait for Him to make the first move. He wants us to seek Him as our Bridegroom. Jeremiah 29:13 says, "You will seek him and you will find him when you seek him with all your heart."[45]

There is more than one princess in this story. We all can marry the prince. There is room in His kingdom for all of us. We can all become the bride of Christ.

"Hallelujah! For the Lord God almighty reigns! Let us rejoice and be glad and give him glory! For the wedding of the Lamb has come, and his bride has made herself ready. Fine linen, bright and clean, was given her to wear." (Fine linen stands for the righteous acts of the saints.) Then the angel said to me, "Write this: Blessed are

---

[45] NIV.

those who are invited to the wedding supper of the Lamb!"(Revelation 19:6b-9 NIV)

I love this beautiful metaphor of Christ as the Bridegroom and the church as His bride. It was the exact visual He gave me when I sought His cleansing touch. He made me brand new, dressed me in fine linen, bright and clean, designating my righteousness in Him. Finally, shame and pride could no longer reside inside.

Who can find a virtuous woman? Christ can! She will be seated with Him in heaven. When we surrender ourselves totally to Christ, as a bride commits herself to her bridegroom, we *all* can be seated at the wedding supper of the Lamb.

In the words of Cinderella, when she was dreaming of going to the ball, "I can just imagine the whole thing: wearing the most beautiful dress you have ever worn in your life and to be on your way at last to the ball."

I hope that in your heart, your dream is to prepare for Christ's return by wearing fine linen, bright and clean because of your righteousness—the most beautiful dress you have ever worn in your life!

WHAT DID JESUS WEAR?

For most women, this subject of clothing is an important one. We want to wear the prettiest dress. An outfit can totally change how we feel about ourselves. Pride and shame rear their ugly heads. Taking pride in what we wear causes us to be overly concerned about impressing others and receiving compliments, and we become dismayed if no one notices. Being financially unable to dress as well as others or just being inept in putting together an outfit can induce shame. Whether we want to impress others, or we just don't care how we look, our outfits make an impact, whether we like it or not. Since we're talking about this theme of clothing and our desire to be more like Jesus, let's give some thought to what Jesus wore.

We are familiar with the Christmas story in Luke 2. When Mary gave birth, she wrapped Jesus in "swaddling cloths" and placed him in a manger. We have a clearer picture of what a swaddling cloth is because swaddling your baby has become popular in recent years. Swaddling cloths are blankets used to wrap babies up tightly so they feel secure and sleep better, as though they are in the womb. Having welcomed a new grandson into the world just two years ago, this conjures feelings of love and joy. There's nothing like holding a swaddled infant in your arms and admiring that new little face—especially when it's your grandbaby!

For us, a swaddling cloth is a blanket. For Jesus, it was strips of cloth. Once the umbilical cord was cut and tied, the baby was washed, rubbed with salt and oil, and wrapped with strips of cloth tied together like bandages. These strips kept the babe warm and secure—swaddled. The Israelites believed this was important because it helped the baby's arms and legs to grow straight.

For most of His life, Jesus wore a robe. That sounds really good to me because I am most comfy and content in my robe! At the end of the day, I cannot wait to put on my robe. Some days, when I get up early to write, I find myself still in my robe past noon. I am working—but in my robe. If Jesus wore a robe all day, then I guess I don't have to feel guilty about staying in my robe all morning.

Even though most of us like to make a statement with what we wear, Jesus preferred to blend into the crowd. He was the Son of God, but He certainly did not wear the royal clothing of a king. Mark 15 takes us to the scene of the trial where Jesus received the death sentence. The soldiers taunted Him by dressing Him in a purple robe. They mocked Him by calling, "Hail, king of the Jews!" They made a crown of thorns and placed it on His head. Then the beatings began. They struck Him on the head with a staff, spit on Him, and bent down on their knees and made fun of Him.

Then, Mark 15:20 says, "They took off the royal robe and put his own clothes back on him and led Him to be crucified." It doesn't really say that they took His clothes off, but it says they put His own clothes back on Him. Imagine how humiliating it must have been for them to dress and undress him in public, as though he was not even a person but an inanimate rag doll.

Mark 15:24 tells us His executioners divided up His clothing. Once they had nailed Him to the cross, it was legal for the execution squad to divide the personal belongings of a prisoner being executed. In Jesus's case, His only belongings were the clothes on His back. We can only imagine how important His clothing was to Him, considering it was the only thing He really owned.

There were four Roman soldiers, so they equally divided the garments, which would have been just a belt, sandals, a head covering, and robe. There was one extra item, and it was Jesus's most personal item: His undergarment. John 19:23 says, "This garment was seamless, woven in one piece from top to bottom." It was like a shirt that started at the neck and reached his knees or ankles.

> "Let's not tear it," they said to one another. "Let's decide by lot who will get it."

At this point, we don't know if Jesus was completely naked as He hung on the cross. If He had been a Roman, He would have been stripped naked. Since Jesus was a Jew, He most likely wore a loin cloth, in accordance with the public decency laws of the Jews.

After His death, His body was released to Joseph of Arimethea, a member of the Sanhedrin who was secretly a follower of Jesus. He lovingly wrapped Jesus in linen cloths. We can picture this as being like an Egyptian mummy—His entire body wrapped tightly in strips of white linen cloths. It's interesting to note that in His death, Jesus was essentially dressed in the same way as He was at birth—in swaddling cloths; strips of cloth wrapped tightly around His body. This is significant because even though He was dead, He was about to be reborn.

After wrapping Him, Joseph placed Jesus's body in a tomb

cut out of rock. He rolled a stone against the entrance. Jesus was dead, but God was not! The Father God was actively doing what only God can do. The metamorphosis began: three days and three nights in the transforming presence of God. Like a butterfly emerging from a cocoon, the only thing found in the tomb was the burial linens Jesus had been wrapped in.

What Jesus wore had spiritual significance. Clothes are often a reflection of our pride, hang-ups, low self-esteem, love of self, or concern for what others think. What was Jesus's attitude toward clothing? Jesus wanted to blend in, to live among the people and develop genuine relationships. He was humiliated on the cross, with no clothes, for our sake. The strips of linen in the empty tomb were the sign that He was no longer dead. He was alive!

Jesus didn't just disappear; He reappeared several times to several people.

Read these Jesus sightings in John 20, and think about how you have experienced Jesus.

- In his first appearance as the risen King, Jesus anonymously comforted Mary. He was so humble in His approach that she thought He was just the gardener. Ironically, it was Jesus's death over which she was overwhelmed with grief. It was not until Jesus called her by name that she recognized this man that she loved.
- Through locked doors, Jesus entered into the very room where the disciples were hiding, praying and waiting. He boldly announced his arrival: "Peace be with you!" He pointed to the wounds in His hands and side to prove that it really was Him. He had been crucified and had risen from the dead.
- One of the disciples, Thomas, was absent and didn't believe the eleven when they shared this grand news. His words became famous: "unless I see … I will not believe" (John 20:25). One week later, Jesus honored his request. He appeared to Thomas and said, "Put your fingers here; see my hands. Reach out your hand and

put it into my side. Stop doubting and believe" (John 20:27). Thomas said to him, "My Lord and my God!" He believed.

- Peter and John were actually the first ones to enter the empty tomb. John said that when he saw the evidence all around him, he believed. And what was the evidence? "He saw the strips of linen lying there, as well as the burial cloth that had been around Jesus's head. The cloth was folded up by itself, separate from the linen" (John 20:6-7).

GETTING TO KNOW YOU

I hope you have developed a habit of having your journal with you when you pick up this book. If not, please hurry to get it. I have some questions to ask, my friend. I want you to hear from God.

Got it? Great! Now take another look at the Jesus sightings in the previous section. Does your moment of belief align with one of these scenes? What did it or would it take for you to "see" the risen Christ?

- Did Jesus come to you quietly and humbly in your grief, as He came to Mary?
- Did He come boldly as He did to the disciples and announce His grand entrance?
- Were you/are you a "doubting Thomas"? Do you demand that Jesus prove His existence to you?
- Are you like John? You believe based on seeing the evidence of the resurrected Christ all around you.

Reflect on your own journey of belief.

- Write down your doubts and struggles.
- Write down your Jesus sightings, the times you saw Jesus at work in your life.

- Write about the moment you believed and were born again. Write everything you can remember, using all five senses, about this experience.
- If you have not believed and accepted Christ, will you pray and seek Him now?

GETTING TO KNOW GOD

This chapter has caused me to reminisce about my wardrobe over the expanse of my life. That's a lot of clothing! The way I dressed reflected how I felt about myself and who I was at the time. My outfit changed as my relationship with God changed. I still remember a dress I wore to church when I was in sixth grade. It had a dropped waist and was made of white lace, with a purple satin ribbon and bow just above the skirted section. The dress was a wee bit short. It drew attention, and the attention drew shame. Though I loved that pretty dress and I knew it looked nice on me, the stares were unbearable.

I see a thread woven throughout the wardrobes of my life. There were times I wanted to be noticed and times when I just wanted to be invisible. In high school in the '70s, I found freedom in being me. I wore the halter tops and bare midriffs and miniskirts. I enjoyed the attention, but the attention made me feel vulnerable. In my second marriage I wore bland colors, like white or ivory blouses, with jeans. My heart just wanted to hide. I wanted to be invisible. Sometimes I even wore men's clothing. Though it was trendy, it really wasn't flattering. But it built a wall of security, made me feel stronger, and gave me a sense of control.

After my husband's suicide, I wore loose-fitting clothing. The last thing I wanted was for men to take notice of me. I was fragile and hurting and seeking God with all my heart.

One thing has been consistent: I've always loved clothing. I started making my own clothing when I was ten years old. What I love about my life now is that I feel totally free to be me. I'm not hung up on what others think about my outfits.

If I like it, if it expresses who I am and doesn't flaunt my body parts, then it's all good! I dress to enhance the person God made me to be. My spirit soars, and my eyes shine like polished stones when I do because Christ is glorified from the inside out. I am being free to be me—the *me* He created me to be.

A virtuous woman knows her inner beauty is more valuable and more beautiful than the most expensive piece of clothing she could ever purchase. She is looking forward to the day when Christ will clothe her in the "most beautiful dress she has ever worn in her life"—a robe of righteousness.

Write about your spiritual journey:

- How has your wardrobe reflected your spiritual and emotional journey over the span of your life?
- Has the Lord become your Bridegroom?
    o Are you so in love with Him that He satisfies your need for love?
    o Has He clothed you in robes of righteousness—a spiritual virgin in His eyes?
    o Ask God to show you the areas in your life to which you are clinging, things that have replaced Him as your means of security, as your first love.
- Have you discovered your God-given destiny?
    o Do you know who you are and what you were made to do?
    o Are you operating in the gifts and graces and talents that He has woven into the depths of your being?
- Are you free to be the person God created you to be? "And who knows but that you have come to royal position for such a time as this?"[46]

---

[46] Esther 4:14 (NIV).

What is God calling you to do? I'm praying for you, my friend! I want all of these things for you. I long for you to know your "true you" so you can fulfill your God-appointed destiny.

A PRAYER FOR YOU

O LORD, you have examined my heart and know everything about me. You know when I sit down or stand up. You know my thoughts, even when I'm far away. You see me when I travel and when I rest at home. You know everything I do.

You made all the delicate, inner parts of my body and knit me together in my mother's womb. Thank you for making me so wonderfully complex. Your workmanship is marvelous—how well I know it.

You watched me as I was being formed in utter seclusion, as I was woven together in the dark of the womb. You saw me before I was born. Every day of my life was recorded in your book. Every moment was laid out before a single day had passed.

How precious are your thoughts about me, O God. They cannot be numbered! I can't even count them; they outnumber the grains of sand! And when I wake up, you are still with me.

Search me, O God, and know my heart; test me and know my anxious thoughts. Point out anything in me that offends you, and lead me along the path of everlasting life.[47]

[47] Psalm 139:1-3, 13-18, 23-24 (NLT).

In Jesus's name, amen.

What is God asking you to surrender to Him? Write these things down and prayerfully surrender them, one by one. This may take more than one sitting. Keep working on this as the Spirit continues to reveal truth in your innermost being. As you surrender, ask God to fill you with more and more of His Spirit.

"JUST KNOCK"

I was alone in my suffering. No one came to my rescue. I cried, but there were no tears. I opened my mouth to scream, but there was no sound. Like a rag doll, I was tossed aside.

Though I couldn't see Him, Jesus was there. He heard my silent screams for help. He saw the unformed tears in my eyes. He promises never to leave us, never to forsake us, and to answer the door when we knock. Just knock.

WHAT DOES SHE DO?

5

I am a human being, not a human doing.
My worth is who I am, not what I can
do or how I am seen by others.
This is the truth of my existence.
—David G. Benner[48]

"**W**hat have I done?" We ask ourselves this question, but it has several connotations. I've had those "Oh no!" moments of "*Now* what have I done?" Those are moments when what I did was not a good thing. Whether it's backing my car out of the garage and smacking into my husband's car; or scraping my bumper a second time on the stone wall in our drive; or discovering I cannot find my keys because I left them in the ignition with the car doors locked or left my purse in a restaurant; or saying the wrong thing at the wrong time—I know you understand that feeling of dread, my friend. (You're probably feeling sorry for my hubby now too. Thankfully, I did not accomplish all of these in one day.)

There are other times when just rearranging the question as "Now, what have I *done*?" brings an entirely different type of stress. It's the sense that time is flying by, and you are searching for a sense of accomplishment. When I journal my prayers, the first thing I do is write the day and date at the top of the page. It's crazy how many times I think, *Wow! Is it really that far along in the week already?* When Thursday arrives I

---

[48] David G. Benner, *The Gift of Being Yourself: the Sacred Call to Self-Discovery* (Downers Grove, Illinois: InterVarsity Press, 2004).

almost always feel like I have lost a day somewhere. How can the days sift by so quickly, like sand through an hourglass? These thoughts usually bombard me with things on my to-do list that I still need to do. I tend to reevaluate how I spent yesterday. What did I do with an entire day? Looking back over my week, I search for satisfaction in what I have done.

Being wired to think that productivity equals time well spent, my values have been a bit off. God is reminding me that people time *is* productive time. Having something to show for your time is important, but people are more important than products. Quality time with people is taking priority over my list of to-dos. Investing in friends and family, pouring into my grandsons and helping my daughter, "spurring one another on"[49] as friends and initiating new relationships—these are the measure of a life well spent.

I'm discovering God in the midst of these interactions. "As iron sharpens iron, so one person sharpens another."[50] We encourage one another and build each other up.[51] We hold each other accountable and carry one another's burdens.[52] Oh, the richness of experiencing life through diverse personalities! Others open our minds to new possibilities and differing perspectives. Relationships lift us from our inclination to make gods of our professions and day planners and from our temptation to put time in a capsule to hoard it for ourselves.

The reward is the beautiful friendships we acquire along the way. Kathleen is a precious friend who has brought depth and color to my tapestry of life. She shares this history of our relationship.

> Just when life was going great, my family faced an unexpected curve in the road. As parents with a fifteen-year-old, our future was readjusted from the joy and anticipation of our hopes and dreams for the future to simply trying to find

---

[49]   Hebrews 10:24 (NIV).
[50]   Proverbs 27:17 (NIV).
[51]   1 Thessalonians 5:11.
[52]   Galatians 6:2.

ways to cope with day-to-day living. One of the adjustments was to be careful not to share our story with just anyone.

Years later, after our son got married, my husband and I moved to a small town to be closer to him and his new wife. All of us were still suffering, as we had been through so much.

Facing new church relationships left me feeling uncomfortable, invisible. I learned to be more reserved, which is very different from my outgoing personality. On Sundays, I started sitting quietly in the back during the church service. I served in the nursery where I felt safe—being careful not to get too personal.

One Sunday a bubbly blonde introduced herself as Cindy. She invited me to a women's event—a Woven Weekend. I was hesitant to go, but something felt different. I decided to chance it and attend. That weekend my healing journey began.

This beautiful woman stood before a large group of women and shared her shattered heart. Cindy spoke about how she, like me, had to find a new way of life. She applied the promises of God; then took me by the hand and introduced me to women who became a source of encouragement. I was "woven into a tapestry of love."

Finding a group of women who love Jesus and love each other helped me grow stronger in the things of the Lord. They love me through times when I feel disenchanted with life, removing the power of isolation.

I no longer feel invisible. The voice of God's love speaking gently but with power and authority, along with the encouragement I receive from my Woven girls has allowed me to embrace the high-spirited Irish personality I was born with. They accept me as I am and give me permission to be everything God intended me to be.

—Kathleen, a Woven Woman of virtue

How will we spend eternity? Watching the clock and posting perfectly edited selfies on a screen? Will we text our conversations without speaking a word? Will we be concerned about trying to produce something valuable each day, something that boosts our ego or creates a greater income? No! If our destination is heaven, we will spend eternity in unity with each other. Our relationships will be holy, authentic, and Christlike.

Life is wonderful here on earth when we invest in relationships. It would be sad to spend our final years listening to the tick-tock of the clock, alone in our own homes. We need others to talk to and to share memories and laugh with. We are made for relationships. This is why God wants us "woven into a tapestry of love."

This type of living may sound ideal, but it's difficult to pull it off in the midst of our hectic lifestyles. After all, we have so much to do!

WHAT DO YOU DO?

One of the first questions we usually ask when we meet someone new is "What do you do?" We are constantly confronted with this question. A college graduate is asked, "What are you going to do?" When a stay-at-home mom shares her status, she may get the response "Oh, so you don't work?" (That deserves a punch in the nose!) If your occupation is unconventional, such as owning your own business or leading a ministry, you may get a blank look, implying the thought, *Does she really do anything?*

When you reach for an introductory handshake, the question "What do you do?" can bring sweaty palms of anxiety. We feel pressured and fear being judged or pigeon-holed according to our occupations.

How do *you* feel when asked what you do? Your reaction depends on your situation. If you are in between jobs, unhappy with your work, or not proud of what you do, you may feel nervous or awkward. If you have the job of your dreams and have worked hard to get there, talking about it gives you confidence and makes you feel important and proud. In that case, you could go on and on, talking about what you do. That person may wish he or she had never asked!

There is no question that society places a high priority on what we do, but maybe it's not the best question to ask when we first meet someone. We need a new intro, such as "Tell me about your family or the people closest to you," or "How do you like to spend your time?"

We pose a similar question to children. "What do you want to be when you grow up?" We are already planting the seed that doing and being are interconnected. Is this true? Do we really have to *do* something to *be* someone? Is our value as a human based on what we do?

We put such a high value on what we do or don't do. Yet this culture of busyness takes the best years of our lives and exhausts our creative energy. Just when we think life is perfect, we're thrown a curve ball that brings us back to reality. We reach a point of burnout, and it is impossible to continue doing what we do. The following passage in James is a great illustration:

> Prosperity is as short-lived as a wildflower, so
> don't ever count on it. You know that as soon as
> the sun rises, pouring down its scorching heat,
> the flower withers. Its petals wilt and, before
> you know it, that beautiful face is a barren stem.
> Well, that's a picture of the "prosperous life."
> At the very moment everyone is looking on in
> admiration, it fades away to nothing.[53]

---

[53]   James 1:9–11 (the Message).

Imagine having an occupation that brings the deepest degree of shame, a lifestyle judged as being sinful or disgusting. We are about to meet a woman who would shudder if faced with the question, "What do you do?" Take a few minutes to read about this courageous woman in Luke 7:36-40. This passage is one of the most beautiful and emotional scenes in the New Testament. Allow yourself to enter this story as an eyewitness.

> Now one of the Pharisees invited Jesus to have dinner with him, so he went to the Pharisee's house and reclined at the table. When a woman who had lived a sinful life in that town learned that Jesus was eating at the Pharisee's house, she brought an alabaster jar of perfume, and as she stood behind him at his feet weeping, she began to wet his feet with her tears. Then she wiped them with her hair, kissed them and poured perfume on them.
>
> When the Pharisee who had invited him saw this, he said to himself, "If this man were a prophet, he would know who is touching him and what kind of woman she is—that she is a sinner."
>
> Jesus answered him, "Simon, I have something to tell you."
>
> "Tell me, teacher," he said.
>
> "Two men owed money to a certain moneylender. One owed him five hundred denarii, and the other fifty. Neither of them had the money to pay him back, so he canceled the debts of both. Now which of them will love him more?"

Simon replied, "I suppose the one who had the bigger debt canceled."

"You have judged correctly," Jesus said. Then he turned toward the woman and said to Simon, "Do you see this woman? I came into your house. You did not give me any water for my feet, but she wet my feet with her tears and wiped them with her hair. You did not give me a kiss, but this woman, from the time I entered, has not stopped kissing my feet. Therefore, I tell you, her many sins have been forgiven—for she loved much. But he who has been forgiven little loves little."

Then Jesus said to her, "Your sins are forgiven."

The other guests began to say among themselves, "Who is this who even forgives sins?"

Jesus said to the woman, "Your faith has saved you; go in peace."

WHAT DID SHE DO?

Luke says this woman "lived a sinful life," which likely means she was a prostitute. Imagine her shame if Jesus had initiated a conversation asking, "What do you do?" It may have stopped her from completing her mission of love.

Obviously, the host was not happy with this uninvited guest. It is surprising she was not booted out based on her occupation. Considering the judgmental attitude of Simon the Pharisee, I wonder how she was able to get that close to Jesus. The Pharisees were a religious sect concerned with separating themselves from anyone or anything considered unclean according to Jewish law. In spite of this, it was culturally acceptable to have meals open to the public. The door was open; there were extra chairs seated around the outside of the room where people could sit and chat while those at the table dined.

Jesus reclined at the table. The woman arrived promptly, intent on anointing Him with perfume. She discovered His feet had not yet been washed. Customarily this would have been tended to immediately when the guest arrived. Standing behind Jesus, she began to kiss His feet, dirt and all. In the tenderness of that moment, she could not hold back her emotions. Long-held tears began to flow, more than enough to wash Jesus's feet and dry them with her hair. These cleansing tears, pent up for years, were significant. While she was cleansing Jesus's feet, Jesus was cleansing her heart from sin, pain, and shame.

She carried with her an alabaster jar filled with perfume. This perfume was used in her profession to prepare her body and her room where she met with clients. It was her love potion. Offering it to Jesus expressed her love and devotion. She was leaving her former life behind, ready to follow Him.

This three-step process of washing, wiping, and anointing Jesus's feet is significant. Jesus did the same three things to the heart of this woman.

He washed her sins away. "Your sins are forgiven."

He wiped her slate clean. "Your faith has saved you."

He anointed her with His words. "Go in peace."

What did she do? She made an example of Simon the Pharisee and all who shared his judgmental attitude. They were concerned about her occupation, her reputation. Jesus's concern was the condition of her heart. He saved her not because of what she did; not because she anointed His feet. He saved her because she chose to be a different person. She left her life of sin instead of continuing as a sinner. This was an invitation for Jesus to come into her heart and life and provide her the strength and power to do the right thing, to live a new life.

WHAT WOULD JESUS DO?

Most likely you have been confronted with the acronym WWJD, meaning *What would Jesus do?* You may even have a bracelet to remind you to do what Jesus would do as you go about your day. Though it's not as trendy as it was in the 1990s, WWJD is still an important prompt to guide us in our words, thoughts, and actions.

The story of the woman living a sinful life brings to the table an important question for our time. Reading her story, we already know what Jesus would do if she showed up at our local church. He would welcome her, partly because she did a very brave thing, demonstrating she was ready for a new life. What the story doesn't share is the time of preparation.

The sinful woman came to a point of decision before she crashed the Pharisee's party. She followed the crowds from afar, listening to what Jesus said and watching what Jesus did. What did Jesus do? He demonstrated by words and deeds that God's love is for every person—even her. Love emanated from the very core of His being. To do what Jesus would do is to be His ambassador of love by following His commands: "Love the Lord with all your heart, soul, mind, and strength; and love your neighbor as yourself."[54]

LOVE LOOKS DEEPER

When we look through the eyes of love, we see the story behind the story. We come to the realization that attitudes and appearances are just smokescreens for the wounded human beings we all are. All sin is the same in the fact that it separates us from God, but there are differing degrees of the seriousness of sin. There is a particular type of sin singled out in 1 Corinthians 6:18 because it affects us differently.

---

[54] Matthew 22:37.

Flee from sexual immorality. All other sins a man commits are outside his body, but he who sins sexually sins against his own body. Do you not know that your body is a temple of the Holy Spirit, who is in you, whom you have received from God? You are not your own; you were bought at a price. Therefore, honor God with your body.

Let's look for the story behind the story of this woman living a sinful life. First, we acknowledge that she could not have been a prostitute without customers. Men were "sinning against their own bodies" by buying sex from her. Yes, she was sinning against her own body as well, but perhaps she had no choice.

We live in a culture that exploits the weak and vulnerable. Pornography, sexual abuse, and human trafficking will go down in history books as the social disgrace of this era. Most women and children trapped in this lifestyle did not choose it; it chose them. They are trapped in the web of someone else's sin. This breaks God's heart. Will you allow it to break your heart too?

Stop for a moment of silent prayer, asking Jesus to present Himself to these helpless, hopeless victims. Imagine yourself in this situation; truly empathize with them and intercede on their behalf. Ask God to rescue them, to send help and hope.

Now consider the source of this problem. Pray for God to convict the hearts of those who solicit and support this worldwide atrocity. It is as close as your neighbor and as far as the opposite ends of the earth and everywhere in between. Begin with this prayer as a power-booster for God to answer our prayers for the victims:

Lord, bring these traffickers, pimps, perpetrators, and their clients to their knees before You. Shine the light of truth into their dark worlds. Overwhelm them with the shame and conviction of their sin. Remove the veil from their eyes, let them see evil as You see it, and turn them from their wicked ways. We pray they choose to follow You.

Abba Father, bring a halt to this activity and confront them at every turn. Let all victims come to know You as their rescue and lover of their souls. May they never escape Your watchful, loving eyes. We praise You for victory in Jesus's name. Amen.

Are you looking deeper when you meet someone who isn't living up to par according to your standards? Are you seeking to see the story behind the story? Do you look through the lens of the Pharisee or the lens of Jesus? The Pharisee sees the sins of others but is blind to her own. Jesus sees the sin but looks deeper to see the heart of the sinner. Jesus loves every heart no matter what the person has done. He sees what the person can become.

GETTING TO KNOW ME

Thank God that He looks beyond our sins because all of us are sinners! We have all been there—we have all been "a woman who has lived a sinful life." Romans 3:23 makes that perfectly clear.

> There is no difference, for all have sinned and have fallen short of the glory of God, and are justified freely by his grace through the redemption that came by Christ Jesus. (NIV)

Hello, sister! I was right there with her—the woman whose body was sinned against and who sinned against her own body. Did you realize one of every three girls and one of every six boys will be sexually abused before their eighteenth birthdays? If there were a roster of female children, my name would have an asterisk beside it as the one in three.

This is such a trap of the enemy, a setup for sexual sin. My approach to life and relationships was birthed from sexual brokenness. Lacking love and affection in my home, I sought it elsewhere. Listening to my father's repetition of lies that he believed about himself soaked into my brain until I began to believe the same.

"I'm no good. I won't amount to anything. Nobody cares."

Being the fifth and last child, I was given no boundaries, no curfew, and the car keys. By then my parents were just trying to survive in the same house together. The best thing they did was to teach me to be honest and hardworking, to attend church, and to serve God. Their advice was "Do what I say, not what I do." I guess my father realized he was not the best example. In high school, I often had to leave for school an hour early to drive my dad to work. He was a repeat DUI offender, and his license was often suspended.

This is not a pity party. It is my broken road that led me home. These hardships were the very things God used to inspire me to rise above my circumstances, to *be* someone better than what life had handed me. I was busy doing things to forge a better future, a different pedigree. I worked hard, was an honor student, and graduated fifth in my high school class. I was involved in extracurricular activities, was a class officer, and crowned queen of FFA, Homecoming Attendant, Miss Business & Office Education, and vied for district and state titles. Most of my life I had wished for a new family, a new home, an escape from the chaos of my own. I vowed I would never drink, smoke, or curse and would never marry a boy who did. I vowed I would marry a Christian and never divorce. I dated the same boyfriend throughout high school. Steve[55] met all of my criteria, and his family was the type I had always dreamed of having. We were married six months after my graduation.

Can I tell you how sneaky Satan is? He planted a sick plan in the heart of a married man. Vince met me when I was sixteen, and he was twenty-four and had two children.

---

[55] Not his real name.

Steve's mother hosted him as the speaker at a youth event in her home. Fast-forward four years: Vince began working his way into Steve's and my life. He invited us, as newlyweds, to a Bible class. Steve was very interested and was quick to sign us up. Next thing I knew, Vince was driving us in his pickup truck to the weekly class. I was in an uncomfortable position, physically, squeezed between the two of them for the forty-minute drive. I kept sensing Vince was purposely swerving to toss me his way. He laughed. I felt confused, ashamed, and dirty again.

After completing the class, he continued his pursuit. Vince recruited my husband to join his direct sales business. Vince was also a lay pastor and led a home church; he kept inviting us to attend. He was looking for the perfect opportunity to make his premeditated move.

It was in the spring, just months before my baby's first birthday. Vince asked if I would help him shop for a gift for his wife—my best friend, Mary[56]. There was nothing I would have enjoyed more than selecting a gift for this woman I loved, who had mentored me in mothering. Yet I felt reluctant, awkward, and unsafe. I spoke with Steve, asking what he thought about it. He encouraged me to go.

I remember that day so well. Vince picked me up in his pickup truck. My baby girl went everywhere I did, so she was with us. He had other stops to make along the way. Waiting in the truck, I recall watching him and thinking he was strange and awkward, but I couldn't really identify why he made me so uncomfortable. In the mall, I tried not to get too close to him, as I felt embarrassed to be seen with him and didn't want anyone to think we were a couple. We did our shopping and returned home. I was blessed to be a blessing to my friend. Other than that, I breathed a deep sigh of relief that it was over, and I wouldn't have to do that again.

Shortly after, Vince showed up at my house unexpectedly. I was alone with my babe. He said some pretty weird things to me about going shopping again because he needed help

---

[56] Not her real name.

buying socks. It was uncomfortable, and I later shared this with my husband. It seemed this man knew my schedule better than I did. He started showing up when I was buying groceries and walked through the aisles with me, developing his scheme. I told him my life was going perfectly, as planned, and he was not a part of the plan. I also would find him waiting in the parking lot after I got my hair done. It seemed no matter where I went he was there; no matter how much I said no, *no* was not an option.

Vince continued to pressure me and manipulate my thinking until I was so confused I could no longer think. He made me feel responsible for his happiness. He made me feel wanted, desirable, beautiful, and needed. He had a way of turning every thought over to his advantage. Eventually, his manipulation worked. He cunningly tunneled his way into my brokenness. I caved, and the rest is history.

Within a few months of that birthday shopping trip, Vince had totally won me over. It is still unbelievable, but I left my husband. Vince left his wife. It was a horrible, ugly mess. Never ever in my wildest dreams would I have seen myself as a main character in this hideous scene. It was the biggest "what have I done?" moment of my life!

Once we were together, Vince told me that when he first saw me at that youth event when I was sixteen years old, he was jealous of my boyfriend, Steve (who of course became my husband). The sequence of events that led to Vince and me being together had not "just happened." It was an intensely thought-out plan in the sick mind of a sexual predator. He made it his goal to have me. Satan was in control of his soul.

I share this now in hindsight. In the midst of his control and manipulation, I was blind to what was really happening. I was only twenty-four years old; he was thirty-two. My insight now is the result of years of seeking God and receiving healing, insight, and understanding.

In spite of it all, there was good in our life together. It is such a dichotomy and hard to explain or comprehend. Vince treated me like the most beautiful woman in the world, but he also manipulated and controlled me. He is the husband who sexually abused my daughter—the worst thing I could ever imagine happening—and he sexually and emotionally abused me.

I want to see as God sees. God is an expert at looking beyond the ugly to see the beauty in every person. We need only to open the eyes of our hearts and allow Him to show us His view. God's view will heal us, revive us, and prepare us to be the person He needs us to be in order to do what He has called us to do. Recently, God has taken me to a new level of healing by revealing the positive influence Vince added to my life. He taught me social skills and business practices, and he helped me build a profitable business doing what I loved. Vince was the biggest fan when my daughter played sports and the biggest supporter of my business.

Why am I sharing all the ugly of my life? Believe me, I am asking God that same question. It's not because I want to. This comes as a warning—this could happen to you! I have witnessed it so often. Once a woman is pulled into this web, she doesn't want anyone telling her what she is doing is wrong. She gets in too deep; he is meeting her needs and fulfilling her fantasy. If you are that woman, I pray this comes as a wake-up call and that God will use it to prevent you from making a terrible mistake.

This is also for those who have been in my shoes. God redeemed my life for His glory. He can do that for you too! Whatever your situation, I pray that by sharing the story behind my story, you will learn to look deeper, to see others through the eyes of love and compassion—the eyes of Jesus. This is the making of a Christ-like leader.

Perhaps you are battling with sin in your life even now. It shouldn't come as a surprise. Satan is constantly knocking at the door of our minds, tempting us to sin. This is a battle of the mind, but if we entertain those thoughts, it becomes a battle for our hearts. Lust settles in, overcomes us, and we find ourselves on a path we never imagined traveling. We become so enslaved by lust that we even convince ourselves God is in it. James describes this process best.

When tempted no one should say, "God is tempting me." For God cannot be tempted by evil, nor does he tempt anyone; but each one is tempted when, by his own evil desire, he is dragged away and enticed. Then after desire has been conceived, it gives birth to sin; and sin, when it is full-grown, gives birth to death. (James 1:13–15 NIV)

Satan knows our weaknesses. He looks at our history and plans his attack. He waits for just the right timing to set the trap. He plants the thought and feeds it to keep it alive. Even if we dismiss it, he will continue to try. We entertain the thought, playing out different scenes in our heads. We find our minds traveling there more and more, which makes it grow. Next thing we know, tempting thoughts consume us and weaken our resistance.

Unless we come to our senses or God intervenes, it's too late to turn back. We find ourselves doing something we never imagined we were capable of doing. It always brings pain to other people—people that we love. If this speaks to your life situation, it is not too late to do the right thing. I urge you to stop and truly seek God's forgiveness and His strength to fight this battle. Another unhealthy relationship is not the remedy to the one you are already in.

Satan is sly. He knows that people are more important than products. He knows God created us for a relationship with Him and with each other. That is exactly why he intends to kill, steal, and destroy our relationships, which ultimately destroys us.[57] He especially wants to separate us from God and keep us searching for love from other sources, which leads us into unhealthy relationships.

To many, I must have seemed like a lost cause. To God, I was His girl. After Steve and I divorced, I rented a home for my precious baby girl and me. It felt as though someone had

---

[57] John 10:10.

flipped a switch and turned off the light of my life. Darkness, loneliness, and failure weighed me down.

It was the first time I felt separated from God, who had been my companion in my earliest memories. In that moment of aloneness, God came near. He convicted my heart of the wrong I had done. His presence was stronger than I had ever experienced. I could not get low enough to express how ugly I felt, how sorry I was, or how much I wanted His forgiveness. I fell facedown, spread-eagled on the bedroom floor. In that one-on-one transaction, God turned my darkness into light. It was His way of saying, "I know the story behind your story. I know you, and I see your heart."

He washed my sins away. "Your sins are forgiven."

He wiped my slate clean. "Your faith has saved you."

He anointed me with His words. "Go in peace."

THE VIRTUOUS WOMAN: WHAT DOES SHE DO?

Take a look at Proverbs 31 again. This time, let's search for things this woman does. What the woman of virtue does is the very thing that intimidates us. You name it—she does it! What does she do? She is a wise shopper, seamstress, cook, entrepreneur, businesswoman, laborer, and community leader, as well as manager, mother, nurturer, and supportive wife of a successful man. Whew! This woman has quite a résumé! But is she really much different from you or me? Isn't this what we women do, in some form or another, at some time or another throughout our lives?

We are going to look at a woman who shares these skills. In the book of Acts, we meet Lydia, who lived hundreds of years—possibly a thousand years—after the woman of virtue passage was written. Yet Lydia personifies the woman in Proverbs.

> On the Sabbath we went outside the city gate to
> the river, where we expected to find a place of

prayer. We sat down and began to speak to the women who had gathered there.

One of those listening was a woman named Lydia, a dealer in purple cloth from the city of Thyatira, who was a worshiper of God. The Lord opened her heart to respond to Paul's message. When she and the members of her household were baptized, she invited us to her home.

"If you consider me a believer in the Lord," she said, "come and stay at my house." And she persuaded us.[58]

Lydia was a prosperous businesswoman. She lived in Philippi and sold dyed goods as far away as Thyatira. She didn't sell just any fabric; she sold purple cloth—the most expensive, royal cloth. Like the woman of virtue, she even may have dressed in purple and fine linen occasionally.

Lydia worshiped God as a proselyte, which means she was not a Jew but a Gentile who had converted to the Jewish faith. When Paul shared the good news of Jesus with her in Philippi, Lydia believed in Christ. She was the first convert to Christianity in all of Europe.

It seems Lydia was leading her own Woven Women group at the river. The women gathered there to pray. Lydia, a follower of God and a leader in the community, was mentoring these women. There are three ways she is identified. She was "a dealer in purple cloth" and "a worshiper of God," and after her baptism she refers to herself as "a believer in the Lord." I find it beautiful that only one of these is her occupation—what she does. The other two refer to the person she chose to be.

The woman of virtue overwhelms us if we focus on all that she does. The passage refers to a multitude of things she is busy doing. Some sound very enterprising and imply

---

[58]   Acts 16:13–15 (NIV).

she is a businesswoman, wife, and mother. But those titles are not given to her. If we look for words to describe who she is or strives to be, we find only two. She is a "woman of virtue" and she is "a woman who fears the Lord." It seems her occupation—what really occupies her heart and mind, what her life is really about—is walking in step with the Holy Spirit.

The woman of virtue needs no title, position, or occupation according to the world's standards because her identity and worth are found in Christ.

GETTING TO KNOW THE VIRTUOUS WOMAN

"She can laugh at the days to come"[59] is my favorite verse describing the Proverbs 31 woman. This woman is not caught up in "What have I done?" because she is not living in the past. She lives in the moment, totally present and loving every minute of life. She is absolutely living, loving, and laughing her way through the day-to-day.

How does she do it? How can she take life so casually and not become a casualty of worrying about tomorrow, being frustrated with today, and stressed about yesterday? This woman is learning to just *be*. She takes God's word literally—and we can too.

This Woven study of the virtuous woman has impacted so many women. I have had the honor and privilege to witness God's work. This is Cheryl's story of getting to know the virtuous woman.

My Journey from Doing to Being

It was at the altar several years ago on a Sunday morning that I first met a lovely lady named Cindy Stiverson. She was seeking God's guidance and wisdom in her life that day. I quickly found that is *life* for her, to be in complete submission to the Lordship of Jesus, seeking His will and His way in all things.

After building a relationship with her, I joined a group of ladies one summer afternoon at Cindy's home. It was there that she introduced us to Woven and to a life-changing study on the Proverbs 31 woman.

At that time in my life, I was keeping a strenuous schedule of teaching sixth graders. After a full day of the joys and challenges characteristic of eleven- to twelve-year-olds, I would head for the church, where I cared for the daily needs of the local congregation as care pastor. The to-do list each day was long. My body and spirit were growing increasingly unbalanced. To say I was busy was an understatement indeed.

Despite the schedule, I knew I hungered for fellowship with women. To be able just to sit and rest in their company once a month filled my life in a powerful way. I was learning to be transparent, to be open, to share and to laugh. Proverbs 31 became alive to me as I learned the teachings in an applicable way that made sense and allowed women to share their hearts, their joys, and their struggles.

There is a new chapter of calmness in my life. To be able to slow down is what my soul was longing for. Busyness was stealing peace that comes from being still and allowing God to be first priority. To seek God each moment I am awake and to know that His moments are pure and holy are wonderful and extravagant gifts that I deeply treasure. I am able to listen and be alert to receive the gift hidden within each personal encounter. I can see God's infinite creations in a new way. I feel I can breathe, I can worship, and it is wonderful.

I am truly thankful for the Woven Women in my church, and the Proverbs 31 study that has been such a blessing to my life. I sing praises in recognition of this as another of God's gifts.

"Charm can mislead and beauty soon fades. The woman to be admired and praised is the woman who lives in the Fear-of-God" (Proverbs 31:30 the Message).

—Cheryl, a Woven Woman of virtue

GETTING TO KNOW YOU

So, my friend, what do you do? Who do you want to be when you grow up? Let's take some *you* time—journal required!

The passage below has greatly impacted my life. Please write it in your journal and think about each phrase as you copy it down. Then, write a response to God about the things that concern you.

Look at the birds, free and unfettered, not tied down to a job description, careless in the care of God. And you count far more to him than birds … What I'm trying to do here is get you to relax, to not be so preoccupied with getting, so you can respond to God's giving. People who don't know God and the way he works fuss over these things, but you know both God and how he works. Steep your life in God-reality, God-initiative, God-provisions. Don't worry about missing out. You'll find your everyday human concerns will be met. Give your entire attention to what God is doing right now, and don't get worked up about what may or may not happen tomorrow. God will help you deal with whatever hard things come up when the time comes. (Matthew 6:26, 31–34 the Message)

Think about your priorities. Respond to these questions in your journal.

- Have you been giving more priority to productivity or to people?
    - Look at your schedule. How can you create more space for relationships?
    - Could you replace social media/texting with more one-on-one time?
    - Are you guilty of making a god of your time, not being available for others? Confess and discuss this in your journal with God.
    - Imagine being less time-focused and more spontaneous.
    - Reflect in your journal: would you feel freer or less critical of yourself? Would it change your attitude toward others?
- Perhaps you are at the other end of the spectrum. Relationships are draining you of productive time. You're giving too much of yourself; others are expecting too much of you.
    - How can you create healthier boundaries with those who are consuming your time and energy?
    - If you are drained due to incessant worry or fear, will you surrender the person(s) to God and trust Him to look after them and their needs?
    - Will you place their hands in the hands of the Savior and confess that you are powerless to save others?

"The need is not the call." These were powerful words my counselor spoke over and over to me. As women, we want to meet the needs of others. As compassionate caregivers, our hearts and eyes are keenly aware of the hurting around us. We easily confuse it as our *calling*. If there is a gaping need in front of us, we assume we must *do* something about it.

God is in the miracle-working business, and He will reach into the depth of this person's being. Often we need to just step aside so the person can grow through this trial with God. Our role is to pray, encourage, and comfort, but stay out of God's way. There is only one Savior. His name is Jesus. Only He can change us at the core of our beings.

What is your current status? Evaluate your life using the list below, and write about it in your journal. You might discover you fit into more than one of the categories.

1. Needy of someone to come alongside you; feeling alone and adrift
2. Exhausted, running on empty, critical of others, and close to burnout
3. Dissatisfied, longing for change, feeling a bit lost
4. Comfortable but lacking a sense of adventure; life is bland
5. Passionate about what you do; confident of who you have become
6. Other:_____

Referring back to the story behind the story in the *Love Looks Deeper* and the *Getting to Know Me* sections, will you muster the courage to write your deepest, darkest moment in life?

It was a big deal for me to share mine in this book. I was nervous, and I battled with spiritual warfare. Satan didn't want me to share with you. It was empowering to write it down. I feel so much stronger and more solid in my walk with God for having confessed it to you, my friend! Thank you for not judging me.

If I can write it for everyone to read, I know you can do this—just between you and God. It will "strengthen you in your inner being, so that Christ may dwell in your heart through faith."[60]

---

[60] Ephesians 3:16–17 (NIV).

- Where was God in the midst of that event?
- Have you allowed Him to come into that scene and speak His truth about who you are in His eyes?
- Will you please seek and accept His forgiveness?

Follow the three-step process and hear these words of Jesus on your behalf:

Your sins are forgiven.
Your faith has saved you.
Go in peace.

GETTING TO KNOW GOD

In chapter 3, we discussed that knowing God is more than just knowing what the Bible says about Him, what the preacher preaches about Him, or reading the latest devotional. To know God is to enter into a two-way conversation with Him. This may seem mystical or magical, but this is a miracle, a gift from God! His Holy Spirit lives in us when we are born again in Christ. He is the still small voice who speaks to our minds and gives wise advice. My heart's desire is for you to become adept at recognizing, listening, and responding to this heavenly voice of God.

If I had recognized God's voice, I would have known what God wanted me to do. If I had recognized God's voice, I would have known who God wanted me to be. I still remember sitting in church, sensing a call to ministry around the age of ten. "Who, me?" I asked. The only women I had seen in ministry were pictures of missionaries on prayer cards. They didn't look anything like the person I expected to be. I decided perhaps I could become a pastor's wife, but it seemed impossible—I couldn't play the piano! (Do you see how Satan twisted that, years later, when I was approached by Vince, my lay pastor?)

In the passage below, James advises us to be as concerned about our inner being as we are about what we're doing. We are to mirror God. The only way we can do that is to listen for His voice and obey what He tells us to do.

> Don't fool yourself into thinking that you are a listener when you are anything but, letting the Word go in one ear and out the other. Act on what you hear! Those who hear and don't act are like those who glance in the mirror, walk away, and two minutes later have no idea who they are, what they look like.
>
> But whoever catches a glimpse of the revealed counsel of God—the free life!—even out of the corner of his eye, and sticks with it, is no distracted scatterbrain but a man or woman of action. That person will find delight and affirmation in the action.[61]

It's like looking in the mirror and noticing you have broccoli in your teeth, your hair is sticking straight up, your mascara is smeared, and your dress is on backward. You can plainly see you are a hot mess, but you totally forget about it and walk right out the door—broccoli and all. The point: this is not just a two-way conversation of praying and listening. Obedience requires an action step. When you see broccoli in your teeth, you waste no time removing it. If God is pointing to something spiritual that needs to be cleaned up, surrender and ask His forgiveness. God wants our spiritual selves in good working order before we go about our day.

To know God's voice is to distinguish the difference between the voice of God and the voice of Satan. Satan is waging a battle for your soul, but don't let him frighten you. God in Christ Jesus already won the battle for you. In fact, the choices you make every day determine who is in control of your life.

---

[61] James 1:23–25 (the Message).

KNOW THE DIFFERENCE

Spend some time in God's Word. With your journal and Bible in hand, process the voices in your head. Allow God's voice to be heard. Take your time with this. You may want to do one of these each day in your prayer time until you have completed all of them.

- Confusion vs. peace? Satan loves to keep us in a state of confusion, but God is a God of peace.
    - o   Read 1 Corinthians 14:33; James 3:16.
- Guilt vs. conviction? There is a difference between guilt and conviction. Guilt is crippling and is Satan's way of stirring up our past sins. Conviction instructs the heart. It is God's way of disciplining us and leading us to freedom from sin.
    - o   Read John 16:8-10; 1 Thessalonians 1:4-5.
- Tempting vs. testing? James 1:12-15 describes the difference between tempting and testing. God reserves the right to allow us to grow through various trials. These are tests of our faith. Satan is the tempter. His goal is to cause us to sin. His voice is the negative thought or temptation that keeps circling viciously in our heads. If we begin to entertain that thought, it turns to lust and gains power over our will.
    - o   Read James 1:1-4 to learn more about the value of God's testing.
- Condemnation vs. discipline? Satan just loves to heap guilt upon guilt to remind us of and condemn us for what we have done wrong. If he is successful, this separates us from God and distances us from other people.

    God forgives. Jesus took our condemnation to the cross. God disciplines us like beloved children. He rewards our obedience.
    - o   Read Romans 8:1, 33-38; Hebrews 7:7-12.
- Doing vs. being? Satan is a slave driver, a taskmaster. His goal is to run us down, wear us out, and keep us

so busy doing good things that we miss the point of God's plan for us. He exhausts us to steal our joy and rob us of loving relationships.

God has all the time in the world. He's more interested in the person that we're becoming because we accomplish more for the kingdom if we become more like our King. Our dependence upon Him will accomplish more than anything we can do in our own strength.

  o   Read Ephesians 2:4–10; 3:20.
- Fear vs. reverence? The word *fear* is often used in the Old Testament in relationship to God. There is reason to fear God because He is all-powerful, all-knowing, and always present. To fear God is to revere Him, respect His awesomeness, and to come before Him in reverence of who He is. Sometimes we can be a bit too casual and take God for granted.

  Satan wants us to fear God in a different way. He convinces us that God is always angry, constantly judging, and waiting for us to mess up. This is not the character of God. God is love.

  o   Read 1 John 4:7–19.

If you consider the overall nature of these characteristics, it becomes obvious that the difference between the voice of Satan and the voice of God is a negative versus positive influence. God's voice is that soft, still whisper introducing new thoughts, new ways of doing things, the tug of the heart prompting you to be or do something not typically on your radar. This is God's way of directing your day—perhaps to visit or correspond with someone or to go here or go there.

When I begin to argue with that inner voice, I know I am arguing with God Himself because it is something I don't want to do. His voice is fatherly and instructional. There have been many times when I did not listen or obey. In hindsight, I saw that if I had followed His prompt, I could have avoided a hardship or misunderstanding. When I do follow Him, the blessing is amazing!

A PRAYER FOR YOU

This is a beautiful prayer of submission written by John Wesley, founder of Methodism. Read it with appreciation for every phrase, and use it as an avenue to submit more fully to God.

A Covenant Prayer

I am no longer my own, but Yours.

Put me to what you will. Rank me with whom You will.

Put me to doing. Put me to suffering.

Let me be employed by You or laid aside for You;

exalted for You or brought low by You.

Let me have all things. Let me have nothing.

I freely and heartily yield all things to
Your pleasure and disposal.

And now, O glorious and blessed God,
Father, Son, and Holy Spirit,

You are mine and I am Yours.
So be it.

And the covenant which I have made on earth,

let it be ratified in heaven.
Amen.

"A QUESTION OF SIN"

She was accused. Caught in the act of adultery. Robed in the scarlet letter. Shame was her companion. She was silent before her accusers.

They pressed in around her, hearts as hard as the stones in hand. Poised to punish, to kill.

Jesus disarmed them with a question of sin. "If any one of you is without sin, let him be the first to throw a stone at her." Saving words. Forgiving words. Hope for a new life.

We are guilty. Accused. Ashamed. Quick to judge, to throw stones.

Jesus forgives. Forgets. Saves. Gives hope. He knows us by name. Jesus has the last word, the final say: "Go now and leave your life of sin."

WHAT DOESN'T SHE DO?

For you were once darkness, but now
you are light in the Lord.
Live as children of light.
—Ephesians 5:8 (NIV)

When we peruse Proverbs 31, most of us arrive at the same question: Is there anything this woman *doesn't* do? It reads like an itinerary, a day in the life of the perfect Christian woman. We feel inferior and deflated, unable to measure up to God's standard. Do not despair, my friend! Take another look at this passage in search of anything and everything this woman *doesn't* do.

10 Who can find a virtuous woman, for her price is far above rubies. (KJV)
11 Her husband has full confidence in her and lacks nothing of value.
12 She brings him good, not harm, all the days of her life.
13 She selects wool and flax and works with eager hands.
14 She is like the merchant ships, bringing her food from afar.
15 She gets up while it is still dark; she provides food for her family and portions for her servant girls.
16 She considers a field and buys it; out of her earnings she plants a vineyard.
17 She sets about her work vigorously; her arms are strong for her tasks.

18 She sees that her trading is profitable, and her lamp does not go out at night.

19 In her hand she holds the distaff and grasps the spindle with her fingers.

20 She opens her arms to the poor and extends her hands to the needy.

21 When it snows, she has no fear for her household; for all of them are clothed in scarlet.

22 She makes coverings for her bed; she is clothed in fine linen and purple.

23 Her husband is respected at the city gate, where he takes his seat among the elders of the land.

24 She makes linen garments and sells them, and supplies the merchants with sashes.

25 She is clothed with strength and dignity; she can laugh at the days to come.

26 She speaks with wisdom, and faithful instruction is on her tongue.

27 She watches over the affairs of her household and does not eat the bread of idleness.

28 Her children arise and call her blessed; her husband also, and he praises her:

29 "Many women do noble things, but you surpass them all."

30 Charm is deceptive, and beauty is fleeting; but a woman who fears the LORD is to be praised,

31 Give her the reward she has earned, and let her works bring her praise at the city gate (NIV).

SHE DOESN'T FLAUNT HER WORTH

The very first line is important, "Who can find a virtuous woman, for her price is far above rubies."[62] This is a woman who knows her worth but doesn't flaunt it. Like a ruby, she is a rare find. She doesn't need to make a name for herself or parade around trying to impress people. Jesus is the one she

---

[62] Proverbs 31:10 (KJV).

aims to please. The woman of virtue has removed the mask, reclaimed her identity, and she knows her true self is rooted in Christ. Her search is over; her heart is at rest.

God gives her value, shapes her story, and reveals her life purpose. To encounter her is to encounter Him. Everything a virtuous woman does—*and doesn't do*—reflects the God who loves her. There is no need for a holier-than-thou attitude either. He does not demand anything but to love Him and love others. She is adept at doing exactly that. Restoring relationships is her way of life, which makes her a faithful friend and a natural leader.

SHE DOESN'T DEGRADE OR HARM HER HUBBY

Her hubby knows his worth also. How does he know? She doesn't harm him. She reminds him he was created for more, and she helps him set his sights above and beyond this world by pointing him to God.

> Her husband has full confidence in her and lacks nothing of value. She brings him good, not harm, all the days of her life.[63]

Despite what our culture propagates, this virtuous woman is the type that real men want to marry. Virtue chases virtue as a beautiful dance of souls, reaching for heavenly realms on earth. Virtue becomes visible by living it, a vision of sheer white—the bride of Christ. The beauty of virtue appeals to the hearts of men. A woman of virtue is a mystery and yet is the answer to the crossword puzzles of her mate's life. She can lead him to the cross and finish his sentences with an exclamation mark. She is his better half; they both know it, but she doesn't show it with attempts to elevate herself over him.

Her prayers keep her humble and keep him seeking to live up to the value she has placed in him. He rises to the

---

63   Proverbs 31:11–12.

occasion and becomes the man of her dreams. She is his secret to success. The more she prays and honors, the more he models his life after the Bridegroom, Jesus Christ. They set the standard for holy living, and this is the reward: "Her husband is respected at the city gate, where he takes his seat among the elders of the land."[64]

The woman of virtue is thoughtful when she speaks with her husband, choosing her words wisely. More important, she doesn't loosely spout out harmful words in public that will reflect poorly on him. Though things get rocky and frustrating even in a healthy marriage, she chooses not to vent her frustrations to others and cut him to the bone. She shows respect by waiting until things cool down; then she uses discernment as to whether or not the issue needs to be addressed with her other half.

The virtuous woman is not subservient to her man. A marriage relationship is stronger when facing life shoulder to shoulder as equal partners, as God intended. Just as she does not harm her husband, he treats his wife with love and respect. There is no room in this relationship for emotional, physical, sexual, or spiritual abuse. A life of virtue will suffocate in a relationship based on power and control—and so will the marriage. Ephesians 5:21-33 clearly describes how a husband and wife are to interact, and it all begins with this mutual understanding: "Submit to one another out of reverence for Christ."[65]

This wife loves her husband with the love of Christ, and sometimes it takes all the love of Christ she can muster to love her man unconditionally. Rather than focusing on what he is lacking, she looks for the good because she wants the same in return. She doesn't devalue her other half because devaluing him devalues her—and vice versa. The virtuous wife is described in 1 Peter 3:1-4:

---

[64] Proverbs 31:23.
[65] Ephesians 5:21 (NIV).

Be good wives to your husbands, responsive to their needs. There are husbands who, indifferent as they are to any words about God, will be captivated by your life of holy beauty. What matters is not your outer appearance—the styling of your hair, the jewelry you wear, the cut of your clothes—but your inner disposition. Cultivate inner beauty, the gentle, gracious kind that God delights in.[66]

Did you catch this line in 1 Peter? *"There are husbands who, indifferent as they are to any words about God, will be captivated by your life of holy beauty."* This gives hope to those who are unequally yoked.[67] We all know women who stay the course, balancing faithfulness to God and church with faithfulness to "indifferent," unbelieving husbands. This can be quite a juggling act. I have friends who have prayed for decades for their husbands' hearts to turn to God. They are ladies-in-waiting for the man of their dreams to rise up and join the ranks of Christian soldiers.

You know these women too. Maybe you are one of them. These words speak loudly as to how we treat such husbands—they are "indifferent ... to any words about God." In other words, you can talk to them about going to church and/or becoming a Christian until you are blue in the face, but mere words will just push them further away. Turn all those words into power-packed prayers. God will do the wooing of his heart, and your hubby "will be captivated by your life of holy beauty."

Every woman wants to be this woman—captivating, beautiful, holy. My dear friend Connie is this woman. She was willing to share her story with us:

My husband, Chuck, struggled with addictions—lots of addictions—throughout our thirty-six-year marriage. I came to Christ early on,

---

[66] The Message.
[67] 2 Corinthians 6:14.

nine years after taking my wedding vows. The closer I came to Jesus, the less my husband wanted anything to do with Him. We raised two teenagers through this challenging time of being unequally yoked.

It got so bad I often longed for my marriage to end. But instead of seeking an attorney, God nudged me to meet with a pastor. I was certain, once the pastor knew my life situation, he would instruct me to "Get the kids and get out of there."

Instead, I heard three words that would end up changing everything: Love him unconditionally.

It took eighteen long years of being unequally yoked before my husband invited Jesus into his heart. Always, throughout every struggle, God nudged me to "stay and pray," loving him unconditionally. Later, when Chuck was asked to share his testimony as to how he came to the Lord, he replied, "It was the consistent thread of Jesus that I saw in my wife. I could not deny Him any longer."

We forget sometimes that others are watching us. Chuck was watching how I handled life's storms during those eighteen years, including the death of his seventeen-year-old son. My husband heard my prayers every evening at the dinner table for God's provision, and he witnessed the amazing and unexplainable ways God answered those petitions. And Chuck knew he didn't always treat me right, yet still I stayed with him.

God hears the cries of His daughters. His love in us enables us to face the hard stuff … and to love unconditionally.

—Connie, a Woven Woman of virtue

Let's pause and pray for these husbands and for God to soften and claim their hearts as His. Pray for our female friends who are living this "life of holy beauty" alone. May they never give up on Christ, the church, their children, or their husbands, and may they be so "captivating" that their lives point their families to the source of their beauty. This is also a reminder to our unmarried friends: choose one who believes as you do, and captivate your future groom with the beauty of holy living.

We cannot assume the woman of virtue is married. As we discussed in chapter 4, the passage was written describing the woman who qualifies as a suitable bride for the King. She may be single, separated, estranged, a single mother, divorced, or a widow. What makes her virtuous? Her marital status is the bride of Christ. King Jesus must become the love of her life. Then she is qualified to bring "him good, not harm all the days of her life."

SHE DOESN'T EAT BREAD

Say what? "She does not eat the bread of idleness."[68] Now there's an interesting figure of speech. Have you noticed women love to eat bread and men are more apt to be meat eaters? Maybe that's why there is something to be said about "eating bread." In this case, she does not eat it. Fortunately, it's not talking about the bread we consume. We can bask in the scent of bread baking in the oven, partake of every scrumptious morsel, and still be women of virtue (unless you're gluten-and-grain-free, like me).

What pictures come to mind when you think about eating the bread of idleness? The Hebrew word *atsluth*, translated here as *idleness*, means "sloth." We immediately picture someone who is unproductive, slothful, or lazy. Eating the bread of idleness implies a compulsion or obsession with idleness. I visualize a person who is miserably bloated as a

---

[68] Proverbs 31:27.

result of an insatiable appetite for this particular "bread." Her misery affects the lives of everyone around her. This is not a pretty picture! Reading 2 Thessalonians 3:11-13 sheds more light into the predicament of idleness:

> We hear that some among you are idle. They are not busy; they are busybodies. Such people we command and urge in the Lord Jesus Christ to settle down and earn the bread they eat … never tire of doing what is right.

What does Paul say about people who are idle? Don't you love the way he puts it? "They are not busy; they are busybodies." It sounds like he's telling them off! Isn't that our reaction to busybodies? We get fed up with them and the trouble they cause.

He also makes a correlation between idleness and bread— they need to "settle down and earn the bread they eat," rather than becoming like our picture of the miserable glutton stuffing her face with the bread of idleness.

In 1 Timothy 5:13, Paul is more descriptive as to what being idle and being a busybody actually entails. Here, he advises the church in regard to young widows:

> Besides, they get into the habit of being idle and going about from house to house. And not only do they become idlers, but also gossips and busybodies, saying things they ought not to. (NIV)

When lonely, miserable, and idle, we tend to get very busy with our mouths, meddling into other people's business. What picture does he give of a person being idle? What does he say they do? Busybodies go from house to house, stirring up trouble with divisiveness. They "say things they ought not to." Just how idle are these people? They are busy with the affairs of others, overlooking their own.

There are times when gossip and rumors start somewhat

innocently. We attempt to retell something we have heard without remembering all the details. Changing just one word can alter the interpretation of a story. Even our tone of voice can turn an innocent remark into a derogatory one. The further the story goes around the grapevine, the more distorted it becomes. In a world saturated with multiple means of communicating, conversations are more challenging than ever. Texting, email, and social media can be misleading without eye contact, tone of voice, and body language. It is easy to take things the wrong way.

Sometimes women abuse prayer requests by sharing confidential information entrusted to them. This is a subtle yet very damaging form of gossip; an attempt to look important as one whom others entrust with their confidentiality. Yet the opposite is true. This person cannot be trusted. As leaders, we must help her to find her worth in Christ by refusing to be drawn into the details behind her request.

Eating "the bread of idleness" also reminds me of going to a nice restaurant that serves warm bread and butter while your meal is being prepared. If we eat too much bread, our appetites wane before the main dish is served. Our bellies are full. In the same way, we quickly get our fill of gossip and idle talk. We hunger for the main course, for life-giving work and light-bearing words. We are starving for virtue.

As Woven Women, God has enlisted us to satisfy these hungry hearts. When we gather together, the conversation is focused on scripture, prayer, and personal stories. There is no room at the table for gossip or belittling our husbands or others. We can be confident in knowing every person has equal opportunity to share, no one has liberty to dominate the table talk, and what we say will not go beyond this circle of friends.

SHE DOESN'T CALL IT QUITS

When darkness comes and things get ugly, she keeps her lamp burning. "She sees that her trading is profitable, and her lamp does not go out at night."[69]

The woman of virtue gains momentum and gets results in her prayer life—her trading is profitable.[70] Ever vigilant, she believes God will accomplish all He has promised according to His timing. She knows this from experience. God has been faithful to her in the past; this strengthens her faith for the future.

Her lamp does not go out at night. Some of you are ready to flip that light switch! Those who are energy-conscious are distracted with thoughts of their electric bill. But this lady's lamp stays lit by keeping company with the Lord. He is her energy source! She stays focused on Him as her life, love, and light. Jesus shares this metaphor about keeping our lamps on:

> Keep your shirts on; keep the lights on! Be like house servants waiting for their master to come back from his honeymoon, awake and ready to open the door when he arrives and knocks. Lucky the servants whom the master finds on watch! He'll put on an apron, sit them at the table, and serve them a meal, sharing his wedding feast with them. It doesn't matter what time of the night he arrives; they're awake—and so blessed![71]

Jesus is referring to our spiritual status: to be spiritually "awake" and expectant for His return, not allowing our spiritual lives to grow dim or dull but keeping our lights burning and bright by being in constant communion with Christ. His Spirit living in us is the lamp, our source of light. We keep the lamp burning by spending time with Him and

---

[69] Proverbs 31:18.
[70] Refer back to chapter 3.
[71] Luke 12:35–38 (the Message).

seeking His plans and direction. By clinging to His promises in the Bible and being quick to confess any disobedience or wrong turn, we stay on track. Our love connection with Christ determines our readiness for His return. The methods He uses to continually point us to Jesus Christ, who never leaves us, are our sensitivity to His Spirit nudging our hearts, His soft still voice whispering wisdom into our thoughts, His continual signs of affirmation along the way, and an inner sense of confidence or direction. Our readiness is simply our awareness of His presence and obedience to His Spirit by being tuned into Him at any and every given moment.

Years ago, a prayer partner gifted me with a wooden sign to hang in my laundry room: "A day hemmed in prayer will never unravel." Every time I read it, I felt challenged. I prayed every morning but not at night. Jesus asks us to pray early in the morning *and* late at night. This doesn't mean we become insomniacs! What about when we can't sleep? There is no point in counting sheep. God urges us to pray at any and all times of the day because He is always present and listening:

> Evening, and morning, and at noon, will I pray,
> and cry aloud: and he shall hear my voice.
> (Psalm 55:17 KJV)

Do you see the correlation between these passages? We are to be tightly bonded to God through Jesus Christ, continually aware and prepared to respond to His Holy Spirit. There is nothing like being on call for God. We can be women God trusts by being women who trust God.

Jesus is instructing us to be expectant in prayer and in the way we live our lives because He will return and we, as Woven Women of virtue, will be dressed in robes of righteousness, seated at the wedding banquet of Christ. I just cannot wait to be seated at the table with *you*!

> This is the promise of God, spoken by angels,
> when the risen Jesus ascended into heaven:

They were looking intently up into the sky as he was going, when suddenly two men dressed in white stood beside them. "Men of Galilee," they said, "why do you stand here looking into the sky? This same Jesus, who has been taken from you into heaven, will come back in the same way you have seen him go into heaven."(Acts 1:10–11 NIV)

I love this question: "Why do you stand here looking into the sky?" Girlfriend, God has work for us to do before Jesus returns. There is a huge, wide world waiting to be reached. Let's keep our lamps burning—morning, noon, and night—so He can count on us to be first responders. We are Woven Women—reaching the world!

SHE DOESN'T FEAR OR FRET

This woman is ready for whatever comes her way. She is not afraid. "When it snows, she has no fear for her household; for all of them are clothed in scarlet."[72] She is so confident, in fact, that "she can laugh at the days to come."[73]

This does not mean she doesn't take life seriously. It illustrates an ability to look life in the face without fear of the future. Instead of focusing on faults and failures, she appreciates how God made her and allows Him to change her. Not taking herself too seriously, her free spirit is able to laugh at her idiosyncrasies. This exemplary friend is obedient to the command, "Don't worry about anything; pray about everything."[74]

God cleansed her past, called her for a specific purpose, and holds the plan for her future.[75] She listens, waiting for

---

[72] Proverbs 31:21.
[73] Proverbs 31:25.
[74] Philippians 4:6 (NLT).
[75] Jeremiah 29:11-13.

His voice of direction before taking the next step.[76] Christ could return at any given moment,[77] and this bride is ready to meet her Bridegroom. She is one of the "smart virgins" Jesus speaks about in the following parable:

> God's kingdom is like ten young virgins who took oil lamps and went out to greet the bridegroom. Five were silly and five were smart. The silly virgins took lamps, but no extra oil. The smart virgins took jars of oil to feed their lamps. The bridegroom didn't show up when they expected him, and they all fell asleep. In the middle of the night someone yelled out, "He's here! The bridegroom's here! Go out and greet him!"
>
> The ten virgins got up and got their lamps ready. The silly virgins said to the smart ones, "Our lamps are going out; lend us some of your oil."
>
> They answered, "There might not be enough to go around; go buy your own."
>
> They did, but while they were out buying oil, the bridegroom arrived. When everyone who was there to greet him had gone into the wedding feast, the door was locked. Much later, the other virgins, the silly ones, showed up and knocked on the door, saying, "Master, we're here. Let us in."
>
> He answered, "Do I know you? I don't think I know you."
>
> So stay alert. You have no idea when he might arrive.[78]

---

[76] Proverbs 3:5–6.
[77] Matthew 24:30–36.
[78] Matthew 25:1–13 MSG

When you first read this scripture, you might think the "smart virgins" are smart alecks. They are unwilling to share their oil with the "silly virgins." It may seem unfair for the silly virgins to be rejected because they had to go get oil. Jesus is illustrating that not everyone will be welcomed into heaven. The silly ones were not taking God's Word or their relationship with Him seriously. They were not prepared.

There is a misconception today that being "a good person" will get you to heaven. Jesus said, "I am the way and the truth and the life. No one comes to the Father except through me."[79] We all know people who only come around when they need their lamps lit, don't we? They live a vicarious life, teetering on the dark side. When rebellion or carelessness leaves them in a pit, they come back around for support, pretending to be Christians but not living the life. They are drawn back to the light, seeking just enough oil to get by. Our role is to always point them back to the only one who can save them.

The moral of the story is to be ready to meet Jesus—the Bridegroom—when He arrives. We prepare by believing He died on the cross to save us from sin, confessing our sinfulness, accepting His forgiveness, and living a life of commitment to Christ, loving Him as a bride loves her bridegroom.

If we are "smart," like five of the ten virgins in the story, we are alert and prepared. Our future is brighter than our past because we go to God for the answer to every life question. He is our future, the oil which keeps our lamps burning. In fact, His Spirit is the lamp that shines from within us. We are His ambassadors to the world.

> Here's another way to put it: You're here to be light, bringing out the God-colors in the world. God is not a secret to be kept. We're going public with this, as public as a city on a hill. If I make you light-bearers, you don't think I'm going to hide you under a bucket, do you? I'm putting you on a light stand. Now that I've put you there

---

[79] John 14:3–6 (NIV).

on a hilltop, on a light stand—shine! Keep open
house; be generous with your lives. By opening
up to others, you'll prompt people to open up
with God, this generous Father in heaven.[80]

Wow—this woman! She is a "light-bearer ... bringing
out the God-colors in the world." She is a Woven Woman,
reinventing leadership by being generous with her heart, her
home, her life; a beautiful reflection of Christ. Her light is so
bright it reaches the world. Could this woman be *you* shining
so brightly?

GETTING TO KNOW ME

As I surrender and grow deeper in love with the Lord, I notice
people are drawn to my eyes and offer compliments. I know
it's not based so much on physical appearance as it is the light
shining through them. They are attracted to Christ in me. I
smile and thank Jesus for placing His lamp in this earthen
vessel of mine. It hasn't always been so. It's taken me years
to grow.

Are you glowing as you're growing? Are you walking in
the light? John recounts a life-changing scene when a woman
met Jesus. Please take a few minutes to carefully read the
details in John 8:1–12. Allow it to soak into your heart before
continuing.

Now, visualize this woman's introduction to Jesus. Her
sin—not her virtue—was her claim to fame. Amid the people
wanting to meet Jesus, she was introduced as the woman
caught in adultery. I can't imagine any woman wanting that
title. We all know that both a male and a female are required
to commit adultery, but they only presented the woman. In
my opinion, a "woman who was a prisoner of men" seems a
more fitting description.

In truth, she was used as a pawn in the hands of the

---

[80]   Matthew 5:14–16 (the Message).

Pharisees. By appealing to Jesus's compassion, they hoped to catch Him betraying the law by using this vulnerable woman as a scapegoat. Humiliating her before the entire group, they announced,

> "Teacher, this woman was caught red-handed in the act of adultery. Moses, in the Law, gives orders to stone such persons. What do you say?" They were trying to trap him into saying something incriminating so they could bring charges against him.[81]

Jesus lingered. All eyes were on Him as He wrote something in the sand. Time stood still. Itching ears awaited His words. Perhaps He was giving her accusers time to reflect on their evil scheme before He thoughtfully responded,

> "If any one of you is without sin, let him be the first to throw a stone at her." One at a time, her accusers put down their rocks and walked away. Jesus looked up and asked her, "Woman, where are they? Has no one condemned you?"
>
> "No one sir," she said.
>
> "Then neither do I condemn you. Go now and leave your life of sin."

In that moment of pardon, the weight of every person's sin must have felt so heavy; the burden was too much for each of them to bear. The Pharisees had incriminated this woman. Jesus brought charges against them all. Not one person was innocent. This signifies what Jesus did for us on the cross. He felt the ugliness, the sin of the people and their eagerness to point out the sin of the downcast and the used and abused. Despite how despicable they were, Jesus responded with grace and offered a brighter future.

---

[81] John 8:4–6 (the Message).

> When Jesus spoke again to the people, he said,
> "I am the light of the world. Whoever follows me
> will never walk in darkness, but will have the
> light of life."[82]

Like the woman caught in adultery, I was a prisoner of men. After discovering that my daughter had been sexually abused, I wanted to learn everything I could about childhood sexual abuse. Reading the legal definitions and descriptions, I realized I also had been sexually abused as a child. My wrong choices began to make sense. It was my way of coping with pain, of filling my love tank. The power of saying *no* had been stolen from me. I couldn't cry real tears or scream out loud until I was in my forties. Silenced by fear, I was held captive all those years.

When I came to my dead end road, Jesus was right there waiting for me, forgiving and encouraging me.

"I don't condemn you. Go on your way, and don't sin."

Not only did He not condemn me, but He didn't blame me. Jesus pointed to the very source of my sin: the sins committed against me and the odds stacked against me. In the darkest time of my life after my husband's suicide, God's answers to my endless questions led me to the light. I know from personal experience His words are true:

> I am the light of the world. Whoever follows me
> will never walk in darkness, but will have the
> light of life.[83]

When Jesus spoke these words to the crowd that day, He was also speaking to you and me. He offers us the same opportunity as the woman caught in adultery—a new beginning, a new life. We have a choice to choose light, a life without sin. My life is a testimony of the power of following Jesus Christ, *the light of the world*. He gave me power over sin and turned my darkness to light.

---

[82] John 8:12 (NIV).
[83] John 8:12 (NIV).

My husband, Mark, was a forty-year-old bachelor when we met. His waiting for the right person was quite a contrast to my two failed marriages. From the beginning of our relationship, I made clear my intention to remain spiritually and sexually pure until I married, *if* I were to marry again. He had made the same commitment to Christ in his younger years.

Of the three marriages, this was the only time I was a virgin on my wedding day. You may find that statement contradictory, considering my history, but God cleansed me from my past before I met Mark. Jesus made me a spiritual virgin, His righteous bride. I didn't have to continue to wallow in my past sins. Just because I'd already had sex with others did not mean I couldn't be pure for this man of my dreams. It's never too late in God's eyes to choose purity. It makes all the difference. Our relationship is built on a strong foundation of mutual love, trust, and equal partnership. I thank God for this beautiful life.

GETTING TO KNOW THE VIRTUOUS WOMAN: WHAT DOESN'T SHE DO?

Let's review what this woman of virtue doesn't do. She doesn't throw stones, doesn't condemn, doesn't get caught up in wrong relationships—but if she does, did, or has, she accepts God's forgiveness, goes on her way, and stops sinning. She forgives herself and doesn't wallow in self-condemnation.

She does not harm her husband and doesn't call it quits. She chooses not to fear or fret. She doesn't "go from house to house" to stir up trouble because she is busy taking care of her own business and family. She does not poke her nose into other people's business or "eat the bread of idleness" by wasting time gossiping or saying things she ought not say. Instead, "she speaks with wisdom and faithful instruction is on her tongue."[84]

You might be thinking, *Everything she doesn't do just adds*

---

[84]   Proverbs 31:26 (NIV).

to her virtue. There are a multitude of things she does not do because her heart is focused on pleasing God, not people. Isn't it easier to see how she manages to accomplish such noble things? She uses her energy on what matters most. This is a beautiful way to sum up her life:

> This is the message we have heard from him and proclaim to you, that God is light, and in him is no darkness at all. If we say we have fellowship with him while we walk in darkness, we lie and do not practice the truth. But if we walk in the light, as he is in the light, we have fellowship with one another, and the blood of Jesus his Son cleanses us from all sin.[85]

The woman of virtue is not an elitist. She is you. She is me. She is a woman who fell down but applied every ounce of strength she had to rise back up again ... and again. She is the woman at the well, the woman with the issue of blood, the woman living a sinful life, the woman caught in adultery. These are the Esthers seated at our table—Cinderella stories in process.

They are Woven Women who have been at the bottom and have risen to the top. They are the cream of the crop. Having met Jesus face-to-face, they've looked into His eyes of love and allowed Him to penetrate the depths of their hearts and change their lives forever. We have the privilege of being their Lydia—gathering women, growing in our knowing of each other, of our true selves, and of God. All the while, we are being woven into a beautifully diverse tapestry of love. The following letter was written by one such woman:

> Ever since I have been in a relationship with Cindy Stiverson, I have grown closer and closer in my walk with the Lord. Her writings and friendship have meant a great deal to me. She

---

[85]   1 John 1:5-7 (ESV).

is an extremely positive and godly influence in my life.

The biggest impact has been through her Woven Quiet Retreats. Cindy's writings for the prayer stations have been profound and very introspective, as though God was speaking directly to me. I was able to look back at my life and see this painful time I have been going through as being directed by God—He wanted me to put Him first in my life.

In order to humble me so I would look to Him as my ultimate, God took my husband away. This was the most powerful circumstance He could have used to get my attention. God needed to be my top priority. The only one I could truly trust. My ultimate!

I have learned through these retreats that no one person is ever enough for another person here on earth. Realizing that I was never enough for my husband is what turned me to God, who is the source of enough.

God and God alone made me enough! It truly fills my soul to realize the King of kings will never leave or abandon me. He is my source of joy. I am ever so thankful to be part of the Woven ministry and for Cindy's words that have helped me on this journey with my Savior. This is a quote from one of her stations that really resonated with me:

"The woman I was yesterday, introduced me to the woman I am today, which makes me very excited about meeting the woman I will become tomorrow!"

After reading her words, I wrote in my journal:

I am Strong.

I was made on purpose.

You, Lord, chose me.

You, God, make me Enough.

Even if …

—Corky, a Woven Woman of virtue

GETTING TO KNOW YOU

Friend, I hope you have your journal ready. It's time to process all the nudges of the heart you have felt while reading this chapter. Relax and allow your mind to travel to new thoughts and insights as the Holy Spirit leads.

Have you ever caught fireflies and placed them in a jar? I think of memories as fireflies, tiny flashing rays of light we try to capture in our thoughts so that we might hold them there and enjoy them awhile. Some memories are spontaneous, fun-loving, joyous beams of light. Others can lead us into a dark and dreary night.

Memories of pain, anguish, and distress become heavy. They trap, enslave, depress, and immobilize us. These life events can serve as a line drawn in the sand—a total change of direction, where everything prior becomes history, and the future is suddenly a huge question mark. Everything you thought you would be doing tomorrow or next week or next year is obsolete, and you become aware that every single moment in time, every single breath you take, and every decision you make is of crucial importance.

Like the woman caught in adultery, most of us have experienced a major crisis in our lives, a turning point that forever changed our courses. Have you had a life-defining moment with Jesus?

- Can you muster the courage to retrieve these memories? Take your time and begin writing whatever comes to the surface.
- Allow these memories to become a spiritual mile marker in your life, right here in this moment, as you ask God to speak healing, hope, and truth into those situations. Write your plea, your prayer.

- Have you accepted the invitation of Jesus to follow Him and live in the light?

Precious friend, God uses your past and your pain to help define your passion and purpose. Our most difficult situations are the very things God uses to create change in this world.

- Identify your passion.
  - o What stirs your soul, makes you cry, or even makes you righteously angry?
  - o What lights your fire? Is there something you wish you could change about this world?
  - o How is God preparing you? What do you feel He is calling you to do?
- Who has helped you on your journey?
  - o Take a moment to pray and thank God for that person or persons.
  - o Read Jeremiah 29:11-13 in your Bible.
  - o Ask God to share His vision for your future.

GETTING TO KNOW GOD

Go back and review the subheadings of this chapter.

- Which section spoke to you the loudest? Write about it, place it before God, and allow Him to use it to shed light on your relationships.
- Read the parable of the ten virgins[86] again in the *She Doesn't Fear or Fret* section.
- Then join me below.

There are five smart and five silly virgins in the story, and all ten of them fell asleep while waiting for their Bridegroom to

---

[86] Matthew 25:1-13 (the Message).

arrive. After sharing this parable, Jesus advised His disciples to "stay alert."[87]

• How can we apply this to our prayer lives?

Our prayer lives are vital signs of our spiritual health. We stay alert by spending quality time with God, hungry to learn more from His Word, and allowing Him to transform us by surrendering more and more of our lives. The word *alert* means to be wide awake. Prayer is our wake-up call with the Lord. He awakens our spirits, convicts our hearts, and guides us on the right path. This is how we gain power over sin.

• Why do you think Jesus shared this particular story as a warning to be alert?

Jesus was reminding his disciples that God is building His kingdom. We have to be alert because the devil is building his kingdom too.

> Stay alert. The Devil is poised to pounce, and would like nothing better than to catch you napping. Keep your guard up. You're not the only ones plunged into these hard times. It's the same with Christians all over the world. So keep a firm grip on the faith. (1 Peter 5:8–9 the Message)

Jesus was alert to the tricks of the devil. He was alerting his disciples to not allow Satan to get a grip on them. We must keep a firm grip on our faith in God and not become spiritually lazy.

Jesus was also aware of his own personal need to stay alert in prayer. He needed the prayers of His disciples as He fulfilled His call to the cross. It is uncanny how the story of the ten virgins resembles the scene described in Matthew 26, just hours before Jesus was arrested:

---

[87] Matthew 25:13 (the Message).

Then Jesus went with them to a garden called Gethsemane and told his disciples, "Stay here while I go over there and pray." Taking along Peter and the two sons of Zebedee, he plunged into an agonizing sorrow. Then he said, "This sorrow is crushing my life out. Stay here and keep vigil with me."

Going a little ahead, he fell on his face, praying, "My Father, if there is any way, get me out of this. But please, not what I want. You, what do you want?"

When he came back to his disciples, he found them sound asleep. He said to Peter, "Can't you stick it out with me a single hour? Stay alert; be in prayer so you don't wander into temptation without even knowing you're in danger. There is a part of you that is eager, ready for anything in God. But there's another part that's as lazy as an old dog sleeping by the fire."

He then left them a second time. Again he prayed, "My Father, if there is no other way than this, drinking this cup to the dregs, I'm ready. Do it your way."

When he came back, he again found them sound asleep. They simply couldn't keep their eyes open. This time he let them sleep on, and went back a third time to pray, going over the same ground one last time. When he came back the next time, he said, "Are you going to sleep on and make a night of it? My time is up, the Son of Man is about to be handed over to the hands of sinners. Get up! Let's get going! My betrayer is here." (Matthew 26:36-46 the Message)

- What advice does Jesus give His disciples—and us—about being alert?

We have to pray in order to "stay alert." This is how we remain strong in the Lord's power and resist the temptations of the devil.

A PRAYER FOR YOU

Oh, Lord Jesus,

I want to be Your ambassador of light in this dark world. Show me what is lacking in me. Shine Your light on my path. I don't want to be caught sleeping when You arrive. Awaken my weary soul that I may be alert and ready when You come to me, daily aware of Your presence and Your plans for my life.

Today I ask You, Lord, to draw a line in the sand. Make this day a turning point in my life, a spiritual mile marker in my journey. Cut me free from my broken road of failure, fear, spiritual neglect, and the many vices I have used to cope with my pain, shame, and disappointment. I recognize these as worthless substitutes for the love and freedom You offer.

Dear Jesus, You spoke these words to the multitudes, and You are speaking to me: "if the Son sets you free, you will be free indeed."[88] I ask You to set me free from my past and present problems. Protect me from the enemy's plans for destruction and darkness. Point me on the right path. Shine Your light on the next step in my walk with Jesus. Help me to recognize Your Spirit's voice and the many ways You guide me. Lead me to Your will in everything I do, whether it is a menial task or a large vision. I want to be prepared and ready when You arrive, fully alert to Your Spirit every day from now to eternity. Make me free indeed!

I am declaring You as my first love, the only love that completes me. Thank you for loving me, and continue to fill

---

[88] John 8:36 (NIV).

me with more of Your love so that I can love You and truly learn to love myself and others.

I pray this in the name of Jesus Christ, who died to set me free.

Amen.

"RADIANT DAISY"

"Those who look to Him are radiant; their faces are never covered with shame."
—Psalm 34:5

He loves us!
Saving, forgiving, redeeming,
rebirthing, regenerating,
unending, unwavering,
unfathomable,
unconditional,
indescribable
love!

A FINAL PLEA

There comes a special moment in everyone's life,
a moment for which that person was born.
That special opportunity, when she
seizes it, will fulfill her mission—
a mission for which she is uniquely qualified.
In that moment, she finds greatness. It is her finest hour.[89]
—Winston Churchill

Well, my friend, we're coming to the end of our journey. Congratulations! The fact that you are reading this final chapter proves your commitment, tenacity, and desire to grow personally, spiritually, and relationally. If you have been faithfully journaling and reflecting after each chapter, you are embracing your personal story, discovering your true self, perceiving other women more positively, and recognizing their—and your—many virtues. There is no need for further introduction to the Proverbs 31 woman. You are her—she is you!

We have asked a lot of questions about this woman of virtue and applied them to our lives: "What makes this chick tick?" and "What is she laughing about?" We've questioned, "Who does she think she is?" and "Where did she get that outfit?" We even probed her private life as we took a deeper look, asking "What does she do?" and "What doesn't she do?"

Our focus now is the last verse:

---

[89] Masculine pronouns in Churchill's quote have been changed to feminine.

> Honor her for all that her hands have done, and
> let her works bring her praise at the city gate.[90]

A final plea at the end of the passage, it comes as a last tribute or epitaph. The word *epitaph* means "to say or do something that is likely to bring some endeavor to an end."[91] This verse seems to be that sort of statement—it brings closure or proclaims this woman's work has come to an end. It gives the impression we are putting this woman to rest; her life is over. We are praising her for her good deeds and moving on. Pause a few minutes to do what this verse is urging us.

- *Honor her* for all she has done to point us to a higher rule of living—as daughters of the King of kings and sisters in Christ.
- *Praise* our blessed woman of virtue for how God has used her to change our perspective of ourselves, of each other, and of God.
- *Thank* our heavenly Father for this passage of scripture that describes the type of women we can become when we choose to accept His invitation of love.

FROM LIFE TO DEATH

Do you ever feel like you spend more time in the future than you do in the present? As a visionary leader, much of my time is spent looking ahead. I predict the outcome so I will know how to prepare. Promoting the next event, preparing the next lesson I will teach or the next message I will speak, organizing an upcoming trip, deciding which new paintings I will market or the next article I will write requires planning months or even years in advance.

I am guessing you live in the future too. Whether it's forecasting, marketing, event planning, networking, educating,

---

[90] Proverbs 31:31 (NIV).
[91] *Collier's Dictionary* (Macmillan Publishing Co., 1986).

scheduling, or meal planning, we are compelled to keep one foot in the future for the sake of success.

What happens when we come to the end of our lives and one foot in the future becomes the metaphorical "one foot in the grave"? Planning and preparing take on a whole new spin. Things that seemed so important when we were young and active are no longer pertinent.

A few years ago, I walked this journey with my mother. She had been diagnosed with pulmonary fibrosis in August. In the following months, her health rapidly deteriorated. Along with her health, her memory and cognitive functioning decreased. We were faced with many decisions. The most difficult were how and where she would spend her last days. Her possessions were reduced to what would fit into a shared room in the nursing home. Her remaining belongings were in her house, but nobody was home.

Those concerns paled on the morning of January 3, when I received a call from the nurse, notifying me that my mother was unresponsive. At this point, she could not even speak. I called my siblings, and we gathered there at her bedside. As we sat in a circle quietly conversing, my brother was the first to notice—silence. Her entire body had given up the fight. She had breathed her last breath and moved into her eternal home.

In those months of caretaking, I had been praying she would go peacefully, hopefully in her sleep. My prayers were answered. She never really woke up that morning. She was at rest. Admiring her breathless body, I suddenly realized this was the last time I would speak to her, kiss her warm body, or touch her soft skin.

When I knelt to kiss her one final time, the smell of her hair transported me to my childhood. After all those years, the scent was still the same. I found a pair of scissors and cut a lock from the back of her head. It was the only piece of *her* I could keep with *me*. Sometimes when I am looking for something else, I come across an envelope containing a lock of black hair. I pause to take a look. The smell has faded, but the love and memories remain.

The following passage expresses the brevity of life compared to the length of eternity:

> Love never fails. But where there are prophecies, they will cease; where there are tongues, they will be stilled; where there is knowledge, it will pass away. For we know in part and we prophesy in part but when completeness comes, what is in part disappears. (1 Corinthians 13:8–10 NIV)

The things of this life pass away, as I witnessed with my mother. Predicting, preparing, planning, speaking, prophesying—they will cease as the life within us passes. Knowledge fades with age. Our minds grow dim. Our eyesight weakens. Our bodies and minds are forced into stillness, but "Love never fails."[92]

Love goes with us to the heavens and greets us at the pearly gates in its completeness! Love is God, and God is love.[93] He never leaves or forsakes us.[94] His love is the legacy we leave on earth beyond our grave. It's what I miss most about my mother and what my heart speaks in her loss.

A few months later, as we began cleaning out her home, I found the following poem in my mother's bedroom. She had cut it from an old magazine, framed it, and placed it on her nightstand. I have no idea how long it had been there, but I discovered it exactly when I needed it most. Whether she planned it or not, it served as a final love note from our mother to her children, grandchildren, and great-grandchildren. Now I pass it on to you because love is your legacy too!

> When I am gone, let me go, so I can move into my afterglow.

---

[92] 1 Corinthians 13:8.
[93] 1 John 4:16.
[94] Deuteronomy 31:6.

You mustn't tie me down with your tears, let's be happy that we've had so many years.

I gave you my love, you can only guess how much you gave me in happiness.

I thank you for the love you each have shown, but now it's time I traveled on alone.

So grieve me for a while if grieve you must, then let your grief be comforted with trust.

It's only for a while that we must part, so bless the memories within your heart.

And then, when you must come this way alone, I'll greet you with a smile and a "Welcome Home."[95]

HONOR HER

Last week our two older grandsons, Isaac (age six) and Jude (age eight), spent the night with us. They brought their brand new Bibles along. On the drive home, they were strapped in the back seat with their Bibles spread open across their laps. My hubby gave them scriptures to look up. He began with John 3:16. Jude was first to read it and was challenged to explain it. Isaac read it too.

Then Grampy told them to look up Proverbs 31, saying, "This is your Grammy's chapter. I want you to read it." I directed them to verses 10 and 11, giving them a break from reading the entire thing. While Isaac was still searching the index, Jude read aloud:

Who can find an excellent woman? She is worth far more than rubies. Her husband trusts her

---

95   Marian Wootton.

completely. She gives him all the important things he needs.[96]

Our deep thinker allowed the words to soak in, quietly studying what he had just read. Then he said emphatically, "That is so true!"

And my heart is still melting. Even an eight-year-old can identify the truth of God's word. "An excellent woman" is hard to find.

In some ways, this question—"Who can find a virtuous woman?"—would appear to just reinforce the lack of appreciation many women feel and the many tasks that go unnoticed and unappreciated. Just being female sometimes seems like a thankless station!

In every household, there are certain things that eventually have to be done, and someone has to do them. As a young newlywed, I suddenly discovered what these things were and who does them. Who washes the pan left in the sink because it was too hard to scrub? Who throws out moldy food in the fridge that smells worse than anything you ever imagined? Who cleans up the throw-up? Who scrubs the toilet and the bathtub ring? Who actually dusts the furniture instead of writing their names in the dust? Yes, it was a rude awakening! Upon discovering all this dirty work, I grew a new appreciation for my mother.

I suppose this is a small glimpse of why the poem introduces this woman as one who is *hard to find*—and closes with the salutation to *"Honor her ... praise her."* It reflects the first of the Ten Commandments.

> Children, obey your parents in the Lord, for this is right. Honor your father and mother—which is the first commandment with a promise—so that it may go well with you and that you may enjoy long life on the earth.[97]

---

[96] Proverbs 31:10–11 (NIRV).
[97] Ephesians 6:1–3.

A few years before my mother's death, this command stalked me. I continually heard these words spoken and saw them written, even in gift shops. My father had been gone for years. My stepfather also had passed. My mother was living alone, and it became hard to communicate with her. She was very hard of hearing, even with two hearing aids. As a widow, she was drawn into a habit of sharing information on the family grapevine, usually with inaccuracy due to her hearing. I tried to keep phone conversations light and my visits less frequent in an attempt not to become the latest inaccurate news. Yet God was obviously trying to tell me— *honor her!*

As a pastor and her youngest daughter, I helped plan the details of her funeral. I really struggled with feelings of not living up to this command of honoring my mother. Though I had given her special attention in the nursing home and throughout her sickness, I regretted the years she spent home alone and how difficult it was to share life with her. It led me back to this beloved poem and that last line: "Honor her. Let her works bring her praise at the city gates."

When family and friends gathered around the casket for one last farewell, I took the opportunity to do exactly that. I honored my mother for the many ways she sacrificed her life for her five children and for helping me through the ugliest time of my life. Mom was known for her distinctive and contagious laugh, so I praised her for her ability to "laugh at the days to come," even when she didn't know what tomorrow would bring.

At the end of my tribute, I asked everyone to stand. I shared how I didn't praise my mother enough when she was living, and I invited them to join me in this one last chance to "let her works bring her praise at the city gates." With everyone standing, we put our hands together and applauded my mother. It was a sight I will not forget. I can only imagine the reception she received at the gates of heaven!

FROM DEATH TO LIFE

I see this final plea from another perspective.

> Honor her for all that her hands have done, and
> let her works bring her praise at the city gate.[98]

Maybe the reference to the *city gate* is the gate of her heavenly home. There, she will be highly honored and immensely rewarded for partnering with God to help build His kingdom.

This leads us to an important question, "Where will I spend eternity?" It's a serious question, isn't it? God's Word is quite clear. There are only two choices: heaven or hell. Heaven is eternal paradise. Hell is eternal torment and damnation.[99]

Jesus shared the way to heaven by pointing out that He is the route. "I am the way, the truth, and the life. No one will see the Father except through me."[100] His death and resurrection is our invitation to heaven. How do we get there? We follow the path provided in God's Word.

- "For God so loved the world that he gave his one and only Son, that whoever believes in him shall not perish but have eternal life."[101]
    - o   Believe that Jesus died to give you eternal life.
- "For all have sinned and fall short of the glory of God."[102]
    - o   Recognize your need for a Savior.
    - o   Confess, "I am a sinner."
- "As far as the east is from the west, so far has he removed our transgressions from us."[103]
    - o   Ask God to cleanse you from your sin.

---

[98]   Proverbs 31:31 (NIV).
[99]   2 Peter 2.
[100]   John 14:6 (NIV).
[101]   John 3:16 (NIV).
[102]   Romans 3:23 (NIV).
[103]   Psalm 103:12 (NIV).

- o   Accept His forgiveness.
- "And all are justified freely by his grace through the redemption that came by Christ Jesus."[104]
  - o   Receive God's grace, His unmerited favor.
  - o   Believe you have been "justified freely." To be "justified" is to stand before God without guilt or shame, just as if you've never sinned.
  - o   Celebrate your redemption. Jesus took the sin of the world upon Himself to exchange our life of sin for a life of freedom from sin.
- "For the wages of sin is death, but the gift of God is eternal life in Christ Jesus our Lord."
  - o   Receive His gift of eternal life.
- "But God demonstrates his own love for us in this: While we were still sinners, Christ died for us."[105]
  - o   Thank Jesus for dying for you.
  - o   Receive God's love into your heart with gratitude for this great gift.
- "If you declare with your mouth, 'Jesus Is Lord,' and believe in your heart that God raised him from the dead, you will be saved."[106]
  - o   Pray with your whole heart, expressing your belief in Jesus and the salvation that comes through Him.
  - o   Declare your acceptance of Jesus as Lord of your life from this day forward.
- "Be still, and know that I am God; I will be exalted among the nations, I will be exalted in the earth."[107]
  - o   Begin a relationship with God.
  - o   Take time daily to be humble and silent before your Maker.
  - o   Read and study God's Word.
  - o   Exalt God in your life by giving Him first place.

---

[104]   Romans 3:24 (NIV).
[105]   Romans 5:8 (NIV).
[106]   Romans 10:9 (NIV).
[107]   Psalm 46:10 (NIV).

- o Pray. Serve. Fellowship in a Christian community of faith.
- "Search me, God, and know my heart; test me and know my anxious thoughts. See if there is any offensive way in me, and lead me in the way everlasting."[108]
  - o Allow God to reveal your blind spots and your need for change.
  - o Continually surrender as God points to areas of life to which you are clinging.
  - o Ask Him to help you break repetitive patterns of sin.
- "'Love the Lord your God with all your heart and with all your soul and with all your mind.' This is the first and greatest commandment. And the second is like it: 'Love your neighbor as yourself.'"[109]
  - o Love Him first and foremost.
  - o Love others in the way that you want to be loved

> "The world and its desires pass away, but the man/woman who does the will of God lives forever" (1 John 2:17).

The will of God is to *love*! As you fall more in love with Him, your desire will be to praise Him. Live a life of love!

LIVING A LIFE OF LOVE

> Honor her for all that her hands have done, and
> let her works bring her praise at the city gate.[110]

Let's approach this final plea in a different way. Perhaps this tribute is not at the end of her life but at the height of her influence. The city gates are where businessmen gathered to discuss important issues and where decisions

---

[108] Psalm 139:23–34 (NIV).
[109] Matthew 22:37–38 (NIV).
[110] Proverbs 31:31 (NIV).

were made, a place where commerce took place and important announcements were proclaimed. The writer is applauding the woman of virtue as a woman of influence who has earned her place among the leaders of the city.

As women, we assume she worked relentlessly to arrive at such a position. The world in which we live was and is a man's world. We have come a long way from biblical days, but most of us still feel the stigma of being female in a male-dominated society. With God by her side, she lifted the glass ceiling, breaking the stereotypical job description of her gender. It marks the point in time where she came to the end of herself and invited Jesus to be center stage in her story.

Her success is so much bigger than time invested or lucky breaks. This woman is tight with the one who has a huge design for her life. She "made the most of every opportunity"[111] God sent her way. He is to be praised, and she gives Him all the credit and glory.

Winston Churchill's words at the opening of this chapter are powerful and express the keys to a life of fulfillment:

- to recognize the "special moment" for which you were born
- to "seize" that "special opportunity"
- to "fulfill ... the mission for which you are uniquely qualified"

Churchill concludes, "In that moment, [she] finds greatness. It is [her] finest hour."

Whether he realized it or not, Winston Churchill was sharing a great truth. God designed each of us for a specific mission for which we alone are qualified and created perfectly to do. If we are in tune with His Spirit and know His voice, God will lead us to that special moment, guide us in seizing the opportunity, and empower us to fulfill our missions. If we continue to walk according to God's leading, we eventually arrive in our finest hour.

---

[111] Colossians 4:5 (NIV).

Using my personal story as an example, my life-defining moment was discovering my daughter was being abused by my husband. Instead of blaming God or being angry with Him for allowing such evil to happen to my daughter, I seized the opportunity to seek God and do what was necessary to protect my daughter. This led both Nicole and me to the individual God-designed missions for which He created us. Fulfilling our missions has given us an incredible sense of purpose. Together and separately, God has used our stories for His glory to impact millions of lives.

So you see, our "special moment" will likely not be glorious or glamorous when it arrives. It may be the ugliest, most heart-wrenching event of our lives. We may be compelled to run from it or turn away and pretend it never even happened. However, if we face it head-on and follow the call of the Holy Spirit, God will do everything in His power to use it for His glory. He will send us on missions of love that will become our legacies.

> No one has ever seen God; but if we love one another, God lives in us and his love is made complete in us.[112]

How do we, as Christ-followers, follow in His footsteps? What does it mean to follow Jesus? How is His "love made complete in us"? We model our lives after the beautiful heroines of faith who have gone before us and who have set the pace.

We follow the path of the woman with the issue of blood, who overcame every obstacle to reach out to Jesus, doing whatever was necessary to get close to Him, and she was healed. Like the Samaritan woman, we listen to Jesus's words, wholeheartedly receive His invitation, and share our transformation with everyone we know. We surrender our most valuable possessions, our false loves, for the sake of loving Jesus, like the woman living a sinful life, who poured

---

[112]   1 John 4:12 (NIV).

out her precious perfume to clean His dirty feet. We join the woman caught in adultery, who walked away from the dark and ugliness of her sin and into the light of a pure life in Christ.

Maturing in our faith, we mentor other women, as Lydia did. She modeled how to worship God as she possibly led the first Woven Women group along the river—gathering women, growing leaders, praying, teaching, and sharing the news of Jesus. She publicly announced her commitment by being baptized in the river.

We become Esthers—women who are willing to "Speak up for those who cannot speak for themselves; ensure justice for those being crushed."[113] We fast and pray and then seize our special moment and become God's vessel to change the course of history and fulfill the mission for which we are uniquely qualified.[114]

We are Woven Women, women of virtue who walk in the strength and anointing of God's purpose for our lives. We may never be great in the eyes of the world, but we can accomplish something great for the kingdom of God. Our greatest joy is to embrace and fulfill the God mission assigned to us.

And who knows but that you have come to your royal position for such a time as this?[115]

A LASTING LEGACY

In all my years spent in Proverbs 31, I've overlooked the verses that precede the poem of the virtuous woman:

> Speak up for those who cannot speak for themselves; ensure justice for those being crushed. Yes, speak up for the poor and helpless, and see that they get justice.[116]

---

[113] Proverbs 31:8–9 (NLT).
[114] Winston Churchill.
[115] Esther 4:14 (NIV).
[116] Proverbs 31:8–9 (NLT).

These verses bring a fresh appreciation for this mother who wrote chapter 31 of Proverbs. She challenges us to take a deeper look at our motives, our actions, and the advice we give to others. How many of us seriously share this mother's concerns? She forces us to ask ourselves, "Who am I trying to please?"

It is so easy to get caught in the trap of working our way into heaven. We can serve on committees, boards, and events throughout the week and take on multiple responsibilities on Sunday mornings. We may attend church every time the doors open. We can perform religious deeds and put on a good show, hoping to be noticed, accepted, or even glorified by our church family. We work to be good enough in God's eyes. While we are busy with our juggling routine, we neglect family, miss our true calling, and wear ourselves out without ever applying our gifts to the plan God has for our lives. We lose sight of the very heart of Christ.

The two-sentence plea of the king's mother in Proverbs 31:8–9 reveals the heart of Christ long before He was born as a babe in Bethlehem. Her words resemble Jesus when He stood in the temple and announced His call to ministry, reading from the prophecy of Isaiah:[117]

> The Spirit of the LORD is upon me, for he has anointed me to bring Good News to the poor. He has sent me to proclaim that captives will be released, that the blind will see, that the oppressed will be set free, and that the time of the LORD's favor has come. (Luke 4:18–19 NLT)

Jesus not only fulfilled the prophecy of Isaiah, but He was also the answer to this prayer of the king's mother. Jesus was definitely not trying to impress religious leaders. His ministry was not aimed at making friends in high places. Jesus went to the outcast, the poor, the wounded, and sinners.

---

[117] Isaiah 61.

His life and ministry remain, two thousand years later, as a legacy of love and grace.

> For it is by grace you have been saved, through faith—and this is not from yourselves, it is the gift of God—not by works, so that no one can boast.[118]

We cannot work our way into heaven. Salvation is a gift—a gift of God to a lost and hurting world. It is our inheritance in Christ Jesus, a gift we can share with anyone we choose and that can be received by anyone who chooses to believe. That brings up another question: "What type of legacy am I leaving for my children, my grandchildren, nieces, nephews, and people with whom I come in contact every day?"

God longs for us to leave a lasting mark on this world. Sometimes it means going out of our comfort zones to love people who are very different from us. Sometimes it is simply to embrace the people who surround us every day; to be a godly example of prayer, support, wise counsel, and commitment to God. At our Woven Hour of Prayer, a woman shared, "God used the prayers of my mother and grandmother to light my path that led me to Him."

Are you making an eternal difference in this world? When our lives are transformed by Christ, our priorities line up with His. The difference He has made in us spurs a desire to make a difference in the lives of others, which becomes evident in our words and actions. Our hearts hurt for the hurting. We pray unselfish prayers. We love even the least of the least. We point others to our heavenly home.

We can be gift givers without any financial cost. God has chosen *us* to distribute His gift of grace—the offer of salvation, eternal life to those who will take a step of faith and accept it. Our only eternal imprint on this world is to share the love and message of Jesus. That is how we leave a lasting legacy.

---

[118] Ephesians 2:8-9 (NIV).

GETTING TO KNOW ME—AN EXTRAVAGANT REWARD

Those who look to him are radiant; their faces are never covered with shame.[119]

At the age of thirty-six, I stepped foot on a Christian campus to pursue a four-year degree in the field of education, having no idea how this community of faith would change me on every level. I received much more than a bachelor's degree!

The required daily chapel services were medicine for my soul. In the splendor of the stained-glass auditorium, I was transfixed through praise and worship and transformed by God's Word, His love, and the godly men and women whom God called to teach and train disciples. God was poised to do "immeasurably more than I could ask or imagine."[120]

It had only been seven months since my husband's suicide. Every morning as I drove the twenty-five-minute route to campus, the tears of pain and shame flowed gently. But one particular day, that changed. I had wandered in the desert long enough.

It was common to have guest speakers in chapel from across the country. This particular day, a missionary couple from France shared the platform. I can't remember much about their message, though I am certain their stories inspired me. God was stirring the pool of my heart as they spoke. They closed the service by availing themselves to students who were interested in speaking with them after chapel, inviting us to make an appointment in the chaplain's office.

I felt a tug on my heart—a need to speak to them. But what would I say? Why did I need to talk to them? I had no idea. Timid and broken as I was, I decided to pray about this "appointment" over lunch. I drove down the street to Burger King, ordered via the drive-through, and drove back to the chapel parking lot to eat. It was hard to swallow a Whopper Jr. amid my sobbing. I went to the chaplain's office and arrived just in the nick of time.

---

[119] Psalm 34:5 (NIV).
[120] Ephesians 3:20 (NIV).

The missionaries were gathering their belongings and putting on their coats, ready to go to lunch. Instead, they graciously invited me into the office to talk. I cried so much that I couldn't speak, so they did most of the talking. He shared how freeing it is to live a life of transparency—nothing to hide behind, living without secrets of hidden sin or past failures.

His wife shared about living a life of constant surrender, turning everything over to God and being set free from worry and fear, pain and shame. She demonstrated how she uses the motion of rotating her hands from palms down to palms up as she lifts her burdens to God. The raising of her hands, palms open, expresses her surrendering to allow God to be in control of her life and future. Then they gathered around me and prayed for me, and we went on with our schedules.

That night as I lay in bed, I did what they said. I made an eternal transaction with God, surrendering my burdens of sorrow, shame, and pain. Little did I know I was being sanctified and cleansed by the blood of Jesus Christ. He was making me holy in His sight. In that moment, I had a vision of myself dressed in a beautiful white wedding gown, a spiritual virgin—the bride of Christ. I had no idea what that meant at the time, but it certainly changed my life forever.

The next morning when I drove to school, tears of joy replaced my tears of dismay. It felt as if God had withdrawn my pain and shame with a giant syringe. Then He injected me with a divine love transfusion—the blood of Christ. I walked on campus that morning, and the next, and the next, feeling so full of love for every single person. It was as if a volcano had erupted in my soul. The lava of love was overflowing. I had to control myself because I wanted to hug every person who passed my way—even complete strangers. It was unbelievable! I had been hearing sermons about love, and I had been reading in 1 John about love, but I had no idea how I could ever love in that way. This is a love that never goes away.

Well, *hello, love*! His love still consumes me. His love has changed everything about me. His love is changing others through me. God filled me with His love so I could love Him and love others in the way that He loves me.

> God is love. Whoever lives in love lives in God, and God in them.[121]

It didn't end there. It was only the beginning. God's love called me into ministry! The beauty of this journey of surrendering to love is that God is still transforming me today. The following passage in Corinthians has become a favorite of mine because it truly describes the reward of living a life of love:

> But whenever anyone turns to the Lord, the veil is taken away. Now the Lord is the Spirit, and where the Spirit of the Lord is, there is freedom. And we all, who with unveiled faces contemplate the Lord's glory, are being transformed into his image with ever-increasing glory, which comes from the Lord, who is the Spirit.[122]

God is never done with us. The "veil" masks our pain and shame because we are so aware of our state of uncleanness before God. But the Spirit has come to set us free, to "unveil" our faces. Isn't this what the groom does for the bride? He lifts the veil to uncover his bride's face in all her glory and then seals his love with a kiss. Arm in arm, veil lifted, they march into their forever future with confidence in this love that is eternally theirs—a love for all to witness and one that beams in the darkest night.

The love of God transforms us into His image. We reflect His glory. He shines through our very countenance. As we surrender more and more to Him, we reflect more and more of His glory, His character, His love, and His holiness ... with ever-increasing glory. In this process we are filled with more

---

121   1 John 4:6 (NIV).
122   2 Corinthians 3:18 (NIV).

of His Spirit, breaking chains of pain and wrapping our hearts around His freedom.

Ever-increasing glory ...I am not the same person I was twenty years ago, ten years ago, two years ago, or even two weeks ago because I choose to embrace this journey of being transformed into the image of Jesus Christ by the Holy Spirit. Someday, when I meet Him face-to-face, I will be made perfect like Him.

The Bridegroom will arrive, the wedding banquet will be served, and He will invite all who are ready to be seated at His table of eternal love, life, and peace—paradise! We don't have to wait until heaven to be changed. The journey begins here on earth, an adventure of continual surrender, transforming glory, increasing joy, and indescribable love. The missionary from France was right on—*this is the best way to live!*

THE POWER OF ONE

I was one lonely woman in 1998 who prayed one consistent prayer for deeper female friendships. I determined to be the one who would remove my mask and seek to restore relationships among the broken rhapsody of women stumbling through life alone.

I had no idea how this one decision would reclaim my identity and create a tsunami of women bowing in prayer and rising up in God's power. I could not have known how our one true God would use one woman to be a catalyst in reinventing leadership for women's ministry.

Through my belief in one God who can do more than I could ask or imagine, He has opened many doors for reaching the world. Our director of Woven Women in Uganda shares just a small window of all that God is doing through Woven in Africa.

Greetings to you all,

This letter brings our love from Uganda to you, our Woven Women friends and supporters. Thank you for the love you have for me and the women in Africa.

Woven Women has helped me discover a number of challenges women in our country suffer in their hearts. This has helped me pray for them. It has given me the chance to venture into various communities indoctrinating them into the Woven ministry, as well as preaching the gospel and winning souls to Christ.

Woven has helped bridge the gap among women in Africa, Uganda in particular. They visit each other, garden together, and [engage in] other activities. This has helped build teamwork among the women, which was not the case before, where everyone would mind her own business.

Our Woven groups have visited women of different dominations, like Moslems and Seventh-Day Adventists, to encourage them and preach the gospel of our Lord Jesus Christ. Many gave their lives to Christ and are now members of our branch churches there.

As director of Woven in Uganda, I was able to buy malaria medicine to distribute to families who cannot access medical services. Due to poverty, many just believe for healing. If healing never comes, then death creeps in.

We believed empowering the women alone couldn't yield much without engaging the men. We taught the men how to make liquid soap, which they can sell and earn income. To help the men's work attitude towards women, we introduced to them the beauty of working together, that it profits more than working in isolation. Together they visited and preached to others and seven men gave their life to Jesus

Christ. We registered forty men and formed the Woven Men group in Kibuku District—the only group of its kind.

Our intention in Kibuku district is to empower the local communities with life skills which can lift them up, change their mind-set and attitude about life. God has not forgotten them but they must put their hands to work so that when they pray to God for a blessing, God will bless the works of their hands.

—Pastor Margaret Nsubuga, Woven Women director, Uganda

GETTING TO KNOW YOU

What if you hold the key to set others free? What if removing your mask of pain and shame is the very thing God can use to bring freedom to another person ... or even to nations?

Though the Jews were looking for a King who would overthrow the Romans, God's answer to reclaiming the identity of His people was not political. He sent a humble servant, His own Son, to restore relationships. Jesus reinvented leadership by mentoring the most unlikely candidates. Through a group of twelve ordinary men, mostly fishermen, His model and message of love has traveled to us and is reaching the world.

One servant, one persistent prayer, one decision, one mask removed, one God, one love, one world, with ever-increasing glory—this is the power of *one*.

- Do you recognize the "special moment" for which you were born?
    - o What is the most life-defining moment you have experienced at this stage of your life?
    - o How did it impact your spiritual journey?
    - o How did it change your view of the past and your hope for the future?
- Did you seize that special opportunity?

- o Did you make a specific decision that altered your path?
- o If so, what was it, and what was the impact?
- o If not, do you have regrets? Ask God to show you how to move forward.
- Have you discovered the mission for which you are uniquely qualified?
  - o Describe your mission thus far.
  - o Ask God to speak to you as you write.
  - o Pray over your mission, and place it before Him.
  - o Be still before God, asking Him to give you vision and direction that will lead you to your purpose and calling. Write down every single word and thought!

I pray you are no longer asking the question, what if? Instead, proclaim with conviction, "I can do everything through Christ who gives me strength."[123]

GETTING TO KNOW GOD

I trust Proverbs 31 has been an incentive for you to be a woman of virtue by challenging you to survey your use of time, energy, resources, and talents. You've heard from Woven Women who have accepted this challenge and applied it to their lives. You have met heroines of faith in the pages of this book, women of the Bible who recognized their special moment and seized it.

There is no need to idolize these women or wish you were one of them. *You* are God's woman to carry forth a legacy of love. He has a mission that only *you* can do! When you embrace it, you will absolutely love your life. In that moment, you will find greatness even in the simple things, the tough times, the victories, and the defeats because you are His, and He is yours.

---

[123] Philippians 4:13 (NLT).

The woman of virtue summons you to become a Woven Woman on a mission—to surrender everything you have and all you are in service and submission to God. This is what I want you to do. Write the statement below in your journal or on a piece of paper. Embellish it, paint it, color it, frame it, or write it in this book—whatever will make it special and meaningful to you. Write the following words and complete the statement:

> My Mission
>
> In order that I may be free to be me and encourage you to be free to be you, God is calling me to …

Sign and date your mission statement.

WOVEN IS FOR EVERY WOMAN—WOVEN IS FOR YOU!

We may be closing this book, but it is clearly not the end of our journey with this woman in Proverbs, nor is it the end of our relationship. It marks a beginning. We have bonded by sharing our stories and discovering how much we are alike. We've become more accepting and understanding of one another's differences; we've prayed and praised God for answered prayers. We've laughed. We've cried. We have experienced life more deeply.

I love Paul's advice in Hebrews 10:24-25:

> Let us consider how we may spur one another on toward love and good deeds. Let us not give up meeting together, as some are in the habit of doing, but let us encourage one another—and all the more as you see the Day approaching.[124]

The upside of this technologically advanced world is that we can easily connect on a personal basis. If you've not yet

---

[124] NIV.

found us on Facebook, I welcome you to our Woven Women page.[125] I invite you to my website for updates on this ministry and to my blog for more reading.[126] Leave a comment, or use the contact page to send me an email. Support our ever-expanding mission to Africa. Shop our line of Woven clothing, international handcrafted jewelry, and "Her Cindyness" artwork.

I would really love to meet you in person! Check out my calendar and come to a Woven Women event. Better yet, let's plan an event together in your area so we can build a team of women who are "woven into a tapestry of love."

We are Woven Women. We love to love.

MY PRAYER OF LOVE FOR YOU, PRECIOUS FRIEND

Grace and peace to you from God, our Father, and the Lord Jesus Christ,

I [will] thank my God every time I remember you. In all my prayers for all of you, I (will) always pray with joy because of [our] partnership in the gospel ... [I am] confident of this: that He who began a good work in you will carry it on to completion until the day of Christ Jesus. It is right for me to feel this way about all of you, since I have you in my heart ... [127]

For this reason I kneel before the Father, from whom every family in heaven and on earth derives its name. I pray that out of His glorious riches He may strengthen you with power through His Spirit in your inner being, so that Christ may dwell in your hearts through faith. And I pray that you, being rooted and

---

[125]   www.facebook.com/WeAreWoven.
[126]   www.WeAreWovenWomen.com.
[127]   Philippians 1:2–14 (NIV).

established in love, may have power, together with all the Lord's holy people, to grasp how wide and long and high and deep is the love of Christ and to know this love that surpasses knowledge—that you may be filled to the measure of all the fullness of God.

Now to He who is able to do immeasurably more than all we ask or imagine, according to is His power that is at work within us, to Him be glory in the church and in Christ Jesus throughout all generations, forever and ever! Amen.[128]

Be blessed. Be true. Be free. Be you!
I truly love you, my friend.

Cindy

---

[128] Ephesians 3:14–21 (NIV).

ABOUT THE AUTHOR

Cynthia Stiverson is pastor and founder of Woven Women, a global organization for uniting and empowering women. Passionate about pursuing God's call as an evangelist, Cindy's gifts of speaking, writing, and artistic expression invite others to embrace freedom, wholeness, and purpose in an environment of inclusiveness.

Cindy would love to meet and encourage the women in your circles with any of these special Woven gatherings or as a guest speaker at your conference:

- Group Leader Training
- Woven Ministry Kick-Off
- Woven Weekend
- Girls' Night Out
- Leadership Retreat
- Creating Quiet Spaces: A Directed Spiritual Retreat

Email Cindy with your inquiries and group needs at www. WeAreWovenWomen.com/contact.

Cindy considers raising her daughter, Nicole Bromley, as her greatest accomplishment. She loves the men in her life: husband, Mark; son-in-law, Matthew; and her three adorable grandsons. Cindy and Mark live in Newark, Ohio, where she serves as pastor to women and South Central Ohio Women's Ministry director in the Church of the Nazarene.

She loves serving breakfast in her 1930s nook to friends new and old from near and far.

LEADER SECTION

HELLO, LEADER!

Welcome to the Woven Women ministry. This section is designed to empower you as a Woven group leader to conduct your small-group gatherings. Each lesson begins with group leader instructions and is followed in sequence with the group handout for your group attendees. The gray highlighted areas of the group leader instructions are your manuscript for leading the women. However, please read and study prior to each session so that you are leading from your heart.

You are invited to register your Woven group on our website at WeAreWovenWomen.com. Look for the link for group leaders. We want you to feel as though this is your website too. Once you have introduced yourself, you will have access to downloadable files for leading your group sessions. The 8½ × 11 pages will be much more convenient to prepare for your group. The larger font will be easier to read and follow the manuscript as you lead. You can print as many full-size copies of the group handouts as you need to distribute in your group. You will also find other free perks to offer your ladies to reinforce the theme of the lessons.

I suggest two leaders per small group of up to twelve women. Each group leader will need her own book. It works well to have an administrative leader and a spiritual leader.

This is discussed in more detail in the *Responsibilities* section. Remember that the focus of the groups is restoring relationships. The vision for Woven is to create an environment where women are warmly embraced and feel safe to remove their masks and share their hearts. Our purpose statement is Colossians 2:2-3:

> I want you woven into a tapestry of love, in touch
> with everything there is to know of God.[129]

This ministry will change the dynamics of your church by healing hearts and producing leaders who become confident models and mentors in ministry by moving freely in their spiritual gifts.

Meeting in homes of the women in your group is important. This creates an environment for open communication, trust, and relationship building. Don't be shy about personally asking women to serve as hostesses or in other areas of leadership. Reassure them that this is not about having a fancy home. Hospitality is simply providing space where others feel at home.

Women need lots of encouragement. Send invitations to your group each month with directions to the hostess's home, the date, and time. Call or text your ladies a day or two prior to each gathering and personally invite them to come.

GETTING STARTED

Reading this book and completing the exercises in each chapter is the best way to prepare to lead a Woven group. The best scenario is to pull together a group of women who could become potential Woven leaders. They may not be serving in a leadership position currently, but look for women who model the characteristics you would want in a leader: trustworthy, loving, humble, committed to prayer ... virtuous women.

Once you have pulled together a group, you can begin

---
[129] The Message.

by reading this book and gather together monthly, every two weeks, or whatever frequency you agree upon. Allow ample time to personally process and apply the chapters between your meeting times. If everyone faithfully works through the *Getting to Know Me* and *Getting to Know God* sections of journaling, you will be personally, spiritually, and emotionally prepared to launch more groups by the time you have completed the book.

I am excited just thinking about the possibilities for you and this group of women. When others see how you are growing, they will be excited for the same opportunity. What a blessing you will be to them!

The following features make Woven unique. Please keep this consistency to preserve the uniqueness of Woven.

Woven is a modeling and mentoring ministry. The women will look to their leader as one who models the virtues and behaviors of a Woven Woman. It is important to remember as a Woven leader, you are mentoring others to be virtuous women. Be sure you are ready to lead. This book is designed to make leaders, so rest assured that God will mold you into the woman He wants for this job! Just be obedient and follow His lead.

Woven is a spiritual formation and friendship ministry. Though you are studying and discussing scripture passages, Woven is not intended as a Bible study. It's important to make this clear. The focus is not to absorb biblical facts and knowledge. The goal is to grow deeper in our relationships with each other and with the Lord. The biblical learning comes naturally as we apply scriptural truths to our everyday lives through experiential learning.

Woven is low commitment. Woven is not intended to add another activity to the long list of responsibilities that we women juggle. Woven is designed to accommodate busy schedules by carving out just one evening per month to let our hair down. It will truly become an oasis in the midst of your busy life. You will find yourself looking forward to this evening of refreshment to recharge your spiritual battery and equip you for the journey.

Remind your group that this is a commitment of only six or seven evenings per year (depending on how you plan your Woven calendar). Schedule your gatherings on the same evening each month. Allow for a summer break and/or holiday break. You will be amazed at the growth that occurs with such small commitment. Encourage them to not miss a single time because they will truly have regrets if they do.

There is no homework. Woven group handouts are distributed when your guests arrive. The material is fresh to everyone, so there is no guilt for not having studied. The discussion is intended to be a spontaneous sharing in response to the lesson. Group leader preparation is minimal as well. The lessons are fully written out for you in manuscript form.

You can lead a group using this book with each woman having her own copy of *Woven* to read and work through the activities; then use the *Group Handout* section when you come together. Another option is to begin your group just using the *Leader* section handouts. Once you begin meeting together, encourage the women to find healing and growth by purchasing their own book for home study. (They will thank you later.)

Woven groups are inclusive. Woven groups are cell groups: living, breathing organisms. The material is designed for women to come and go freely without feeling uncomfortable for not having prepared. Though the lessons continue to build on one another, each lesson can stand alone. This allows for new guests to participate in the discussion, even if they join you midseason.

An important element of Woven is to invite new women to your group. Woven is a perfect connection point for women in the community, women who are new to the church, or women in your neighborhood. This would be quite a gift for women to be introduced to God and connect with godly girlfriends! May the Spirit lead you to those ladies.

Woven Women serve the greater community. Check with local service groups or agencies, or do something special for women staying at a local shelter, visit shut-ins, or take up a collection for women in crisis. You will grow together as a group as you find ways to give to others. It is eye-opening when you discover the needs and begin to truly love your neighbors. As an example, we have a monthly art therapy ministry to women who are recovering from substance abuse. You can also take a look at other ways to get involved with Woven outreach efforts on our website.

Woven groups are covenant groups. There is an openness in sharing that does not usually occur in other small-group settings. It's important for the ladies to covenant together that your sharing will be held confidential within the group. If you want, you could outline the expectations into a covenant to which each woman agrees. However, I have found it unnecessary. If you have trustworthy leaders, the women will likely honor one another's privacy. In the opening of each lesson, you will see this trust issue addressed by simply repeating together, "What happens with the girls stays with the girls!" This is just a sweet and subtle reminder to put every heart at ease.

WOVEN LEADERSHIP

As your group grows and becomes established, you will launch more groups. This will require a group leader team. The team consists of the Woven leaders who will lead their respective small groups. Woven group leaders will be more effective if they commit to their own monthly team gathering, ideally one week prior to your scheduled groups. Each team needs a leader who serves as your Woven Women ministry leader. This may be your women's ministry director. Or you may determine an overall leader, perhaps one of the initial leaders. Most likely, she is the person God called to initiate this ministry in your setting. My best guess—"she" is *you.*

Woven group leader gatherings are meant to prepare you, as leaders, for your monthly group gatherings. Monday evenings seem to work best, as you catch your ladies before they are worn out from their workweek, and it's easier to remember. Connect with your ladies on Sunday mornings or whenever you can as much as possible.

The Woven group leader gatherings will become your own personal oasis. You will become a support and encouragement to each other as you gain insight from one another's perspectives. This learning will be priceless as you partner in leading your groups. Team meetings serve as a practice session, an opportunity for leaders to experience Woven in the same way that ladies in your group do. It will stimulate new ideas and make your ministry to women stronger and more effective. It's also a time of praying for your groups, casting vision for your ministry, sharing successes and failures, and planning events to bring your women together in one place. You will become so attached to one another that you will look forward to this time each month. Oh, the love! This will be contagious! When other women see the relationships your Woven team has, they will be standing in line for the love of it.

ARE YOU READY FOR THIS?

God is about to tremendously bless you as He uses your gifts to grow you. At the same time He will tremendously heal and bless other women through you. You will not believe how God will weave your hearts together in His love.

I am so grateful for you! Thank you for leading a Woven Women ministry.

We are Woven Women. We love to love!

Yours and His,

Cindy

Meet me in my nook at www.WeAreWovenWomen.com.

MORE SUGGESTIONS FOR LEADING YOUR GROUPS

Let your hostess know in advance that refreshments are to be served *after* the discussion time.

- The hostess can become your helpmate in getting started on time.
- If refreshments are served first, you will feel as though you have lost control of the group before you get started.
    - o If you feel you need to eat first, you could start your group while they are eating by doing the Getting to Know Each Other activity.
- Or schedule a half hour meet-and-greet prior to beginning.

Remember that *you* are the leader.

- Keep the *main thing* the main thing! It's up to you to set the pace for your time together.
- Take leadership in directing women's attention to what you are there to do.
- Some of your ladies will already know each other; others will simply be very comfortable engaging in lengthy chit-chat. While it is true that we want to get them talking and communicating, we want the communication to be focused on the point of the lesson.

The lessons are intended to help your women open up and share.

- The questions begin very open and easy to answer and become progressively more intimate.
- You may leave out one or two of the questions that seem redundant or have been covered in the course of conversation. However, omitting more than that will jeopardize the depth of your time together and with the Lord.

- To get the desired results, it is important to move through the entire lesson.

You may need to be aggressive in directing the conversation or discussion to keep on track.

- This may mean doing what feels rude, such as interrupting when others are talking and many other polite conversation rules.
- Leading a discussion sometimes means breaking the rules to bring everyone back on subject. This is a very delicate skill!
    o Do it lightly and with a bit of humor.
    o Do it with a "thank you for sharing".
    o Do it with the guidance of the Holy Spirit.
    o Know the difference between times you need to cut someone short and times you need to allow her to share her heart. Seek God in these situations. Listen to His voice. Follow your instincts.
    o If someone is sharing a genuine, personal, heartfelt need, don't shut her down. Stop and pray over her as a group. Praying for the matter is the best way to handle it and move on.

Pray! Pray! Pray!

- Be prayed up. You will need God's guidance before you ever step foot in your ladies' homes. Pray for your women, yourself, and your coleader, for God to open and heal hearts.
- The closing prayer time is for your women and their personal needs. Ask them to keep their prayer requests more personal rather than becoming overwhelmed with a huge list of extended people. The prayer requests should relate to applying the lesson to their lives.

- Invite and encourage your women to participate by praying at the close of your gathering. Prayer will tie the heart-knot for your time together.
- Encourage your ladies to send cards or give a call to those who are sick or who need encouragement.
- Don't forget to send cards to your ladies.

RESPONSIBILITIES

The following is an overview of tasks and suggestions on how to divide up the responsibilities. You can also engage some of your women by asking them to help in certain areas.
Monthly Hostess

- Getting to Know Your Hostess activity: five minutes to share personally with the group
- Opens her home for the Woven gathering, or provides refreshments, or both
- If the same gals repeatedly host in their homes, you can ask a different woman each month to share about herself so that everyone has an opportunity to share about her life

Group Leaders (two suggested, as follows)

- Administrative Leader
  - Administers communications and paperwork.
    o Schedule and contact hostess.
    o Provide directions to home where you will be gathering.
    o Prepare and mail and/or email invitations.
    o Contact your group members two days prior to monthly gathering as an encouragement to attend (can recruit others to help with this).
    o Keep group list and contact info up-to-date.
  - Introduce hostess.
  - Give announcements.

- Lead Getting to Know Each Other activity (icebreaker).

- Spiritual Leader
  - Introduces topic.
  - Leads Getting to Know the Lord activities.
    - o Studies and prepares to lead lesson.
    - o Facilitates open discussion of scripture and questions.
    - o Leads prayer time.
  - Records prayer requests.

- Both Leaders
  - Send notes to first-timers and visitors.
  - Send thank-you notes to hostesses.
  - Send notes and cards of encouragement to ladies.
  - Connect with your ladies throughout the month and at church on Sundays.
  - Pray! Pray! Pray!
  - Pamper your ladies! You can find some wonderful little hostess gifts and pamper gifts for your gals at the Dollar Tree or Michael's. Many of our ladies rarely receive little tokens of love and appreciation. It's the little added touches that show how much you care.

LESSON 1

WOVEN: FREE TO BE—YOU AND ME

Group Leader Instructions

⊃ **LEADERS**

This opening session can be used as a kick-off event to introduce Woven to the women of your church or community. Schedule your event. Begin promoting it three or four weeks in advance. Designate a place for ladies to sign up to attend. This will help them commit and gives you an idea how many to expect. Be sure to get their contact information (name, phone, email, mailing address) so you can follow up with them. At the event, use response cards with dates/times of potential groups you will be offering. (If you would like to schedule me and/or my team to lead this, contact www. WeAreWovenWomen.com/contact.)

Prepare by reading and meditating on this lesson for several days prior to your group. When it moves from your head to your heart, you will be ready to share with your group.

⊃ Begin on time.
⊃ Open with prayer.

- ⊃ Welcome your guests.
- ⊃ Make sure everyone has a copy of the group handout, scripture, and response card.

⊃ SCRIPT

Welcome to our first Woven gathering! The goal of this session is to introduce you to the purpose and vision of this ministry. Let's begin our journey together!

We will be gathering together *(chosen week, day, time)* each month for *(number of months).*

- ⊃ You may want to provide a calendar handout with your Woven dates to help them remember.

Woven is not just another meeting to add to your calendar.

It's a gathering of women for the purpose of growing in relationship with each other and with the Lord. When we think of going to a meeting, we sometimes feel tense. It can be confrontational, and you may feel you have to defend yourself and hold your ground.

When you think of Woven, you can look forward to belonging to a group where you can relax and enjoy new friends. It will become an oasis in your month, a time and space where you will be nourished and refreshed, where you can be free to be you, and I can be free to be me. So, let's get started.

Woven sessions are divided into three time segments:

- ⊃ Getting to Know Your Hostess
- ⊃ Getting to Know Each Other
- ⊃ Getting to Know the Lord

➲ GETTING TO KNOW YOUR HOSTESS

Our Woven groups will gather in different homes each month. This allows us to remove our "masks" and really get to know one another.

It's really a privilege to be the hostess. One perk is having an awesome group of women praying together in your home. Your home becomes sacred space, and you will sense the fresh presence of the Holy Spirit long after your new friends have gone. The next morning you will awaken to precious memories of love and laughter with your ladies!

We want to offer you the option of opening your home to our Woven group. Please take a look at the sign-up sheet and choose a date that you would like to be our hostess or provide refreshments, or you may want to do both.

➲ Pass around a sign-up sheet for monthly hostesses and refreshments.

Let's take a few minutes to get to know our hostess.

Our hostess tonight is (name). Please come and share a bit about yourself with us!

➲ Allow about five minutes for hostess to share.

➲ GETTING TO KNOW EACH OTHER

Now that we know our hostess a little better, let's get to know each other.

On the count of three, please introduce yourself by shouting your name. One, two, three …

(Use this as an illustration of how, in our culture, we are all so busy keeping up with everything on our schedules that we have no time for relationships.)

Isn't that just how crazy our lives really are?

There are so many voices competing for our attention that we feel pressured and stressed most of the time. We don't have time to know and appreciate each other or to really hear from the Lord and know His desires for us. We struggle to move beyond two-sentence conversations,

"Hi. How are you?" "I'm fine."

We see each other in our Sunday-morning best and begin to judge each other based on outward appearances. We never get to know each other beyond the surface. Our relationships can be as shallow as someone we see every week at the grocery store or the nail salon. We fall into competition mode, analyzing one another according to how we dress, how much we weigh, and how we fix our hair. We fail to see the heart. Yet God's Word tells us in 1 Peter 3:3–4 that our inner selves, our hearts are most important.

> Your beauty should not come from outward adornment, such as braided hair and the wearing of gold jewelry and fine clothes. Instead, it should be that of your inner self, the unfading beauty of a gentle and quiet spirit, which is of great worth in God's sight.

Woven was established in 1998 to encourage women to come to know each other three-dimensionally. During our time together, we will go beyond appearances and look into one another's hearts.

Ladies, isn't this what you have longed for your entire life: for someone to simply see your heart? God made us to be in relationship. He longs to break down the walls and barriers that Satan and society have built between us.

The purpose statement for Woven is Colossians 2:2: "I want you Woven into a tapestry of love, in touch with everything there is to know of God."

This is so exciting! We are going to learn that our appearance is so unimportant. Women share common needs, common desires—we even have a lot of the same issues! We are of one heart. As we share our joys and burdens each month, God will truly weave us together in love. And I don't know of a single woman who doesn't need more God and more girlfriends in her life.

Let's get to know each other by going around the table and, *one at a time*, share

- o   your name,
- o   how you began coming to our church or when you moved to this community (*Reader's Digest* condensed version),
- o   and a little-known fact about yourself.

➲   Allow 10-15 minutes to share, depending on how many are in your group.

Let's get into our lesson by digging into God's Word. This is where our hearts really become woven into a tapestry of love—when we center our conversation and relationships in Christ. When we do, we can confidently share our hearts with each other. There is an element of trust that is a gift. We agree that *what happens with the girls stays with the girls*—let's say that together!

➲   GETTING TO KNOW THE LORD

The scripture for our discussions will stem from the poem of the virtuous woman found in Proverbs 31.

➲   Read aloud or go around room and have each person read one or two verses.

The Virtuous Woman: Proverbs 31:10 (KJV) and Proverbs 31:11-31 (NLT)

10 Who can find a virtuous woman? for her price is far above rubies.

11 Her husband has full confidence in her and lacks nothing of value.

12 She brings him good, not harm, all the days of her life.

13 She selects wool and flax and works with eager hands.

14 She is like the merchant ships, bringing her food from afar.

15 She gets up while it is still dark; she provides food for her family and portions for her servant girls.

16 She considers a field and buys it; out of her earnings she plants a vineyard.

17 She sets about her work vigorously; her arms are strong for her tasks.

18 She sees that her trading is profitable, and her lamp does not go out at night.

19 In her hand she holds the distaff and grasps the spindle with her fingers.

20 She opens her arms to the poor and extends her hands to the needy.

21 When it snows, she has no fear for her household; for all of them are clothed in scarlet.

22 She makes coverings for her bed; she is clothed in fine linen and purple.

23 Her husband is respected at the city gate, where he takes his seat among the elders of the land.

24 She makes linen garments and sells them, and supplies the merchants with sashes.

25 She is clothed with strength and dignity; she can laugh at the days to come.

26 She speaks with wisdom, and faithful instruction is on her tongue.

27 She watches over the affairs of her household and does not eat the bread of idleness.

28 Her children arise and call her blessed; her husband also, and he praises her:

29 "Many women do noble things, but you surpass them all."

30 Charm is deceptive, and beauty is fleeting; but a woman who fears the LORD is to be praised.

31 Give her the reward she has earned, and let her works
   bring her praise at the city gate.

Proverbs 31:10–31 is an acrostic poem, meaning that each
line of the poem begins with the next letter in the Hebrew
alphabet. This was a writing method that made it easier to
memorize. It's believed that in Jewish homes it was a tradition
for men and children to recite this poem around the Sabbath
table on Friday nights.
Why do you think they would have memorized and recited
this poem?

➲ Allow time to discuss in your groups, but keep it
  moving.

The poem of the virtuous woman depicts the value and
importance of the role of women in Israelite society at that
time. She was a business manager, compassionate caregiver,
craftswoman, wise teacher, provider of food and clothing,
hard worker, respected wife, and beloved mother. All of these
qualities are manifested in the woman of virtue because she
is "a woman who fears the Lord" (Proverbs 31:30).
How does the role of the proverbial woman of virtue
compare to our role in society today?

➲ Allow time to discuss in your groups.

What are some of the qualities and virtues that today's
society places value and emphasis upon? Describe the woman
whom our culture would consider perfect, virtuous, or
valuable.

➲ Allow time to discuss in your groups.

What is most frustrating or stressful to you as a woman
in the twenty-first century?

➲ Allow time to discuss in your groups.

What was your first reaction to the woman in this passage of scripture?

*How do you feel about her?

*How does she make you feel about yourself?

This is why Woven is so important; we need to make time to know each other beyond the surface and know each other on a heart level.

> When we make the effort to know, understand, and embrace each other as unique individuals, God truly sets us free! And He empowers us to set each other free.

You have the power to set me free to be me, and I have the power to set you free to be you. That power is God's love being birthed in our hearts. He wants us "woven into a tapestry of love"! That's our theme and our goal for this study.

The woman in Proverbs 31 will be our example. We will learn that this is not another to-do list to make us feel inadequate as Christian women. Nope! She is not trying to fill her day with busyness. The virtuous woman is living in the freedom of being totally surrendered to God. Everything she does flows from His Spirit working through her.

She is free to be who God made her to be and do what He called her to do.

➲ PRAYER

How can we pray for you tonight? Was there something that came to mind in our discussion that you would like to share?

➲ Allow open sharing of personal prayer requests in your groups if you have time.

- Your ladies may be uncomfortable praying aloud this first time.

- You can encourage them to share a one- or two-sentence prayer. If you want to keep it short, go around the room and ask that each woman lift the person on her right in prayer. If they prefer, give them the option to say a silent prayer when it is their turn; then just give a few moments of silence before moving on.

- One leader could open, and the other leader close the prayer time.

- Don't forget to pray God's blessings on the refreshments!

➲ OUTREACH PROJECT

Explain that another aspect of Woven is reaching out to help disadvantaged women in the church or community. This would be a good time to announce or discuss what your group would like to do for a project in this first season of Woven. Take a look at WeAreWovenWomen.com to get ideas or to join us in our efforts globally.

➲ REFRESHMENTS

Give each monthly hostess the option of providing refreshments or having someone else from the group provide them. This is a great time of bonding and fellowship, so allow time and don't rush those who want to linger. Remember you will only have seven evenings with them. If possible, seat the ladies around a table where you are able to fellowship as a group. The room will soon echo with laughter!

LESSON 1

FREE TO BE—YOU AND ME

Group Handout

⮑ **GETTING TO KNOW YOUR HOSTESS**

⮑ **GETTING TO KNOW EACH OTHER**

Share

- o your name,
- o how you began coming to our church or when you moved to this community
    (*Reader's Digest* condensed version), and
- o a little known fact about you.

⮑ **GETTING TO KNOW THE LORD**

THE VIRTUOUS WOMAN: PROVERBS 31

10 Who can find a virtuous woman? for her price is far above rubies.
11 Her husband has full confidence in her and lacks nothing of value.

12 She brings him good, not harm, all the days of her life.

13 She selects wool and flax and works with eager hands.

14 She is like the merchant ships, bringing her food from afar.

15 She gets up while it is still dark; she provides food for her family and portions for her servant girls.

16 She considers a field and buys it; out of her earnings she plants a vineyard.

17 She sets about her work vigorously; her arms are strong for her tasks.

18 She sees that her trading is profitable, and her lamp does not go out at night.

19 In her hand she holds the distaff and grasps the spindle with her fingers.

20 She opens her arms to the poor and extends her hands to the needy.

21 When it snows, she has no fear for her household; for all of them are clothed in scarlet.

22 She makes coverings for her bed; she is clothed in fine linen and purple.

23 Her husband is respected at the city gate, where he takes his seat among the elders of the land.

24 She makes linen garments and sells them, and supplies the merchants with sashes.

25 She is clothed with strength and dignity; she can laugh at the days to come.

26 She speaks with wisdom, and faithful instruction is on her tongue.

27 She watches over the affairs of her household and does not eat the bread of idleness.

28 Her children arise and call her blessed; her husband also, and he praises her:

29 "Many women do noble things, but you surpass them all."

30 Charm is deceptive, and beauty is fleeting; but a woman who fears the LORD is to be praised.

31 Give her the reward she has earned, and let her works bring her praise at the city gate.

- Why do you think they would have memorized and recited the poem?

- How does the role of the proverbial woman of virtue compare to our role in society today?

- What are some of the qualities and virtues that today's society places value and emphasis upon?

  o Describe the woman whom our culture would consider "perfect."

  o What is most frustrating or stressful to you as a woman in the twenty-first century?

- What was your first reaction to the woman in this passage of scripture?

  o How do you feel about her?

  o How does she make you feel about yourself?

> When we make the effort to know, understand, and embrace each other as unique individuals, God truly sets us free! And He empowers us to set each other free.

You have the power to set me free to be me, and I have the power to set you free to be you. That power is God's love being birthed in our hearts. He wants us "woven into a tapestry of love." That's our theme and our goal for this study.

WHAT MAKES THIS CHICK TICK?

Group Leader Instructions

Prepare by reading and meditating on this lesson for several days prior to your group. When it moves from your head to your heart, you will be ready to share with your group.

- ➲ **You will need** pens and paper or sticky notes for the Getting to Know Each Other activity; hostess gifts, pamper gifts
- ➲ **Be organized.** Arrive early and have everything ready (papers, pens, etc.) before your gals arrive. Then you won't waste time with this during the session.
- ➲ **Meet and greet your ladies as they arrive.** Introduce them to each other as much as possible while waiting to begin.
- ➲ **Start on time with a welcome and prayer.** If you have new ladies, introduce yourself and your coleader. Then ask everyone in your group to share only their names.
- ➲ **Make sure everyone has a group handout and self-evaluation.**
- ➲ **Share announcements.**
    - o Sign-ups for upcoming hostesses/refreshments, etc.
    - o Women's events? Opportunities to serve?

➲ GETTING TO KNOW YOUR HOSTESS

- ➲ Introduce your hostess and the person who provided refreshments.
- ➲ Thank them verbally and with a hostess/thank-you gift.
- ➲ Ask your hostess to share about herself and her life. Keep it to five minutes or so.

➲ GETTING TO KNOW EACH OTHER

- ➲ **You will need** pens and paper or sticky notes.

Let's take a few minutes to write down the responsibilities and various roles that we fill, such as mom, wife, daughter. Include current roles and roles throughout your adult life.

- ➲ Allow time for them to make their lists.
- ➲ To make it more fun, give them a pad of sticky notes to write each role on and have them stick the notes all over themselves!

Are you surprised at the number of things you were able to come up with?

➲ LET'S GO AROUND THE ROOM AND SHARE

- ➲ your name and
- ➲ which roles and responsibilities you find fulfilling and which ones really define you as a person, or *what makes you tick as a chick.*

Let's get into our lesson by digging into God's Word. This is where our hearts really become woven into a tapestry of love—when we center our conversation and relationships in Christ. When we do, we can confidently share our hearts with each other. There is an element of trust, which is a gift. We agree that *what happens with the girls stays with the girls—* let's say that together!

➲ GETTING TO KNOW THE LORD

The woman of virtue in Proverbs 31 is the main passage for our lessons this year. By looking beyond the surface of this woman, we will gain deeper insight into our own lives. And in doing that, we will be on the journey of being "Free to Be—You and Me!"

➲ **Read Proverbs 31:10–31** together by asking each lady to read one or two verses. Offer them the option to just pass if they are uncomfortable reading in public.

➲ INTRODUCE TOPIC

This month's lesson is **"What Makes This Chick Tick?"**

When we read this passage of the woman of virtue described in Proverbs 31, it's easy to feel overwhelmed and intimidated. Some of us are even irritated by her and the implication that she seems so "perfect." The implication that we are expected to fit into this perfect example of a Christian woman is a lot of pressure.

What's up with this woman anyway?

What motivates her to do all that she does, and how in the world does she do it?

Tonight our goal is to begin to build a positive relationship with her by searching for these qualities in ourselves. We want to see this woman as someone we can become, someone we can relate to, instead of just an ideal. The goal is to see *ourselves* and each other as virtuous women.

- What roles and responsibilities does this woman in scripture fill?

  Wife, mother, cook, businesswoman ...

- How do these roles/responsibilities reflect the lifetime of a woman?
  - o Can you find different seasons of a woman's life represented here?
  - o Does the idea that this is accomplished over a lifetime make her more approachable and believable?

- What relationships are represented in the passage? Relationship with husband, family, community, children, servants, merchants, the Lord
  - o Do these appear to be healthy relationships?
  - o Which relationship really sums up the entire passage in verse 30?

    Verse 30: "Charm is deceptive and beauty is fleeting; but a woman who fears the Lord is to be praised."

This verse gives glory to God for every attribute, ability, and accomplishment of this woman. The Lord is the source of her stability, strength, and excellence.

Take another look at the list you made earlier.

- How does your relationship with the Lord affect your other relationships and all that you do?

Compare and contrast the many roles/relationships/responsibilities of the woman of virtue in Proverbs with your own list.

- What do you have in common? Could the passage describe you?

➲ **Explain the self-evaluation exercise. Give them time to complete it; then discuss.**

➲ Do these applications of the Proverbs 31 verses help you see her as someone you can become?

➲ Do you know anyone who demonstrates the qualities listed in the self-examination? What does she stir in you? Envy? Respect? Admiration?

➲ What did you learn about yourself by taking this evaluation?

Being a woman of virtue is attainable but only through surrendering to a deeper relationship with God, not through our own striving to be Superwoman or by maxing out our schedules or by trying to impress people by doing good works.

We become virtuous when we allow God to work in us and through us. When we put our relationship with God as first priority, then everything we do becomes an act of worship, a beautifully orchestrated masterpiece of God's choosing, with Him as the director.

➲ PRAYER

How can we support you in prayer, based on tonight's lesson?

➲ Did you discover areas you need to work on in the evaluation?

➲ How can you adjust your priorities to grow deeper in your relationship with God and others?

➲ **Present your ladies with pamper gifts as they leave.**

LESSON 2

"WHAT MAKES THIS CHICK TICK?"

Group Handout

➲ **GETTING TO KNOW YOUR HOSTESS**

➲ **GETTING TO KNOW EACH OTHER**

What happens with the girls stays with the girls—let's say that together!

➲ **GETTING TO KNOW THE LORD**

- What roles and responsibilities does this woman in scripture fill?

- How do these roles/responsibilities reflect the lifetime of a woman?
    - o Can you find different seasons of a woman's life represented here?
    - o Does the idea that this is accomplished over a lifetime make her more approachable and believable?

- What relationships are represented in the passage?

    Relationship with husband, family, community, children, servants, merchants, the Lord

    o Do these appear to be healthy relationships?
    o Which relationship sums up the entire passage in verse 30?

    Verse 30: "Charm is deceptive and beauty is fleeting; but a woman who fears the Lord is to be praised."

- How does your relationship with the Lord affect your other relationships and all that you do?

SELF-EVALUATION

Where are you in your search for virtue?

Rate yourself in the following areas from Proverbs 31, using the scale:

0=not at all; 1=infrequently; ?=sometimes; 3=often; 4=almost always

I. Proverbs 31:10b–11 "She is worth far more than rubies. Her husband has full confidence in her and lacks nothing of value."

____I have confidence in myself.
____Others have confidence in me and trust my word/work.

II. Verse 15 "She gets up while it is still dark."
Verse 18 "She sees that her trading is profitable, and her lamp does not go out at night."

____I spend time in prayer daily.
____I spend time in scripture daily.

____I keep God first in my daily routine.
____I trust the Lord to provide the grace to sustain me in my work.

III. Verse 17 "She sets about her work vigorously; her arms are strong for her tasks."

____Strength: I possess the "inner strength" necessary to tackle a task.
____Endurance: I remain steadfast in my commitment and press on to the goal.
____Commitment: I see things through to completion.

IV. Verse 20 "She opens her arms to the poor and extends her hands to the needy."

____Compassion: I am sensitive to the needs of others and am willing to meet those needs.
____Empathy: I am able to feel what others are feeling; I can relate to them in their circumstances.
____I am active in community service/outreach.

V. Verse 21 "When it snows, she has no fear for her household; for all of them are clothed in scarlet."

____I am thrifty: I am a good provider for myself and/or my family while maintaining a budget.
____I do not live above my means by overspending.
____I love a good bargain!

VI. Verse 22 "She makes coverings for her bed; she is clothed in fine linen and purple."

____I take care of myself and am attentive to my appearance.

VII. Verse 25 "She is clothed with strength and dignity; she can laugh at the days to come."

____Faith: I trust in the Lord to supply my needs.

VIII. Verse 26 "She speaks with wisdom, and faithful instruction is on her tongue."

____I think before I speak.
____I am conscientious in not offending others when I speak to them.
____I give God the glory for what He has done in my life.
____I nurture others in the way of the Lord.
____I seek out opportunities to witness.
____I refrain from using offensive language.
____I refrain from speaking critically of others.

IX. Verse 28 "Her children arise and call her blessed; her husband also, and he praises her"

____I model biblical characteristics as an example for others.
____Next to God, I am careful to keep my family as first priority in my life.

X. Verse 30 "Charm is deceptive, and beauty is fleeting; but a woman who fears the LORD is to be praised."

____It is not a secret that I love the Lord.
____My emphasis and desire is more focused on growing spiritually than on acquiring more "things."

XII. Verse 31 "Give her the reward she has earned, and let her works bring her praise at the city gate."

____My life shows evidence of "good fruit."
____Others recognize the hand of God in my life.
____I have been awarded/rewarded for specific areas of ministry or productivity in my work.

- How do you see yourself in relation to the woman of virtue in Proverbs?
- Does the translation of the verses of Proverbs 31 in the evaluation above help you see the woman of virtue as someone you can become?
- Do you know anyone who demonstrates the qualities listed in the self-evaluation?
- What did you learn about yourself by taking this evaluation?

> We become virtuous when we allow God to work in us and through us. When we put our relationship with God as first priority, then everything we do becomes an act of worship, a beautifully orchestrated masterpiece of God's choosing, with Him as the director.

➲ PRAYER

How can we support you in prayer, based on tonight's lesson?

- What is one specific area you would like to commit to improving based on the evaluation?

- How can you adjust your priorities to grow deeper in your relationship with God and others?

LESSON 2

"WHAT MAKES THIS CHICK TICK?"

Scripture Passage

Proverbs 31:10 (KJV); Proverbs 31:11–31 (NIV)

10 Who can find a virtuous woman? for her price is far above rubies.

11 Her husband has full confidence in her and lacks nothing of value.

12 She brings him good, not harm, all the days of her life.

13 She selects wool and flax and works with eager hands.

14 She is like the merchant ships, bringing her food from afar.

15 She gets up while it is still dark; she provides food for her family and portions for her servant girls.

16 She considers a field and buys it; out of her earnings she plants a vineyard.

17 She sets about her work vigorously; her arms are strong for her tasks.

18 She sees that her trading is profitable, and her lamp does not go out at night.

19 In her hand she holds the distaff and grasps the spindle with her fingers.

20 She opens her arms to the poor and extends her hands to the needy.

21 When it snows, she has no fear for her household; for all of them are clothed in scarlet.

22 She makes coverings for her bed; she is clothed in fine linen and purple.

23 Her husband is respected at the city gate, where he takes his seat among the elders of the land.

24 She makes linen garments and sells them, and supplies the merchants with sashes.

25 She is clothed with strength and dignity; she can laugh at the days to come.

26 She speaks with wisdom, and faithful instruction is on her tongue.

27 She watches over the affairs of her household and does not eat the bread of idleness.

28 Her children arise and call her blessed; her husband also, and he praises her:

29 "Many women do noble things, but you surpass them all."

31 Give her the reward she has earned, and let her works bring her praise at the city gate.

- Can you find different seasons of a woman's life represented here?

- Does the idea that this is accomplished over a lifetime make her more approachable and believable?

- Which relationship sums up the entire passage in verse 30?

- How does your relationship with the Lord affect your other relationships and all that you do?

LESSON 3

"WHO DOES SHE THINK SHE IS?"

Group Leader Instructions

Prepare by reading and meditating on this lesson for several days prior to your group. When it moves from your head to your heart, you will be ready to share with your group.

- ⊃ **You will need** a group handout and a small gift bag with a pen and several small squares of paper for each person, hostess gifts, pamper gifts.
- ⊃ **Be organized.** Have everything ready (papers, pens, etc.) before your gals arrive. Then you won't waste time during the session.
- ⊃ **Meet and greet your ladies as they arrive.** Introduce them to each other as much as possible while waiting to begin.
- ⊃ **Start on time with a welcome and prayer.**
- ⊃ Thank them for coming, and let them know how happy you are that they are here.
- ⊃ If you have new ladies, introduce yourself and your coleader.
- ⊃ **Share announcements.**
  - o Sign-ups for upcoming hostesses/refreshments, etc.

➲ GETTING TO KNOW YOUR HOSTESS

- ➲ Introduce your hostess and the person who provided refreshments.
- ➲ Thank them verbally and with a hostess/thank-you gift.
- ➲ Ask your hostess to share about herself and her life. Keep it to five minutes or so.

➲ GETTING TO KNOW EACH OTHER

- • *Note*: This lesson could take a bit longer than usual. Be sure to get started on time and keep it moving.
- • Each person will need twice as many squares of paper as there are women, including one for herself.

Write your name on your bag and take one piece of paper out of your bag. Without identifying yourself, write two things on that piece of paper that not many people know about you. Then fold your paper in half and hand it to me, without letting anyone see what you wrote.

- • Mix up the papers in a bag or basket.

I'm going to pass the bag around. I want you to pull out one piece of paper. It doesn't matter if you get your own paper, as long as you don't tell anyone. When everyone has a paper we will go around the room, read the papers, and try to guess who it is.

- • Have fun reading the papers and discovering each person's secrets.

Now, take the other papers out of your bag. You should have one for every person. At the top of each paper, write the name of one person in the group until you have a piece of paper for every woman in the group. As we go through the lesson, write a note of affirmation to *each woman* in our group. Tell her what you love and admire about her. This may be the first time you have met some of the ladies. If so, just write some positive things you have noticed about your new friends during our time together.

- After they have written a note for everyone, have them place their notes in one another's bags.

Let's get into our lesson by digging into God's Word. This is where our hearts really become woven into a tapestry of love—when we center our conversation and relationships in Christ. When we do, we can confidently share our hearts with each other. There is an element of trust that is a gift. We agree that *what happens with the girls stays with the girls*—let's say that together!

➲ GETTING TO KNOW THE LORD

INTRODUCTIONI

I have a feeling we can all remember a time in our lives when we've looked at another woman and thought, *Who does she think she is?* How many of you have ever had that thought? Maybe she made us angry, or we were disgusted by her attitude, or maybe we just have a critical spirit toward her. In all fairness, it may be accurate to say that we usually feel this way because she actually did something that offended us.

But there are those other times when you meet a woman who walks so confidently that you just cannot help but think, *Just who does she think she is?*

This time, it's not because she was offensive at all but because she is just so perfect or so at peace with herself, or just so cheerful that it makes you feel insignificant. Maybe you thought, *Boy, she really thinks she's something.*

That is certainly the type of woman we are reading about

in Proverbs 31. She radiates all those qualities that make us feel inadequate. She seems too good to be true.

Our lesson tonight is titled "Who Does She Think She Is?"

Let's read out loud together this selection of verses from Proverbs 31. You have it there on your group handout. Ready? Let's read this together:

> She gets up while it is still dark ... She sees that her trading is profitable, and her lamp does not go out at night ... Her husband is respected at the city gate, where he takes his seat among the elders of the land. (Proverbs 31:15, 18, 23)

What do you think about this woman? Imagine if she were here tonight and wrote these things about herself on her little piece of paper! We probably wouldn't like her very much, would we?

We would be thinking, *Who does she think she is?*

She "sees that her trading is profitable"? What kind of trading is she doing?

She gets up early <u>and</u> stays up late? Most of us do one or the other, but she's doing *both*? Besides, she's even bragging about it! Otherwise, how would anyone know her schedule? So her husband is a bigwig in the city. What makes her think that she had anything to do with that? She must be a snob!

Doesn't this sound like the perfect setup for a woman we want to avoid?

If we have any insecurities, this woman would definitely bring all of those feelings to the surface. The truth is that what we are really feeling in our hearts is, *I wish I were more like her.* And the pain of our hearts is that we see ourselves as not good enough or not as good as this person. Our enemy, the devil, has a field day reminding us of every lie he has ever told us to attack our self-esteem.

How can we arrive at this place of peace in who we are and who God has made us to be?

What can we learn from the woman of virtue in Proverbs 31?

Let's look at her from another perspective!

Suppose this woman's "profitable trading" is with the Lord, and that's why she is up early in the morning and goes to bed late at night. What if she were beginning and ending her day by spending time with God?

➲ Go around the room and have every lady respond to this first question. Are you a morning person, a night person, or are you at your peak in the afternoon?

➲ Open the discussion with these questions:

- If you were to meet this woman, and she spoke the words of the psalmist below, how would that change your attitude toward her?

   "But I call to God, and the LORD saves me. Evening, morning and noon I cry out in distress, and he hears my voice." (Psalm 55:16-17)

- Compare these words to the verses from Proverbs 31 that we read together. What similarities do you see?

   Both are intensely focused; the morning and evening aspects could speak to the fact that the profitable trading is time spent with the Lord in scripture and prayer.

- How do you suppose this dedication to spending time in prayer would affect a woman's life?

➲ Allow time for answers; then offer these thoughts or pose them as further questions:

   ➲ It would make her more confident; would bring peace to her life and countenance.
   ➲ It would affect the success of her husband; she would have a God-given respect for him, which would elevate

his self-esteem and might result in this family being esteemed in their community because of their example and solid foundation.

➲ It would make her "trading more profitable" in all aspects of life as she submits everything to the Lord in prayer.

➲ It would empower the Lord to accomplish through her all that Proverbs 31 describes.

• How could you arrange or rearrange your schedule to spend your personal peak time of the day in prayer?

• Other than the time of day, what is preventing you from spending the quality and/or quantity of time with the Lord that He deserves?

Satan will do everything he can to prevent us from spending time with God.

In John 10:10, Jesus said,

"The thief comes only to steal and kill and destroy; I have come that [you] may have life, and have it to the full."

• When and how can you minimize the distractions in your prayer time?

The only way we can overcome our circumstances and change our attitude is by being committed to prayer and reading God's Word. This is how we fight the enemy. It's also how we discredit all the lies that he uses to destroy our self-esteem.

> The secret to becoming a woman with inner peace and God-confidence is to discover our value to God by spending time in scripture and prayer.

We are fighting a cultural battle that separates and divides us and causes us to look at one another as competition. But God wants to weave our hearts together in love. As Christian women, we are to encourage and uplift one another with our words, and speak truth into each other's lives. That's what this little exercise we did tonight is about.

Have you written all your love notes and distributed all your notes into the bags?

Let's take a few minutes to read our love notes. You may discover that in our eyes and certainly in the eyes of the Lord, you are an amazing and virtuous woman!

➲ PRAYER

- ➲ Give them a few minutes to read their notes and then share a couple of favorites with the group. (You can expect tears here. Have some tissues ready.)
- ➲ Ask them to share their reactions to what others said about them.

Let's close in prayer by asking the most important question: "Lord, who do You think I am?"

- ➲ Allow time for silent prayer.
- ➲ Ask for prayer requests if you have time. If not, close with Psalm 139.

Psalm 139 gives us just a hint of how much God loves us. Let's close by praying together:

Lord God,

> You made all the delicate, inner parts of my body and knit me together in my mother's womb. Thank you for making me so wonderfully complex! Your workmanship is marvelous—how well I know it.

You watched me as I was being formed in utter seclusion, as I was woven together in the dark of the womb. You saw me before I was born. Every day of my life was recorded in your book. Every moment was laid out before a single day had passed.

How precious are your thoughts about me, O God. They cannot be numbered! I can't even count them; they outnumber the grains of sand!

And when I wake up, you are still with me!

⮑ Follow the spirit by either leading in a time of open prayer, or, if it's getting late, simply close by asking God to reveal the truth of His love to each woman.

⮑ **Present your ladies with pamper gifts as they leave.**

LESSON 3

"WHO DOES SHE THINK SHE IS?"

Group Handout

➲ **GETTING TO KNOW YOUR HOSTESS**

➲ **GETTING TO KNOW EACH OTHER**

- ➲ Write your name on your bag and take one piece of paper out of your bag. Without identifying yourself, write two things on that piece of paper that not many people know about you. Then fold your paper in half and hand it to your leader, without letting anyone see what you wrote.
- ➲ Now, take the other papers out of your bag. You should have one for every person. At the top of each paper, write one name so that you have a piece of paper for each woman here. As we go through the lesson, write a note to each woman in our group to affirm her and tell her what you love and admire about her.

➲ **GETTING TO KNOW THE LORD**

Let's read these verses out loud together:

She gets up while it is still dark ... She sees that her trading is profitable, and her lamp does not go out at night ... Her husband is respected at the city gate, where he takes his seat among the elders of the land. (Proverbs 31:15, 18, 23)

- Are you a morning person, a night person, or are you at your peak in the afternoon?

- If you were to meet this woman, and she spoke the words of the psalmist, below, how would that change your attitude toward her?

  "But I call to God, and the LORD saves me. Evening, morning and noon I cry out in distress, and he hears my voice" (Psalm 55:16–17).

- Compare the psalm to the verses from Proverbs 31 that we read together. What similarities do you see?

- How do you suppose this dedication to spending time in prayer would affect a woman's life?

- How could you arrange or rearrange your schedule to spend your personal peak time of the day in prayer?

- Other than the time of day, what is preventing you from spending the quality and/or quantity of time with the Lord that He deserves?

- When and how can you minimize the distractions in your prayer time?

In John 10:10, Jesus said,

  "The thief comes only to steal and kill and destroy; I have come that [you] may have life, and have it to the full."

> The secret to becoming a woman with inner peace and God-confidence is to discover your value to God through scripture and prayer.

➲ PRAYER

"Lord, who do you think I am?"

Psalm 139 gives us just a hint of how much God loves us. Let's close by praying together:

Lord God,

> You made all the delicate, inner parts of my body and knit me together in my mother's womb. Thank you for making me so wonderfully complex! Your workmanship is marvelous—how well I know it.
>
> You watched me as I was being formed in utter seclusion, as I was woven together in the dark of the womb. You saw me before I was born. Every day of my life was recorded in your book. Every moment was laid out before a single day had passed.
>
> How precious are your thoughts about me, O God. They cannot be numbered!
>
> I can't even count them; they outnumber the grains of sand!
>
> And when I wake up, you are still with me.

LESSON 4

"WHERE DID SHE GET THAT OUTFIT?"

Group Leader Instructions

Prepare by reading and meditating on this lesson for several days prior to your group. When it moves from your head to your heart, you will be ready to share with your group.

- ⊃ **You will need** a group handout and a roll of toilet paper for each person (Yes, I'm serious!), hostess gifts, pamper gifts.
- ⊃ **Be organized.** Arrive early and have everything ready before your gals arrive. Then you won't waste time with this during the session.
- ⊃ **Meet and greet your ladies as they arrive.**
- ⊃ **Start on time with a welcome and prayer.**
- ⊃ Thank them for coming and let them know how happy you are that they are there! If you have new ladies, introduce yourself and your coleader.
- ⊃ **Make sure everyone** has a group handout and a roll of toilet paper.
- ⊃ **Share announcements.**
  - o Have you planned an outreach project yet?
  - o Sign-ups for upcoming hostesses/refreshments, etc.

⮊ GETTING TO KNOW YOUR HOSTESS

- ⮊ Introduce your hostess and the person who provided refreshments.
- ⮊ Thank them verbally and with a hostess/thank-you gift.
- ⮊ Ask your hostess to share about herself and her life. Keep it to five minutes or so.

⮊ INTRODUCE THE TOPIC

We have been taking a closer look at the woman of virtue in Proverbs 31. We've searched out many questions about her—those unspoken questions we women often ask about one another. *"Who does she think she is?"* and *"What makes this chick tick?"*

Our goal is to find a kinship with this woman; to make her more realistic and achievable; to see her as three-dimensional rather than just looking at her outward appearance; to see what motivates her and learn from her example; to see ourselves in her; and even to feel the love of the Lord for her as a friend, rather than some superhero or an impossible ideal that we have to measure up to.

This month we want to know,

"Where did she get that outfit?"

We're going to begin with a fun activity that will help us to get to know each other better. That would explain why you have a roll of toilet paper in your hands.

⮊ GETTING TO KNOW EACH OTHER

- ⮊ Ask your ladies to partner with someone. One person will be the receiver and one person will be the giver. Before explaining what they will be doing, ask them to decide who will be the giver and who will be the receiver on their teams.

- ➲ Once each team has a giver and receiver, instruct the *givers* to design an outfit of clothing from the toilet paper on their partner, the *receiver*. The outfit is to reflect her friend's best qualities.
- ➲ Give them ten minutes to finish. The giver will introduce herself and her partner to the group. Then she will explain how her "designer fashion" reflects her partner's best qualities. Have fun!
- ➲ If you have time, they can switch roles and do it again, so that every woman has a designer fashion. You will be amazed at how this exercise will touch hearts.

Let's get into our lesson by digging into God's Word. This is where our hearts really become woven into a tapestry of love—when we center our conversation and relationships in Christ. When we do, we can confidently share our hearts with each other. There is an element of trust that is a gift. We agree that *what happens with the girls stays with the girls*—let's say that together!

➲ GETTING TO KNOW THE LORD

If you were to arrive dressed in toilet paper, people would definitely wonder, "Where did you get that outfit?"

Isn't that a familiar question among females? "Oh, I love your outfit! Where did you get it?" How many of you have ever tried to avoid answering that question? Have you ever purchased something at K-mart or a thrift store and really didn't want to admit it? Or maybe you're thinking, *I don't want to tell where I got this because I don't want to show up somewhere and discover that I have a twin!*

Tonight we are focusing on verses 21 and 22 of the virtuous woman passage in Proverbs 31:

When it snows, she has no fear for her household;

for all of them are clothed in scarlet.

She makes coverings for her bed; she is clothed
in fine linen and purple.

- If you were to meet this woman, what would your first
  impression be, based on what she is wearing?
- Suggested responses:
  - o She may be wealthy; well-dressed; royalty.
  - o She's not afraid to be noticed.
  - o She is prepared.

The color purple is connected to royalty. The color was achieved by making a dye from mollusks, a shellfish in the Mediterranean Sea. It was a pricey dye, as it took 250,000 mollusks to make one ounce. Purple was the color God required in the tabernacle. The color purple was reserved for royal robes and garments of the wealthy.

It is obvious that this woman of virtue was well dressed. But we want to look deeper into this woman of virtue not to focus on her outward appearance and what she was wearing but to look for those inner qualities that speak about who she is as a person.

Let's take a closer look and see how the Lord is at work in her life.

➲ Ask someone to read 1 Peter 3:3-4:

Your beauty should not come from outward adornment, such as braided hair and the wearing of gold jewelry and fine clothes. Instead, it should be that of your inner self, the unfading beauty of a gentle and quiet spirit, which is of great worth in God's sight. (NIV)

Reading the passage in 1 Peter, you may be left with the impression that the woman of virtue is showing too much concern for her outward beauty by wearing linen and purple. It's hard to imagine that a man (Peter) would tell us that he doesn't want us to take care of our outer appearance and to look beautiful on the outside.

The emphasis here is not that we are to follow some kind of dress code. Peter is simply saying that we women need to get our priorities right and spend as much or more time and care of our inner beauty as we do of our outward beauty. Our jewelry, clothing, hair, outward appearance should not be what defines us. The point he's making is that our real source of beauty is the beauty of our heart—the beauty that shines from the inside out.

Imagine if, when we look at one another as women, we were not focused so much on the outer appearance. What would happen if we looked deeper and tried to see how God is at work in each other's lives?

- How would that change your relationships?
    o Do you think you would have more friends?
    o Be more accepting of others? Or more judgmental?
    o Would you be more appealing as a potential friend?
    o Would other women be more comfortable around you?

If we look more deeply at the woman of virtue and not just at her outfit, what clues do the verses of Proverbs 31:21–22 reveal about this woman as a person? (Allow time for discussion.)

- She plans ahead; she is not fearful of the future.
- She takes care of her family's needs; she is productive; she takes care of herself and is well dressed.
- She isn't sloppily put together. Instead, she is thoughtful about how she presents herself and this gives her more confidence.

Jesus speaks directly to our concerns for physical and material needs in the Sermon on the Mount. Listen to what

He has to say about clothing and outward appearances in this passage in Matthew 6:25-34:

25 Therefore I tell you, *do not worry* about your life, what you will eat or drink; or about your body, what you will wear. Is not life more important than food, and the body more important than clothes?

26 Look at the birds of the air; they do not sow or reap or store away in barns, and yet your heavenly Father feeds them. Are you not much more valuable than they?

27 Who of you by worrying can add a single hour to his life?

28 *And why do you worry about clothes?* See how the lilies of the field grow. They do not labor or spin.

29 Yet I tell you that not even Solomon in all his splendor was dressed like one of these.

30 If that is how God clothes the grass of the field, which is here today and tomorrow is thrown into the fire, will he not much more clothe you, O you of little faith?

31 So *do not worry*, saying, "What shall we eat?" or "What shall we drink?" or "What shall we wear?"

32 For the pagans run after all these things, and your heavenly Father knows that you need them.

33 But seek first his kingdom and his righteousness, and all these things will be given to you as well.

34 Therefore *do not worry about tomorrow*, for tomorrow will worry about itself. Each day has enough trouble of its own. (NIV, emphasis added)

- What does Jesus repeat over and over in this passage? *Do not worry!*

Look again at the verses in Proverbs:

> When it snows, she has no fear for her household;
> for all of them are clothed in scarlet. She makes

coverings for her bed; she is clothed in fine linen and purple.[130]

- How do you see the Lord at work in the life of the woman of virtue through the image that these two verses portray?

- Is she worried about tomorrow or about what her family will wear or what she will wear?

The passage says that *she has no fear for tomorrow*, just as Jesus said in Matthew 6:34. It's as though this woman is being obedient to Jesus's words. And because of her obedience, God is dressing her in the finest of fabrics.

She is dressed in royal colors and expensive fabrics because she is resting in the Lord's provision for her.

Proverbs 31:25 says, "She is clothed with strength and dignity; she can laugh at the days to come."

She is not worried about tomorrow if she is laughing at the days to come. The promise that God will dress us more splendidly than King Solomon is beautifully illustrated in the life of the woman of virtue.

So … where did she get that outfit? I believe she got it from the Lord Himself. When we rest in the Lord and focus on our relationship with Him, we become confident in His promises.

The woman of virtue knows that her inner beauty is more valuable and more beautiful than the most expensive piece of clothing she could ever purchase.

---

[130] Proverbs 31:21-22 (NIV).

➲ PRAYER

As we lead into prayer, let's take a few minutes to think and share:

- What are some of the worries and day-to-day realities you face that prevent you from walking in the Lord's promise to clothe you and feed you and take care of you?

- How have you experienced God's care in your life?

Allow quiet time for them to think about the questions and to answer them. You may want to suggest some things they may be facing to help them open up. Pray for the needs presented and for God's provision. Thank God for His ability to meet our every need, and ask Him to enable us to see Him at work, to acknowledge the many ways that He provides for us.

➲ **Send out your ladies with a sweet little pamper gift as they leave. Remind them of your next meeting date.**

LESSON 4

"WHERE DID SHE GET THAT OUTFIT?"

Group Handout

➲ **GETTING TO KNOW YOUR HOSTESS**

➲ **GETTING TO KNOW EACH OTHER**

➲ **GETTING TO KNOW THE LORD**

Proverbs 31:21–22

> When it snows, she has no fear for her household;
> for all of them are clothed in scarlet.
>
> She makes coverings for her bed; she is clothed
> in fine linen and purple.

• If you were to meet this woman, what would your first
  impression be, based on what she is wearing?

> Your beauty should not come from outward
> adornment, such as braided hair and the wearing
> of gold jewelry and fine clothes. Instead, it

should be that of your inner self, the unfading beauty of a gentle and quiet spirit, which is of great worth in God's sight. (1 Peter 3:3-4 NIV)

- Imagine if, when we look at one another as women, we were not focused so much on the outer appearance, but we would instead look at the work of the Lord in one another's lives.

- How would that change your relationships?
    o Do you think you would have more friends?
    o Be more accepting of others? Or more judgmental?
    o Would you be more appealing to them as a potential friend?
    o Would they be more comfortable around you?

- If we look more deeply at the woman of virtue and not just at her outfit, what clues do the two verses in Proverbs reveal about this woman as a person?

25 Therefore I tell you, *do not worry* about your life, what you will eat or drink; or about your body, what you will wear. Is not life more important than food, and the body more important than clothes?
26 Look at the birds of the air; they do not sow or reap or store away in barns, and yet your heavenly Father feeds them. Are you not much more valuable than they?
27 Who of you by worrying can add a single hour to his life?
28 *And why do you worry about clothes?* See how the lilies of the field grow. They do not labor or spin.
29 Yet I tell you that not even Solomon in all his splendor was dressed like one of these.
30 If that is how God clothes the grass of the field, which is here today and tomorrow is thrown into the fire, will he not much more clothe you, O you of little faith?
31 So *do not worry*, saying, "What shall we eat?" or "What shall we drink?" or "What shall we wear?"

32 For the pagans run after all these things, and your heavenly Father knows that you need them.

33 But seek first his kingdom and his righteousness, and all these things will be given to you as well.

34 Therefore *do not worry about tomorrow*, for tomorrow will worry about itself. Each day has enough trouble of its own. (Matthew 6:25–34 NIV, emphasis added)

• What does Jesus repeat over and over in this passage?

Look again at the verses in Proverbs:

When it snows, she has no fear for her household;

for all of them are clothed in scarlet.

She makes coverings for her bed; she is clothed in fine linen and purple.

The woman of virtue knows that her inner beauty is more valuable and more beautiful than the most expensive piece of clothing she could ever purchase.

➲ PRAYER

What are some of the worries you face that prevent you from accepting the Lord's promise to clothe you, feed you, and take care of you?

How have you experienced God's care in your life?

LESSON 5

"WHAT DOES SHE DO?"

Group Leader Instructions

Prepare by reading and meditating on this lesson for several days prior to your group. When it moves from your head to your heart, you will be ready to share with your group.

- ➲ **You will need** a group handout for each person, hostess gifts, pamper gifts, and a variety of fabrics, yarns, ribbons, each approximately 36 inches long and no more than half an inch wide.
- ➲ **Be organized.** Have everything ready before your gals arrive. Then you won't waste time during the session.
- ➲ **Meet and greet your ladies as they arrive.**
- ➲ **Start on time with a welcome and prayer.**
- ➲ Thank them for coming and let them know how happy you are that they are there. If you have new ladies, introduce yourself and your coleader.
- ➲ **Make sure everyone has** a group handout and a strip of fabric.
- ➲ **Share announcements.**
  - o Upcoming events
  - o Sign-ups for upcoming hostesses/refreshments, etc.

➲ GETTING TO KNOW YOUR HOSTESS

- ➲ Introduce your hostess and the person who provided refreshments.
- ➲ Thank them verbally and with a hostess/thank-you gift.
- ➲ Ask your hostess to share about herself and her life. Keep it to five minutes or so.

➲ GETTING TO KNOW EACH OTHER

- ➲ Allow each person to choose a strip of cloth/ribbon. Have a variety of styles to choose from.
- ➲ Once everyone has a piece of cloth, go around the room and ask each lady to give her name and answer the question, "What do you do?" They can also share why they chose their particular fabric and how it reflects their personality or life.

Let's get into our lesson by digging into God's Word. This is where our hearts really become woven into a tapestry of love—when we center our conversation and relationships in Christ. When we do, we can confidently share our hearts with each other. There is an element of trust that is a gift. We agree that *what happens with the girls stays with the girls*—let's say that together!

➲ GETTING TO KNOW THE LORD

Last month we were asked that very female question that we have all been asked at one time or another, "Where did you get that outfit?" In our groups last month, we were asking that question of the woman of virtue in Proverbs 31. We decided the Lord Himself had clothed her in royal purple and fine linen because she trusted Him to provide everything she needed.

This month we want to know: "What does she do?"

"What do you do?" It's one of the first questions we usually ask when we meet someone new. It seems like we are constantly being confronted with this question, and we find ourselves asking it of other people. When you're graduating from high school or college, everyone asks, "What are you going to do?" If you're a stay-at-home mom, you might get the response, "Oh, so you don't work?" Or if your occupation is unconventional, if you own your own business, or do ministry ... people might just look at you with a big question mark on their faces, trying to decide if you really "do anything" or not.

- What about you? How did you feel when we asked you to answer the question, "What do you do?" when we started this evening? Nervous? Hesitant? Confident? Self-conscious? Intimidated? Unimportant? Embarrassed? Ho-hum? Proud?

Somehow the question "what do you do?" often brings anxiety and pressure, because we feel like we will immediately be judged and pigeon-holed according to how we answer. It feels like we are in some sort of competition because according to our American culture, our worth is based on having a title and position. The greater the position, the more valuable and important we are perceived to be. There is no question that our society places a high priority on what we do.

What about this woman of virtue? What does *she* do? When we read this passage in Proverbs 31, "what she does" is the very thing that intimidates us. We wonder, "Is there anything she *doesn't* do?" Let's go around the room and read Proverbs 31.

Proverbs 31:10 (KJV); Proverbs 31:11–31 (NIV)

10 Who can find a virtuous woman? for her price is far above rubies.
11 Her husband has full confidence in her and lacks nothing of value.

12 She brings him good, not harm, all the days of her life.

13 She selects wool and flax and works with eager hands.

14 She is like the merchant ships, bringing her food from afar.

15 She gets up while it is still dark; she provides food for her family and portions for her servant girls.

16 She considers a field and buys it; out of her earnings she plants a vineyard.

17 She sets about her work vigorously; her arms are strong for her tasks.

18 She sees that her trading is profitable, and her lamp does not go out at night.

19 In her hand she holds the distaff and grasps the spindle with her fingers.

20 She opens her arms to the poor and extends her hands to the needy.

21 When it snows, she has no fear for her household; for all of them are clothed in scarlet.

22 She makes coverings for her bed; she is clothed in fine linen and purple.

23 Her husband is respected at the city gate, where he takes his seat among the elders of the land.

24 She makes linen garments and sells them, and supplies the merchants with sashes.

25 She is clothed with strength and dignity; she can laugh at the days to come.

26 She speaks with wisdom, and faithful instruction is on her tongue.

27 She watches over the affairs of her household and does not eat the bread of idleness.

28 Her children arise and call her blessed; her husband also, and he praises her:

29 "Many women do noble things, but you surpass them all."

30 Charm is deceptive, and beauty is fleeting; but a woman who fears the LORD is to be praised.

31 Give her the reward she has earned, and let her works bring her praise at the city gate.

- According to the passage, what does the woman of virtue do?

  Verse 13: selects wool and flax and works with eager hands; verse 14: brings food from afar; verse 15: provides food for her family.

- What are some things she does that, in our society, would bring the response, "Oh, so you don't work?" because they are domestic in nature?

  Providing food for her family and servants; spinning and weaving; sewing and quilting; compassionate ministries and volunteering in the community; seeing that her family's needs are met

- Is there anything that hints of a possible "occupation"? (Verses 16, 18, 24)

In the book of Acts, we read about a woman named Lydia, who lived hundreds of years, possibly a thousand years, after the women of virtue passage was written (Proverbs 31: tenth century BC; Acts: first century AD). Yet Lydia is the personification of this woman in Proverbs. She brings to life many of the activities and qualities of the woman of virtue.

Lydia was a prosperous businesswoman. She lived in Philippi and dealt in dyed goods. She didn't sell just any fabric; she sold purple cloth, the most expensive royal cloth. Just like the woman of virtue, she most likely dressed in purple and fine linen now and then.

Lydia worshiped God as a proselyte, which means she was not a Jew but a Gentile who had converted to the Jewish faith. When Paul shared the good news of Jesus with her in Philippi, Lydia believed in Christ. She was the first convert to Christianity in all of Europe.

READ LUKE'S WORDS IN ACTS 16:13–15:

On the Sabbath we went outside the city gate to the river, where we expected to find a place of prayer. We sat down and began to speak to the women who had gathered there. One of those listening was a woman named Lydia, a dealer in purple cloth from the city of Thyatira, who was a worshiper of God. The Lord opened her heart to respond to Paul's message. When she and the members of her household were baptized, she invited us to her home. "If you consider me a believer in the Lord," she said, "come and stay at my house." And she persuaded us.

- What does Lydia "do" in this passage?
- Compare what Lydia does to what the woman of virtue does.
  - o Lydia prays with other women.
  - o Lydia gathers at the city gate (compare to Proverbs 31:23, 31).
  - o Lydia sells and trades purple cloth (compare to Proverbs 31:18, 22, 24).
  - o Lydia worships God (compare to Proverbs 31:30).
  - o Lydia is baptized.
  - o Lydia opens her home to the disciples (compare to Proverbs 31:20).
- What titles are given to Lydia?
  - o Dealer in purple cloth.
  - o Worshiper of God.
- What title does she give herself after her baptism?
  - o Believer in the Lord.

- Going back to Proverbs, can you find anywhere in this passage a title for the woman of virtue and what she does?

The only title for the Proverbs 31 woman is "woman of virtue" and "a woman who fears the Lord." The passage refers to a multitude of things that she does, some of which sound very enterprising and imply that she is a businesswoman, a wife, and mother. But those titles are not given to her. It seems that her "occupation"—what really occupies her heart and mind, what her life is really about—is just walking in step with the Lord.

> The woman of virtue needs no title, position, or occupation according to the world's standards because her identity and worth are found in Christ.

Looking at these two women's examples, how do you think people would react if, when you are asked, "What do you do?" you responded, "I am a believer in the Lord," or "I am a woman who fears the Lord," or "I am a woman of virtue"?

Imagine how different it would be if our society placed value on our relationship to the Lord rather than worldly positions and titles.

- ⊃ What if, when asked the question "What do you do?," you answered based on your relationship with the Lord?
  - o What would your answer be?
  - o Would it be easier or more difficult to answer?
  - o How would it change your priorities in everyday life?

What if you determined in your heart that your occupation, your livelihood, your career was to work for Jesus Christ? What if you would just enter into a partnership with the Lord and allow everything else to be secondary? How would that change your life?

LET'S DO A LITTLE EXPERIMENT.

- ➲ Take your fabric strip and pull on it to test its strength.
- ➲ Now fold it in half so that you have two shorter strips. One half represents you and the other half represents the Lord.
- ➲ Now twist them together and pull on the twisted strip. Do you see how much stronger the fabric becomes?
  - o Imagine if one strip of the fabric was of infinite strength ... the one representing Jesus.

- ➲ Just think how much different your life would be if you would totally rely on His strength.

Philippians 4:13 says, "I can do everything through him who gives me strength."

Let's say that together: I can do everything through him who gives me strength.

It makes it easier to comprehend how the woman of virtue was able to "do" so much, doesn't it? If she was partnering with the Lord and relying on His strength, it's easy to believe that she was capable of doing all that the passage says she did.

Now imagine how much easier it would be to rely on the Lord's strength if we had someone to partner with us. Ecclesiastes 4:9–12 says:

> Two are better than one, because they have a good return for their work: If one falls down, her friend can help her up. But pity the [wo]man who falls and has no one to help (her) up! Also, if two lie down together, they will keep warm. But how can one keep warm alone? Though one may be overpowered, two can defend themselves. A cord of three strands is not quickly broken. (NIV)

⮕ Divide your ladies into groups of two. It's best if they are paired with someone they don't know very well. Then instruct them to select one more strip of yarn or ribbon from the bag. Now tie all three braid strips together. One of you can hold onto the knot while the other braids them together.

> *It's a good idea to have enough yarn or ribbon for every woman to take a braided strip home as a reminder of this lesson.

See how much stronger this is? Just by adding a third cord, you are able to braid it for even stronger support and strength. This is why we are here tonight: to draw strength from each other; to allow the Lord to knit our hearts together in love. We need the strength of one another in order to strengthen our relationship with God and to face the pressures of the world.

As the scripture says: "Two are better than one ... but a cord of three strands cannot be quickly broken."

PRAYER

We're going to stay in our groups of two for prayer time tonight. Share with each other.

What areas of your life are broken or need repair? In what ways are you needing strengthening right now?

Then take turns praying for each. If you're not comfortable praying, it only takes a sentence or two. It doesn't have to be eloquent. Then when we're done, I will close by praying for us as a group.

Thank them for coming and send them home with a pamper gift.

LESSON 5

THE WOMAN OF VIRTUE: WHAT DOES SHE "DO"?

Group Handout

➲ **GETTING TO KNOW YOUR HOSTESS**

➲ **GETTING TO KNOW EACH OTHER**

   ➲ **"What do you do?"**

➲ **GETTING TO KNOW THE LORD**

How did you feel about answering the question "What do you do?" when we started this evening?

     Proverbs 31:10 (KJV); Proverbs 31:11–31 (NIV)

10 Who can find a virtuous woman? for her price is far above rubies.
11 Her husband has full confidence in her and lacks nothing of value.

12 She brings him good, not harm, all the days of her life.

13 She selects wool and flax and works with eager hands.

14 She is like the merchant ships, bringing her food from afar.

15 She gets up while it is still dark; she provides food for her family and portions for her servant girls.

16 She considers a field and buys it; out of her earnings she plants a vineyard.

17 She sets about her work vigorously; her arms are strong for her tasks.

18 She sees that her trading is profitable, and her lamp does not go out at night.

19 In her hand she holds the distaff and grasps the spindle with her fingers.

20 She opens her arms to the poor and extends her hands to the needy.

21 When it snows, she has no fear for her household; for all of them are clothed in scarlet.

22 She makes coverings for her bed; she is clothed in fine linen and purple.

23 Her husband is respected at the city gate, where he takes his seat among the elders of the land.

24 She makes linen garments and sells them, and supplies the merchants with sashes.

25 She is clothed with strength and dignity; she can laugh at the days to come.

26 She speaks with wisdom, and faithful instruction is on her tongue.

27 She watches over the affairs of her household and does not eat the bread of idleness.

28 Her children arise and call her blessed; her husband also, and he praises her:

29 "Many women do noble things, but you surpass them all."

30 Charm is deceptive, and beauty is fleeting; but a woman who fears the LORD is to be praised.

31 Give her the reward she has earned, and let her works bring her praise at the city gate.

- According to the passage, what does the woman of virtue "do"?
- What are some things she does that, in our society, would bring the response, "Oh, so you don't work?" because they are domestic in nature?
- Is there anything that hints of a possible "occupation"?

- Acts 16:13-15

> On the Sabbath we went outside the city gate to the river, where we expected to find a place of prayer. We sat down and began to speak to the women who had gathered there. One of those listening was a woman named Lydia, a dealer in purple cloth from the city of Thyatira, who was a worshiper of God. The Lord opened her heart to respond to Paul's message. When she and the members of her household were baptized, she invited us to her home. "If you consider me a believer in the Lord," she said, "come and stay at my house." And she persuaded us.

- What does Lydia "do" in this passage? Compare what Lydia does to what the woman of virtue does.
  - o What titles are given to Lydia in this passage?
  - o What title does she give herself after her baptism?

- Going back to Proverbs, can you find, anywhere in this passage, a title for this woman and what she does?

The woman of virtue needs no title, position, or occupation according to the world's standards because her identity and worth are found in Christ.

Looking at these two women's examples, how do you think people would react if, when they asked you what you do, you said, "I am a believer in the Lord," or "I am a woman who fears the Lord," or "I am a woman of virtue"?

Imagine how different it would be if our society placed value on our relationship to the Lord rather than worldly positions and titles. What if, when asked the question, "What do you do?" you answered based on your relationship with the Lord?

- What would your answer be?
- Would it be easier or more difficult to answer?
- How would it change your priorities in everyday life?

I can do everything through him who gives me strength. (Philippians 4:13)

Two are better than one, because they have a good return for their work: If one falls down, her friend can help her up. But pity the [wo]man who falls and has no one to help [her]up! Also, if two lie down together, they will keep warm. But how can one keep warm alone? Though one may be overpowered, two can defend themselves. A cord of three strands is not quickly broken. (Ecclesiastes 4:9–12 NIV)

This is why we are here tonight: to draw strength from each other, to allow the Lord to knit our hearts together in love. We need the strength of one another in order to strengthen our relationship with the Lord and to face the pressures of the world. What areas of your life are broken and need repair? In what ways do you need strengthening?

LESSON 6

"WHAT DOESN'T SHE DO?"

Group Leader Instructions

Prepare by reading and meditating on this lesson for several days prior to your group. When it moves from your head to your heart, you will be ready to share with your group.

- ➲ **You will need** a group handout for each person, hostess gifts, pamper gifts, and a Friendship Bread starter dough for each person.
- ➲ **Be organized.** Have everything ready before your gals arrive. Then you won't waste time with this during the session.
- ➲ **Meet and greet your ladies as they arrive.**
- ➲ **Start on time with a welcome and prayer.**
  Thank them for coming and let them know how happy you are that they are there. If you have new ladies, introduce yourself and your coleader.

- ➲ **Share announcements.**
  - o Sign-ups for upcoming hostesses/refreshments, etc.
  - o Next month's gathering date/place

- ➲ **Give everyone** a group handout.

⮑ GETTING TO KNOW YOUR HOSTESS

- ⮑ Introduce your hostess and the person who provided refreshments.
- ⮑ Thank them verbally and with a hostess/thank-you gift.
- ⮑ Ask your hostess to share about herself and her life. Keep it to five minutes or so.

⮑ GETTING TO KNOW EACH OTHER

Going around the room in turn, each lady should say her name and share something she can't seem to get done. Each person should repeat the name of every woman who has already shared and say the thing those women can't seem to get done before sharing her own.

For a surprise ending, the first person must repeat the names and things of everyone else in the room. (She thought she was off the hook.)

Let's get into our lesson by digging into God's Word. This is where our hearts really become woven into a tapestry of love—when we center our conversation and relationships in Christ. When we do, we can confidently share our hearts with each other. There is an element of trust that is a gift. We agree that *what happens with the girls stays with the girls*—let's say that together!

⮑ GETTING TO KNOW THE LORD

Last month we asked the identifying question of our times: "What do you do?" It's one of the first questions we usually ask when we meet someone new. It seems we are constantly confronted with this question, and we find ourselves asking it of other people. Last month, we not only asked each other that question, but we also asked in reference to the woman of virtue in Proverbs 31, "What does she do?" We discovered that what she does is the very thing that intimidates us. When we read Proverbs 31, we wonder, "Is there anything she *doesn't* do?"

So that is our question this month: "The woman of virtue: what *doesn't* she do?" I'm sure that there are many things she does not do, but in reading this passage, it seems like she's got all the bases covered. Let's look at the passage and see if it actually mentions anything she does *not* do.

Proverbs 31:10 (KJV); Proverbs 31:11–31 (NIV)

10 Who can find a virtuous woman? for her price is far above rubies.
11 Her husband has full confidence in her and lacks nothing of value.
12 She brings him good, **not harm**, all the days of her life.
13 She selects wool and flax and works with eager hands.
14 She is like the merchant ships, bringing her food from afar.
15 She gets up while it is still dark; she provides food for her family and portions for her servant girls.
16 She considers a field and buys it; out of her earnings she plants a vineyard.
17 She sets about her work vigorously; her arms are strong for her tasks.
18 She sees that her trading is profitable, and **her lamp does not go out at night.**
19 In her hand she holds the distaff and grasps the spindle with her fingers.
20 She opens her arms to the poor and extends her hands to the needy.
21 When it snows, **she has no fear** for her household; for all of them are clothed in scarlet.
22 She makes coverings for her bed; she is clothed in fine linen and purple.
23 Her husband is respected at the city gate, where he takes his seat among the elders of the land.

24 She makes linen garments and sells them, and supplies the merchants with sashes.
25 She is clothed with strength and dignity; she can laugh at the days to come.
26 She speaks with wisdom, and faithful instruction is on her tongue.
27 She watches over the affairs of her household and **does not eat the bread of idleness.**
28 Her children arise and call her blessed; her husband also, and he praises her:
29 "Many women do noble things, but you surpass them all."
30 Charm is deceptive, and beauty is fleeting; but a woman who fears the LORD is to be praised.
31 Give her the reward she has earned, and let her works bring her praise at the city gate.

- According to the passage, what does the woman of virtue *not* do?
  See highlights in the passage above.

- How do you suppose these things that she does *not* do help her to accomplish what she *does* do?
  She does "not harm" her husband; they are a team and support to one another.

  She does "not fear"; she walks in faith and trusts the Lord to help her.

  "She does not eat the bread of idleness"; she is on top of things and does not waste time with things that are not profitable.

- Reading between the lines, can you think of some things she probably does *not* do that aren't actually mentioned here?

Consider verse 27, "She does not eat the bread of idleness."

Isn't that an interesting figure of speech? How many of you love to eat bread?

Somehow, it seems like God made women to eat bread and men to eat meat. Maybe that's why the woman of virtue passage has something to say about "eating bread," but in this case she *doesn't* eat it. Fortunately, it's not talking about the same kind of bread that we like to eat. So we can all breathe easier, knowing that we can still eat bread and rolls and be women of virtue!

- What mental pictures do you get when you think about eating "the bread of idleness"?

The Hebrew word *atsluth*, translated here as *idleness*, actually means sloth. We picture a woman who just doesn't do anything, one who is slothful or lazy. But if we carry that thought a bit further, what do you envision?

Eating the bread of idleness makes it sound like a compulsion or an obsession with idleness. I just picture this woman filling up on this bread of idleness and getting bloated and miserable, and her misery begins to affect the lives of everyone around her. Not a pretty picture!

It gets even uglier because when women are miserable and idle, they get very busy with their mouths, saying things they should not say, meddling into other people's business. The following passage in 2 Thessalonians 3:11-13 sheds more light into this predicament of idleness.

Let's read it together:

> We hear that some among you are idle. They are not busy; they are busybodies.
>
> Such people we command and urge in the Lord Jesus Christ to settle down and earn the bread they eat ... never tire of doing what is right.

- What does Paul say about people who are idle? They are busybodies.

Don't you love the way he puts it? They are not *busy*; they are busy*bodies*! Sounds like he's telling them off! Isn't that our reaction, though, to busybodies? We get fed up with them and the trouble they cause. In verse 12, he also makes a correlation to bread; they need to "settle down and earn the bread they eat," rather than becoming miserable gluttons who are stuffing their face with the bread of idleness.

Let's look at a passage from 1 Timothy 5:13, where Paul is giving warnings and advice to the church on how it should deal with young widows:

> Besides, they get into the habit of being idle and going about from house to house. And not only do they become idlers, but also gossips and busybodies, saying things they ought not to.

Paul gets a little more descriptive as to what being idle and being a busybody really entail.

- What picture does he give us of a person being idle? What does he say she does?

    Go from house to house ... perhaps stirring up trouble among people, gossiping,

    Busybodies "say things they ought not to."

Just how idle are these people? Sounds like they are very busy, doesn't it? They're just busy with the affairs of other people and are not taking care of their own.

Do you know anyone like that?

It's pretty easy to think of women who are in the business of eating the bread of idleness, isn't it? And, if we think about it, we don't have to eat very much bread before we become full.

In the same way, it doesn't take much gossip and idle talk for people to get their fill of the busybody.

Contrast that thought with the woman portrayed in Proverbs 31:27.

> She watches over the affairs of her household
> and *does not eat the bread of idleness.*

THE WOMAN OF VIRTUE: WHAT DOESN'T SHE DO?

- ➲ She doesn't "go from house to house" because she is busy taking care of her own business and her own family.
- ➲ She does not poke her nose into other people's business,
  - o And she "does not eat the bread of idleness."

- ➲ She's doesn't become a busybody.
- ➲ She doesn't waste her time gossiping and "saying things she ought not" be saying.

Because she does not eat the bread of idleness, the previous verse, Proverbs 31:26 tells us what the woman of virtue *does* instead:

> She speaks with wisdom and faithful instruction
> is on her tongue.

Look back over the things in the Proverbs 31 passage that the woman of virtue *doesn't do.*

The woman of virtue does not harm her husband. She does not live in fear.
She does not eat the bread of idleness by gossiping. She speaks with wisdom and grace.

Now that you know that she *doesn't* do those things, isn't it easier to see how she is able to accomplish all the things she does? Maybe she is so busy doing good things that she doesn't have time to be a busybody. Avoiding the bread of idleness is *not* to say that we are to be busy all the time.

Remember: the word is translated from a word meaning sloth or laziness. Idleness, slothfulness, or laziness is quite different from resting and being at rest in the Lord.

Think back to our opening exercise of sharing what we do.

It's easy to see how gossip and rumors can get started somewhat innocently. Sometimes we try to retell something someone said, and we just don't get it right, or we say it in a tone of voice that makes it sound derogatory. Even changing just one word can totally change the interpretation of a story. And the further the story goes through the grapevine, the more distorted it becomes.

- Can you think of a time when you were hurt by someone's retelling a story that someone else supposedly said about you? Allow time to share.

- Can you think of a time when you hurt someone by eating the bread of idleness, saying words that were merely idle words, words of no value to others but instead tore someone down and upset her? Allow time to share.

Think of all the energy and emotion wasted by speaking and hearing words of idleness compared to the energy and empowerment we gain from words of kindness and wisdom and faithful instruction.

Let's partner with a person next to you, pray for one another's hurt feelings and emotions, and confess our own sins of "eating the bread of idleness."

LESSON 6
WHAT DOESN'T SHE DO?

Group Handout

➲ **GETTING TO KNOW YOUR HOSTESS**

➲ **GETTING TO KNOW EACH OTHER**

Share your name and something you can't seem to get done.

➲ **GETTING TO KNOW THE LORD**

Proverbs 31:10 (KJV); Proverbs 31:11–31 (NIV)

10 Who can find a virtuous woman? for her price is far above rubies.
11 Her husband has full confidence in her and lacks nothing of value.
12 She brings him good, not harm, all the days of her life.
13 She selects wool and flax and works with eager hands.
14 She is like the merchant ships, bringing her food from afar.
15 She gets up while it is still dark; she provides food for her family and portions for her servant girls.

16 She considers a field and buys it; out of her earnings she plants a vineyard.
17 She sets about her work vigorously; her arms are strong for her tasks.
18 She sees that her trading is profitable, and her lamp does not go out at night.
19 In her hand she holds the distaff and grasps the spindle with her fingers.
20 She opens her arms to the poor and extends her hands to the needy.
21 When it snows, she has no fear for her household; for all of them are clothed in scarlet.
22 She makes coverings for her bed; she is clothed in fine linen and purple.
23 Her husband is respected at the city gate, where he takes his seat among the elders of the land.
24 She makes linen garments and sells them, and supplies the merchants with sashes.
25 She is clothed with strength and dignity; she can laugh at the days to come.
26 She speaks with wisdom, and faithful instruction is on her tongue.
27 She watches over the affairs of her household and does not eat the bread of idleness.
28 Her children arise and call her blessed; her husband also, and he praises her:
29 "Many women do noble things, but you surpass them all."
30 Charm is deceptive, and beauty is fleeting; but a woman who fears the LORD is to be praised.
31 Give her the reward she has earned, and let her works bring her praise at the city gate.

- According to the passage, what does the woman of virtue *not* do?

- How do you suppose these things that she does *not* do help her to accomplish what she *does* do?

- Reading between the lines, can you think of some things she probably does *not* do that aren't actually mentioned here?

- Consider verse 27. It reads, "She does not eat the bread of idleness." Isn't that an interesting figure of speech? What mental pictures do you get when you think about "eating the bread of idleness"?

We hear that some among you are idle. They are not busy; they are busybodies. Such people we command and urge in the Lord Jesus Christ to settle down and earn the bread they eat … never tire of doing what is right. (2 Thessalonians 3:11–13 NIV)

- What does Paul say in 1 Thessalonians about people who are idle?

Besides, they get into the habit of being idle and going about from house to house. And not only do they become idlers, but also gossips and busybodies, saying things they ought not to. (1 Timothy 5:13 NIV)

- What picture does he give us in 1 Timothy of a person being idle? What does he say they do?

- Contrast that with the woman portrayed in Proverbs 31:27.

    She watches over the affairs of her household
    and does not eat the bread of idleness.

Proverbs 31:26 tells us what the woman of virtue does instead:

    "She speaks with wisdom and faithful instruction
    is on her tongue."

> The woman of virtue does not harm her husband. She does not live in fear.
> She does not eat the bread of idleness. She speaks with wisdom and grace.

Can you think of a time you have been hurt by someone retelling a story that someone else supposedly said about you?

Can you think of a time when you have hurt someone by eating the bread of idleness, saying words that were merely idle words, words of no value to others but instead tore someone down and upset her?

Let's pray for one another's hurt feelings and emotions, and confess our "eating the bread of idleness."

LESSON 7

A FINAL PLEA

Group Leader Instructions

Prepare by reading and meditating on this lesson for several days prior to your gathering. When it moves from your head to your heart, you will be ready to share with your group.

- ➲ **Meet and greet your ladies as they arrive.** Introduce them to each other as much as possible while waiting for others to arrive.
- ➲ **Start on time with a welcome and prayer.**

  Thank them for coming and let them know how happy you are that they are there. If you have new ladies, introduce yourself and your coleader.

- ➲ **Make sure everyone has a group handout.**
- ➲ **You will also need** the mission statement, the Virtuous Woman awards, and a long-stemmed rose for each lady.
- ➲ **Share announcements.**
  - o Have you planned an outreach project yet?
  - o Sign-ups for upcoming hostesses/refreshments, etc.

➲ GETTING TO KNOW YOUR HOSTESS

- ➲ Introduce your hostess and the person who provided refreshments.
- ➲ Thank them verbally and with a hostess/thank-you gift.
- ➲ Ask your hostess to share about herself and her life. Keep it to five minutes or so.

➲ GETTING TO KNOW EACH OTHER

Tonight is our final session with the woman of virtue as she is described in Proverbs 31. We've asked a lot of questions about her and applied them to our own lives. We've asked what makes this chick tick, and what is she laughing about. We've wondered, "Who does she think she is?" and "Where did she get that outfit?" And we took a deeper look at what she does and does not do. Let's open up tonight by going around the room.

- ➲ Say your name and share what your opinion or perception was of the woman of virtue *before* beginning this study.

Note: You may want to direct them to look at the passage to stir their thoughts.

Let's get into our lesson by digging into God's Word. This is where our hearts really become woven into a tapestry of love—when we center our conversation and relationships in Christ. When we do, we can confidently share our hearts with each other. There is an element of trust that is a gift. We agree that *what happens with the girls stays with the girls*—let's say that together!

➲ GETTING TO KNOW THE LORD

> Tonight our lesson is titled, "The Woman of Virtue: A Final Plea," and our focus is on the last verse of Proverbs 31:
>
> Give her the reward she has earned, and let her works bring her praise at the city gate.[131]

This verse comes as "a final plea" at the end of the passage. This final plea sounds almost like a funeral or an epitaph on a gravestone. The word *epitaph* is "to say or do something that is likely to bring some endeavor to an end."[132] This verse seems to be just that sort of statement: one that brings closure or proclaims that the virtuous woman's endeavors have come to an end. It gives the impression that we are putting this woman to rest; that her life is over. We are praising her for her good deeds and moving on.

Let's take a few minutes to do what this passage is telling us. Let's praise this woman of virtue and "give her the reward she has earned" for how she has impacted our lives through this study.

➲ Share one thing that you have learned from this remarkable woman, something that really stood out to you about the woman of virtue as we have analyzed her these past months together (e.g., a great revelation from this passage or a new thought, an application that you hadn't thought of before, a new way of looking at other women or yourself).

As we listen to one another share, it's clear that this is not the end of our journey with this woman in Proverbs, and it is certainly not the end of our journey with one another. Instead, it marks a beginning: we've developed new friendships; we've discovered how much we are alike; we've become more accepting and understanding of one another's differences;

---

131   Proverbs 31:31 (NIV).
132   *Collier's Dictionary* (Macmillan Publishing Co., 1986).

and we've shared one another's burdens in prayer and praised the Lord for answered prayers. We've laughed, we've cried, and we've experienced life through one another.

Let's celebrate our group and the relationships we've formed.

➲ Share how being a part of this group has impacted you.

Isn't it amazing the encouragement and companionship that have developed by just spending these few hours a month with one another?

In Hebrews 10:24-25, Paul instructs us:

> Let us consider how we may spur one another on toward love and good deeds. Let us not give up meeting together, as some are in the habit of doing, but let us encourage one another— and all the more as you see the Day approaching. (NIV)

We are going to follow Paul's advice. First, I want to remind you that we will be meeting again _____. So we are not going to give up meeting together; we are just taking a break for _____. (At this point you may want to discuss or announce possible activities/get-togethers for the time when you break from regularly scheduled group sessions or announce the next set of lessons.) And we can continue to encourage one another, even if we don't have our monthly sessions.

➲ What are some practical ways that we can encourage one another?
   o Make phone calls
   o send notes
   o catch up on one another in church
   o invite one another to lunch
   o pray for one another.

Tonight we are going to take a few minutes to encourage one another and spur one another on toward love and good deeds. This is the night you've all been waiting for (*drumroll, please!*)—the Virtuous Woman awards.

We're going to pass out a ballot on which you will cast your vote for each category. You must vote for every woman in the room for one award, including yourself. So, ladies, look around and make sure you don't miss anyone. There are several categories, as you can see, and there are also blank categories. You have the liberty of coming up with your own award for someone if you can think of a more appropriate title. However, it must be biblical as these *loosely* are derived (and must derive) from one of the verses in Proverbs 31. Okay, those are the rules. You each have a ballot, and you may begin casting your votes.

➲ Give them a few minutes to complete their ballots.
➲ *Notes to group leader*:
    o Before the session, assign the award you feel is most fitting for each lady in your group.
    o Using the form in the appendix, copy the awards onto card stock and fill them out with the appropriate names.
    o You could also laminate the awards and make them into magnets.

Hopefully, this passage has become a challenge, an incentive for you to be women of virtue, to continue the legacy of this woman in your personal journey. She challenges us to survey our own use of time, energy, resources, and talents. The woman of virtue is a challenge to become women on a mission, to offer everything that we have and all that we are in service and submission to the Lord and to His divine plan for our lives.

Tonight we've shared what we've learned from the woman of virtue in Proverbs 31. We've shared how this group has impacted our lives, and we've thought about some practical ways to continue to encourage one another toward love and good deeds. Let's take a few minutes and write down at least one thought, one nugget of truth you are going to apply to your life. Write down whatever God has asked of you or revealed to you, and make that your commitment, your mission.

Leaders: Hand out mission statements and give them a few minutes to write. While they do that, prepare the Virtuous Woman awards. Then announce the awards and present them to each lady. It would be lovely to give them each a pink or white rose and have them stand and give an acceptance speech. Their acceptance speech is to share their mission statement. After they have shared their mission statement, let the other women in the group affirm them by sharing which Virtuous Woman award they assigned her and why. They will discover that they have many virtues!

PRAYER TIME

Let's recite the following passage from Philippians as our covenant before closing in prayer tonight. After we read it, feel free to lead out in a short prayer, and then I will close.

> 2 Grace and peace to you from God our Father and the Lord Jesus Christ.
> 3 I [will] thank my God every time I remember you.
> 4 In all my prayers for all of you, I [will] always pray with joy
> 5 because of [our] partnership in the gospel …
> 6 [I am] confident of this: that He who began a good work in you will carry it on to completion until the day of Christ Jesus.
> 7 It is right for me to feel this way about all of you, *since I have you in my heart.* (Philippians 1:2-14 NIV, emphasis added)

Thank everyone for their contributions to the group. Announce when you will be getting together again.

LESSON 7

"A FINAL PLEA"

Group Handout

➲ **GETTING TO KNOW YOUR HOSTESS**

➲ **GETTING TO KNOW EACH OTHER**

- Say your name and share your opinion or perception of the woman of virtue before beginning this study. *Note*: You may want to look at the passage to stir your thoughts.

➲ **GETTING TO KNOW THE LORD**

Give her the reward she has earned, and let her works bring her praise at the city gate. (Proverbs 31:31 NIV)

- Share one thing that you have learned from this remarkable woman, something that really stood out to you about the woman of virtue as we have analyzed her these past months together (e.g., a great revelation from this passage or a new thought, an application that you hadn't thought of before, a new way of looking at other women or yourself).

- Let's celebrate our group and the relationships we've formed. Share how being a part of this group has impacted you.

Let us consider how we may spur one another on toward love and good deeds. Let us not give up meeting together, as some are in the habit of doing, but let us encourage one another—and all the more as you see the Day approaching. (Hebrews 10:24-25 NIV)

- What are some practical ways that we can encourage one another?

THE VIRTUOUS WOMAN AWARDS

Rules: You must vote for every woman in the room one time for one award, including yourself. There are several categories, as you can see, and there are also blank categories.

You have the liberty of coming up with your own award for someone if you can think of a more appropriate title. However, it must be biblical as these *loosely* are derived (and must derive) from one of the verses in Proverbs 31.

Tonight we've shared what we've learned from the woman of virtue in Proverbs 31. We've shared how this group has impacted our lives, and we've thought about some practical ways to continue to encourage one another "toward love and good deeds" (Hebrews 10:24-25).

Let's take a few minutes and write down at least one

thought, one nugget of truth you are going to apply to your life.

Write down whatever God has asked of you or revealed to you. Make that your commitment, your mission.

VIRTUOUS WOMAN AWARD PRESENTATIONS

Let's recite the following passage from Philippians as our covenant before closing in prayer tonight. After we read it, feel free to lead out in short prayers.

> Grace and peace to you from God our Father and the Lord Jesus Christ.
>
> I [will] thank my God every time I remember you.
>
> In all my prayers for all of you, I [will] always pray with joy because of [our] partnership in the gospel ...
>
> [I am] confident of this: that He who began a good work in you will carry it on to completion until the day of Christ Jesus.
>
> It is right for me to feel this way about all of you, *since I have you in my heart.*[133]

---

133 Philippians 1:2–7 (NIV, emphasis added).

PROVERBS 31:10 (KJV); PROVERBS 31:11–31 (NIV)

10 Who can find a virtuous woman? for her price is far above rubies.

11 Her husband has full confidence in her and lacks nothing of value.

12 She brings him good, not harm, all the days of her life.

13 She selects wool and flax and works with eager hands.

14 She is like the merchant ships, bringing her food from afar.

15 She gets up while it is still dark; she provides food for her family and portions for her servant girls.

16 She considers a field and buys it; out of her earnings she plants a vineyard.

17 She sets about her work vigorously; her arms are strong for her tasks.

18 She sees that her trading is profitable, and her lamp does not go out at night.

19 In her hand she holds the distaff and grasps the spindle with her fingers.

20 She opens her arms to the poor and extends her hands to the needy.

21 When it snows, she has no fear for her household; for all of them are clothed in scarlet.

22 She makes coverings for her bed; she is clothed in fine linen and purple.

23 Her husband is respected at the city gate, where he takes his seat among the elders of the land.

24 She makes linen garments and sells them, and supplies the merchants with sashes.

25 She is clothed with strength and dignity; she can laugh at the days to come.

26 She speaks with wisdom, and faithful instruction is on her tongue.

27 She watches over the affairs of her household and does not eat the bread of idleness.

28 Her children arise and call her blessed; her husband also, and he praises her:

29 "Many women do noble things, but you surpass them all."

30 Charm is deceptive, and beauty is fleeting; but a woman who fears the LORD is to be praised.
31 Give her the reward she has earned, and let her works bring her praise at the city gate.

LESSON 7: VIRTUOUS WOMAN AWARDS BALLOT

Virtuous Wife Award: _____

Because "her husband has full confidence in her and lacks nothing of value" (Proverbs 31:11).

Virtuous Prayer Warrior Award: _____

Because "she sees that her trading is profitable and her lamp does not go out at night" (Proverbs 31:18).

Virtuous Mother/Grandmother Award: _____

Because "her children rise up and call her blessed" (Proverbs 31:28).

Virtuous Neighbor Award:_____ _____

Because "she opens her arms to the poor and extends her hands to the needy" (Proverbs 31:20).

Virtuous Domestic Goddess Award:_____

Because "she makes coverings for her bed; she is clothed in fine linen and purple" (Proverbs 31:22).

Virtuous Attitude Award:_____

Because "she can laugh at the days to come" (Proverbs 31:25).

Virtuous Gourmet Award: _____

Because "she is like the merchant ships, bringing her food from afar" (Proverbs 31:14).

Virtuous Entrepreneur Award: _____

Because "she considers a field and buys it; out of her earnings she plants a vineyard" (Proverbs 31:16).

Virtuous Fitness Award: _____

Because "she sets about her work vigorously; her arms are strong for her tasks" (Proverbs 31:17).

Virtuous Early Bird Award: _____

Because "she gets up while it is still dark" (Proverbs 31:15).

Virtuous Leader Award: _____

Because "she speaks with wisdom, and faithful instruction is on her tongue" (Proverbs 31:26).

Virtuous First Lady Award:_____

Because "her husband is respected at the city gate, where he takes his seat among the elders of the land" (Proverbs 31:23).

Virtuous _____ Award:

Because _____

INDEX

Printed in the United States
By Bookmasters